Praise for *Thank You for Your Service*

An Amazon Best Book of the Year
A *Washington Post* Best Book of the Year

"An important piece of work, a deep dive into the psychology of a country where a poor job market and a short national memory mean there is almost nothing left but pity for the men and women returning from conflict."
—*The Globe and Mail*

"An exquisite piece of journalism. . . . It is unflinching, remarkable and guaranteed to further infuriate anyone who has lamented George W. Bush's decision to invade Iraq. That war, Finkel makes clear, will haunt its veterans and their families for lifetimes to come."
—*Maclean's*

"A searingly intimate true chronicle of after-war life for a group of soldiers returning from Iraq. . . . A remarkable, powerful and unforgettable book."
—*Toronto Star*

"This is not—nor should it be—an easy book. But it is an essential one."
—Elizabeth D. Samet, *The New York Times Book Review*

"A heartbreaking book powered by the candor with which these veterans and their families have told their stories, the intimate access they have given Mr. Finkel." —Michiko Kakutani, *The New York Times Book Review*

"Finkel's ability to embed in these trenches, recording remarkably intimate moments between husband and wife, social worker and patient, is no less valuable than when he did so near explosions less metaphorical. He bears witness, seemingly never sugarcoating or judging either the horrors these soldiers are subjected to by ghosts and guilt, or the ones they themselves inflict upon their loved ones. It is a boo⬚ ⬚⬚⬚⬚⬚ should read."

"Books like this aren't likely to bring a ⬚⬚⬚ *Thank You for Your Service* should be manda⬚⬚⬚ people who naively believe all those advertisements promising ⬚⬚⬚⬚⬚ career in the armed forces."
—*Winnipeg Free Press*

ALSO BY DAVID FINKEL

The Good Soldiers

Thank You for
Your Service

David Finkel

Foreword by
Lieutenant-General Roméo Dallaire

Introduction by Carol Off

Anchor Canada

Library and Archives Canada Cataloguing in Publication data is available upon request

ISBN 978-0-385-68954-0

Cover image © 2017 Universal Studios and
Storyteller Distribution Co., LLC. All rights reserved.
Book design by Abby Kagan
Printed and bound in the USA

Published in Canada by Anchor Canada,
a division of Random House of Canada Limited,
a Penguin Random House company

10 9 8 7 6 5 4 3 2 1

www.penguinrandomhouse.ca

Penguin
Random House
ANCHOR CANADA

For Phyllis Beekman,
who taught me about damage and recovery

To Elizabeth Helen Hill
for saying okay

FOREWORD

by Lieutenant-General Roméo Dallaire

War is persistent and universal, and so too is the terrible physical and psychological price paid by the men and women who fight it, and their families. David Finkel has demonstrated an exceptional ability to identify and describe the psychological consequences of modern warfare.

Although *Thank You for Your Service*, like Finkel's earlier book, *The Good Soldiers*, focuses on men from a U.S. Army infantry battalion that served in Baghdad, it could just as easily have been written about Canadians in Afghanistan, or any theatre of war, for that matter. This book has both global and timeless relevance. In the eloquence of the soldier-speak captured by Finkel, "... all wars are the same, only the landscape changes."

Finkel shows us, from an intimate vantage point, the damage done to soldiers, their families and those that command them, and he clarifies how, in military culture, the very concept of a mental injury carries a great deal of stigma. This book is both difficult to read and rewarding. It calls up the full range of emotions: tears at the plight of a young family struggling with the baggage of war, anger at the shortage of therapeutic help for the injured and their resulting overreliance on medication, and even occasionally laughter at the unique humour soldiers use to mask their emotions.

Finkel does find some signs of hope. He depicts the unflagging courage and determination of the injured, and the strong desire on the part of a number of senior generals to overcome the mental health challenges of modern warfare. Most encouragingly, he sees signs of success in some of the many programs that now exist for the returning injured. And their predecessors from earlier wars? As Finkel writes, "Most of them came home from their wars to no help at all."

INTRODUCTION

by Carol Off

A different person came home." That's a lament I've heard so many times. A husband or wife, a son or a daughter went off as a soldier to Afghanistan or Bosnia or Rwanda but never really returned. Oh, they came back physically—they even looked the same after the tour in Medak or Sarajevo or Kandahar—but they were fundamentally altered. And never in a good way.

How is it possible? How can decades of a person's development become rewired in a matter of six months or a year? A relatively happy and well adjusted man or woman comes back from a military mission morose and withdrawn. A solid, loving father and husband becomes a monster, capable of abuse and violence. A dependable, mood-steady warrior returns sullen and paranoid, and soon after hangs himself or smashes his car into a brick wall. What happened "over there" to change everything?

Thank You for Your Service is a journey into the lives of those who returned to the United States from war in Iraq but could no longer fit into the space that they had occupied before deployment. The men of U.S. 2-16 Infantry Battalion who David Finkel follows so intimately are angry, disengaged and frightened of themselves and others. Wives do not recognize these men, and eventually the women run out of patience and love, or they are forced to flee the violence and chaos that now surrounds the man they married. Then there are the soldiers who simply give up trying to make sense of it all and take their own lives, leaving partners, parents and children bewildered.

The majority of post-deployment soldiers in the United States and Canada do not report the psychological problems described as Post-Traumatic

Stress Disorder (PTSD) or, in military language, Operational Stress Injuries. But no country's defence department is really keeping an adequate score. One Canadian military analysis claims that 13 per cent of our troops suffered from mental and emotional problems within five years of returning from Afghanistan. But that doesn't begin to tell the story. Soldiers are reluctant to disclose their mental health issues, fearing reprisal or mockery, and governments are loath to gather full statistics out of a concern for the costs of compensation.

Many stress injuries are explained as the obvious consequences of extreme violence. Soldiers get bashed around when their armoured carriers are ambushed and, if the men and women inside survive, their brains are often bruised. They sustain concussions in everything from combat to car accidents. They also see colleagues blown up, and then must overcome their fear in order to return to duty the next day. Given the ordeals, it is surprising that there aren't more stress injuries. But the Canadian experience with PTSD poses more troubling and complex questions about the origins of these injuries. Why do so many soldiers suffer PTSD when they return from so-called peacekeeping missions?

Throughout the 1990s, an unprecedented number of Canadian Forces personnel headed off to United Nations–sponsored missions, principally in Africa and the former Yugoslavia. Many soldiers came back severely traumatized. Canadians were led to believe that these missions were benign and friendly and included no combat role, but the troops who took part in the operations discovered that there was often no peace to keep. They were under orders to maintain the UN mandate of "neutrality" in the midst of ethnic cleansing and genocide. Some Canadian units disobeyed the higher command in order to intervene, notably in Croatia and Rwanda. Here was their dilemma: How can a soldier, well armed and well trained, simply observe while women are raped, children murdered and whole families driven from burned and looted homes?

These acts of mutiny, as some soldiers called them, were rarely documented or reported, with one extraordinary exception: the 1993–94 United Nations Assistance Mission for Rwanda (UNAMIR), led by Canada's General Roméo Dallaire. His poorly equipped force attempted to stop the genocide, and Dallaire tried to assist the media in reporting the inadequacy of his UN mission. But Dallaire's full disclosure did not end with the war in Rwanda.

No other person in Canada, or perhaps anywhere, has done as much as General Dallaire to reveal the psychological effects of conflict on soldiers. He volunteered the deepest, darkest secrets of his postwar trauma and warned the Canadian government that it faced an epidemic of Operational Stress Injuries from these allegedly benign peacekeeping missions.

In the early 1990s, the crippling disease was already taking its toll. In just one rotation through Croatia so many Canadian soldiers suffered illnesses that, in 1999, the Department of National Defence launched a Board of Inquiry to determine if the men and women had been exposed to some environmental toxin. Soldiers suffered skin rashes and hair loss; some had impaired eyesight or impotency; many developed cancer. But, digging deeper, the inquiry discovered that the soldiers suffered depression; their marriages had failed; their careers had crumbled; and an unknown number had taken their own lives. The board's conclusion: they suffered from the curious and underestimated condition of Post-Traumatic Stress Disorder.

Canada has long been in denial about the extent of PTSD in the ranks. Military doctors and advocates for the troops have been able to shame the government into giving more assistance to veterans, but many working soldiers struggle to hold on to their jobs as they return to lives into which they no longer fit. And there is pathetically little known about the emotional and psychological condition of the thousands of reservists who supplemented these missions.

Like the professionals in David Finkel's account, Canadian mental health workers hoping to understand PTSD often look to the experiences of the Vietnam War. That was perhaps the first conflict in which doctors began to diagnose and document the range of debilitating pathologies that were once simply written off as "shell shock." Yes, there are long-term effects of concussions sustained in combat, and damage sustained from fearing for one's life each day. But those who study the nuances of PTSD identify a distinct set of common emotions—guilt, feelings of powerlessness and futility—that become exponentially more potent under extreme duress. Soldiers carry an overwhelming sense of responsibility for the lives of others, not just their colleagues but also the civilians they are supposed to protect and the civilians they end up killing because they can't distinguish them from the enemy. In addition, there is a sense of impotence, as Canadian troops discovered in peacekeeping, when they have the means but not the mandate to protect innocent people. And, finally, there is the despair that comes from being involved in a mission that you—or, worse, your society—might regard as wrong or futile.

War—and its often carefully disguised sister, peacekeeping—is an encounter with evil. Those who are exposed to it see the worst of what humans are capable of, and they learn what they themselves are capable of, all in the most extreme circumstances. It changes you forever. And it is almost impossible for families to understand what afflicts these returning troops.

The same soldier didn't come back from Iraq or Afghanistan. Nor did he return from the World Wars, from Vietnam, Bosnia, Rwanda . . . or Troy. In Homer's *Iliad*, the warrior Achilles despairs:

Fate is the same for the man who holds back, the same if he fights hard.
We are all held in a single honour, the brave with the weaklings.
A man dies still if he has done nothing, as one who has done much.

Over the years, soldiers have shared with me some of their fear and pain, but I don't know of any account that is as intimate and searing as *Thank You for Your Service*. As devastating as the stories are, there is a thread of hope here: Finkel shows what it takes to bring a soldier back from the brink. It's a long and painful process, and only some of the wiring is restored. And, in dollars-and-cents terms, it's also very expensive.

Perhaps when the psychological effects of military missions are finally tabulated, the crass price tag will force governments to confront the real cost of a mission, and that might discourage them—rightly or wrongly—from intervening. Through the stories of the wounded but still dedicated warriors in these pages, David Finkel poses the question that has endured over all the ages of war: Is it worth it?

Carol Off has been a host of CBC Radio's *As It Happens* since 2006. She was previously a documentary reporter for *The National*. Her books on the Canadian military include *The Lion, the Fox, and the Eagle* (2000) and *The Ghosts of Medak Pocket: The Story of Canada's Secret War* (2005).

PROLOGUE

Y ou could see it in his nervous eyes. You could see it in his shaking hands. You could see it in the three prescription bottles in his room: one to steady his galloping heart rate, one to reduce his anxiety, one to minimize his nightmares. You could see it in the screensaver on his laptop—a nuclear fireball and the words FUCK IRAQ—and in the private journal he had been keeping since he arrived.

His first entry, on February 22:

Not much going on today. I turned my laundry in, and we're getting our TAT boxes. We got mortared last night at 2:30 a.m., none close. We're at FOB Rusta-miyah, Iraq. It's pretty nice, got a good chow hall and facilities. Still got a bunch of dumb shit to do though. Well, that's about it for today.

His last entry, on October 18:

I've lost all hope. I feel the end is near for me, very, very near. Darkness is all I see anymore.

So he was finished. Down to his final hours, he was packed, weaponless, under escort, and waiting for the helicopter that would take him away to a wife who had just told him on the phone: "I'm scared of what you might do."

"You know I'd never hurt you," he'd said, and he'd hung up, wandered around the FOB, gotten a haircut, and come back to his room, where he now said, "But what if she's right? What if I snap someday?"

It was a thought that made him feel sick. Just as every thought now made him

Adam Schumann on his last day of war

feel sick. "You spend a thousand days, it gets to the point where it's Groundhog Day. Every day is over and over. The heat. The smell. The language. There's nothing sweet about it. It's all sour," *he said. He remembered the initial invasion, when it wasn't that way.* "I mean it was a front seat to the greatest movie I've ever seen in my life." *He remembered the firefights of his second deployment.* "I loved it. Anytime I get shot at in a firefight, it's the sexiest feeling there is." *He remembered how this deployment began to feel bad early on.* "I'd get in the Humvee and be driving down the road and I would feel my heart pulsing up in my throat." *That was the start of it, he said, and then Emory happened, and then Crow happened, and then he was in a succession of explosions, and then a bullet was skimming across his thighs, and then Doster happened, and then he was waking up thinking,* "Holy shit, I'm still here, it's misery, it's hell," *which became,* "Are they going to kill me today?" *which became,* "I'll take care of it myself," *which became,* "Why do that? I'll go out killing as many of them as I can, until they kill me.*

"I didn't give a fuck," *he said.* "I wanted it to happen. Bottom line—I wanted it over as soon as possible, whether they did it or I did it."

The amazing thing was that no one knew. Here was all this stuff going on, pounding heart, panicked breathing, sweating palms, electric eyes, and no one regarded him as anything but the great soldier he'd always been, the one who never complained, who hoisted bleeding soldiers onto his back, who'd suddenly begun insisting on being in the right front seat of the lead Humvee on every mission, not because he wanted to be dead but because that's what selfless leaders would do.

He was the great soldier who one day walked to the aid station and went through the door marked COMBAT STRESS *and asked for help and now was on his way home.*

Now he was remembering what the psychologist had told him: "With your stature, maybe you've opened the door for a lot of guys to come in."

"That made me feel really good," *he said. And yet he had felt so awful the previous day when he told one of his team leaders to round up everyone in his squad.*

"What'd we do now?"

"You didn't do anything," *he said.* "Just get them together."

They came into his room, and he shut the door and told them he was leaving the following day. He said the hard part: that it was a mental health evacuation. He said to them, "I don't even know what I'm going through. I know that I don't feel right."

"*Well, how long?*" one of his soldiers said, breaking the silence.

"*I don't know,*" he said. "*There's a possibility I won't be coming back.*"

They had rallied around him then, shaking his hand, grabbing his arm, patting his back, and saying whatever nineteen- and twenty-year-olds could think of to say.

"*Take care of yourself,*" one of them said.

"*Drink a beer for me,*" another said.

He had never felt so guilt-ridden in his life.

Early this morning, they had driven away on a mission, leaving him behind, and after they'd disappeared, he had no idea what to do. He stood there for a while alone. Eventually he walked back to his room. He turned up his air conditioner to high. When he got cold enough to shiver, he put on warmer clothes and stayed under the vents. He packed his medication. He stacked some packages of beef jerky and mac 'n' cheese and smoked oysters, which he wouldn't be able to take with him, for the soldiers he was leaving behind and wrote a note that said "*Enjoy.*"

Finally it was time to go to the helicopter, and he began walking down the hall. Word had spread through the entire company by now, and when one of the soldiers saw him, he came over. "*Well, I'll walk you as far as the shitters, because I have to go to the bathroom,*" the soldier said, and as last words, those would have to do, because those were the last words he heard from any of the soldiers in his battalion as his deployment came to an end.

His stomach hurt as he made his way across the FOB. He felt himself becoming nauseated. At the landing area, other soldiers from other battalions were lined up, and when the helicopter landed, everyone was allowed to board except him. He didn't understand.

"*Next one's yours,*" he was told, and when it came in a few minutes later, he realized why he'd had to wait. It had a big red cross on the side. It was the helicopter for the injured and the dead.

That was him, Adam Schumann.

He was injured. He was dead. He was done.

1

Two years later: Adam drops the baby.

The baby, who is four days old, is his son, and there is a moment as he is falling that this house he has come home to seems like the most peaceful place in the world. Outside is the cold dead of 3:00 a.m. on a late-November night in Kansas, but inside is lamplight, the warm smell of a newborn, and Adam's wife, Saskia, beautiful Saskia, who a few minutes before had asked her husband if he could watch the baby so she could get a little sleep. "I got it," he had said. "I got it. Get some rest." She curled up in the middle of their bed, and the last thing she glimpsed was Adam reclined along the edge, his back against the headboard and the baby in his arms. He was smiling, as if contentment for this wounded man were possible at last, and she believed it enough to shut her eyes, just before he shut his. His arms soon relaxed. His grip loosened. The baby rolled off of his chest and over the edge of the bed, and here came that peaceful moment, the baby in the air, Adam and Saskia asleep, everyone oblivious, the floor still a few inches away, and now, with a crack followed by a thud, the moment is over and everything that will happen is under way.

Saskia is the one who hears it. It is not loud, but it is loud enough. Her eyes fly open. She sees Adam closed-eyed and empty-armed, and only when he hears screaming and feels the sharp elbows and knees of someone scrambling across him does he wake up from the sleep he had promised he didn't need. It takes him a second or two. Then he knows what he has done.

He says nothing. There is nothing he can say. He is sorry. He is always

Adam Schumann at home

sorry now. He has been sorry for two years, ever since he slunk home from the war. He watches his wife scoop up the baby. He keeps watching, wishing she would look at him, willing her to, always so in need of forgiveness, but she won't. She clutches the crying baby as he dresses and leaves the room. He sits for a while in the dark, listening to her soothe the baby, and then he goes outside, gets into his pickup truck, and positions a shotgun so that it is propped up and pointed at his face. In that way, he starts driving, while back in the house, Saskia is trying to understand what happened. A crack. A thud. The thud was the floor, and thank God for the ugly carpet. But what was the crack? The bed frame? The nightstand?

This baby. So resilient. Breathing evenly. Not even a mark. Somehow fine. How can that be? But he is. Maybe he is one of the lucky ones, born to be okay. Saskia lies with him, then gets up and comes back with a plastic bottle of water. She drops it from the side of the bed and listens to the sound it makes as it hits the floor.

She drops a pair of heavy shoes and watches them bounce.

She finds a basketball and rolls it off the edge.

She fills a drink container with enough water to weigh about as much as the baby, and as Adam continues driving and considering the gun, not yet, not yet, not yet, not yet, she rolls that off the edge, too.

Two years. He is twenty-eight now, is out of the army, and has gained back some weight. When he left the war as the great Sergeant Schumann, he was verging on gaunt. Twenty-five pounds later, he is once again solid, at least physically. Mentally, though, it is still the day he headed home. Emory, shot in the head, is still draped across his back, and the blood flowing out of Emory's head is still rivering into his mouth. Doster, whom he might have loved the most, is being shredded again and again by a roadside bomb on a mission Adam was supposed to have been on, too, and after Doster is declared dead another soldier is saying to him, "None of this shit would have happened if you were there." It was said as a soldier's compliment—Adam had the sharpest eyes, Adam always found the hidden bombs, everyone relied on Adam—but that wasn't how he heard it then or hears it now. It might as well have been shrapnel, the way those words cut him apart. It was his fault. It is his fault. The guilt runs so deep it defines him now. He's always been such a good guy, people say of Adam. He's the one people are drawn to, who they root for, smart, decent, honorable, good instincts, that one. And now? "I feel completely broken," Adam says.

"He's still a good guy" is what Saskia says. "He's just a broken good guy."

She says it as an explanation of why on some days she has hope that he will once again be the man he was before he went to war. It's not as if he caused this. He didn't. It's not as if he doesn't want to get better. He does. On other days, though, it seems more like an epitaph, and not only for Adam. All the soldiers he went to war with—the 30 in his platoon, the 120 in his company, the 800 in his battalion—came home broken in various degrees, even the ones who are fine. "I don't think anyone came back from that deployment without some kind of demons they needed to work out," one of those soldiers who was with Adam says.

"I'm sure I need help," another says, after two years of night sweats and panic attacks.

"Constant nightmares, anger issues, and anytime I go into a public place I have to know what everyone is doing all the time," another of them says.

"Depression. Nightmares of my teeth falling out," another says.

"I get attacked at home," another says. "Like I'm sitting in my house and I get attacked by Iraqis. That's how it works. Weird-ass dreams."

"It has been more than two years, and he's still beating me," the wife of another says. "My hair is falling out. I have a bite scar on my face. Saturday he was screaming at me about how I was a fucking bitch because I didn't have the specific TV he wanted hooked up."

"Other than that, though," the one who might be in the best shape of all says with an embarrassed laugh, after mentioning that his wife tells him he screams every night as he falls asleep. He sounds bewildered by this, as do they all.

"I have to admit a day doesn't go by that I don't think about those days, the boys we lost, and what we did," another says. "But life goes on."

Out of one war into another. Two million Americans were sent to fight in Iraq and Afghanistan. Home now, most of them describe themselves as physically and mentally healthy. They move forward. Their war recedes. Some are even stronger for the experience. But then there are the others, for whom the war endures. Of the two million, studies suggest that 20 to 30 percent have come home with post-traumatic stress disorder—PTSD—a mental health condition triggered by some type of terror, or traumatic brain injury—TBI—which occurs when a brain is jolted so violently that it collides with the inside of the skull and causes psychological damage. Depression, anxiety, nightmares, memory problems, personality changes, suicidal thoughts: every war has its after-war, and so it is with the wars of Iraq and Afghanistan, which have created some five hundred thousand mentally wounded American veterans.

How to grasp the true size of such a number, and all of its implications, especially in a country that paid such scant attention to the wars in the first place? One way would be to imagine the five hundred thousand in total, perhaps as points on a map of America, all suddenly illuminated at once. The sight would be of a country glowing from coast to coast.

And another way would be to imagine them one at a time, starting with the one who is out in the middle of a Kansas night, driving around and around unseen. Toward dawn, he returns home. He doesn't mention to Saskia where he has been, or what he had been thinking, and she doesn't ask. Instead, the shotgun is put away, the baby awakens for his next feeding, their other child, who is six and anxious and has begun wetting her bed, awakens after doing so again, and a breaking family whose center has become Adam's war wounds gets on with another day of trying to recover, followed by another day after that.

He doesn't believe anything is wrong with him. That's part of it. He stares at himself in a mirror, ignores what his red eyes look like except to see with continuing regret that he still has two of them, does the inventory. Two eyes, two ears, two arms, two legs, two hands, two feet. Nothing missing. Symmetrical as ever. No scarred-over bullet holes. No skin grafts over bomb burns. Not even a smudge in the tattoo covering his right forearm, needled into him between deployments as a display of undying love, which says SASKIA in letters constructed of stick figures in various poses of having sex. He is physically unmarked, so how can he be injured? The answer must be that he isn't. So why was he sent home with a diagnosis of severe PTSD? The answer must be that he's weak. So why was that diagnosis confirmed again and again once he was home? Why does he get angry? Why does he forget things? Why is he jittery? Why can't he stay awake, even after twelve hours of sleep? Why is he still tasting Emory's blood? Because he's weak. Because he's a pussy. Because he's a piece of shit. The thoughts keep coming, no way to stop them now, and yet when he goes into the living room and sees Saskia, he gives no indication of the pandemonium under way.

"Good morning," he says, an act of civility that some days takes all of his might. Not that she doesn't know, but he betrays nothing until he goes outside and sees that the neighbors have once again tied up their dogs on short leashes and that the dogs are tangled up and howling.

"God. People," he says with disgust, and that is enough to loosen this morning's version of the leash that Saskia finds herself bound by every day. Now her own storm begins over what her life has turned into, and there's no sure way to stop hers, either.

"They have a forty-thousand-dollar car, and they live like shit," she says, getting into the driver's seat of their car, an aging SUV with a cracked windshield and balding tires. "That's what this town is, forty-thousand-dollar cars and people who live like shit."

The town, called Junction City, population twenty-five thousand or so, is adjacent to Fort Riley, the post where Adam deployed from and returned to three times during his seven years in the army. It is in the part of Kansas between the populated east and the wide-open rest of the state, a geography that tends to evoke in people who don't live there idealized notions of America's heartland and the poetry of the plains. As for Junction City itself, it has long had a reputation as a scruffy place, and the downtown neighborhood where Adam and Saskia live bears that out. Across the street is a convicted sex offender—a pedophile, Saskia suspects. Nearby is a drug dealer, and a few doors down is a parolee who keeps coming over and asking to use the phone. Poetry in the heartland: while Adam was gone, Saskia slept with a gun.

Their own old house is small for four people and two big, sweet, sloppy dogs, but it is what they can afford. It cost a little over a hundred thousand dollars. It has two small bedrooms on the main floor, and another bedroom in the basement, carved out of the grungy furnace room. Their bedroom is the one with three hidden guns. The baby, whose name is Jaxson, sleeps down the hall, and the basement is for Zoe, the six-year-old, who at bedtime has to be coaxed again and again to go down the steps.

Saskia found the house and bought it during Adam's final deployment, the one that wrecked him. This was where they would claim the life they both had expected to have by his enlisting in the army: house, kids, dogs, yard, money, stability, predictability. She knew he was coming home ill, but she also knew that he would be better once he was away from the war and back with her, that just by her presence he would heal. "That fairy-tale homecoming" is how she thought of it. "Everybody's happy. Kind of like an it-never-happened kind of thing." When he got home and wasn't happy, she told him she understood, and when he said he wasn't yet ready to be around a lot of people, she understood that, too. Her patience, she had decided, would be bottomless. They rented out the house she had fixed up for him and moved to a vacated farmhouse out in the country. It was beautiful there in autumn, but less so in winter, when the fields turned to stubble and the gray sky lowered on them. The isolation finally became too much when one of their cars broke down, so they came back to Junction City, and Saskia decorated the bedroom with a wall stenciling that said "Always Kiss Me Goodnight."

He did. Then, dulled by prescriptions for anxiety and depression and jitteriness and exhaustion and headaches, he didn't. And then she didn't, either, not always, and gradually less than that, and one day she confided to a friend, whose own husband had also come back ill from the war: "My mood changes every day. One day, it's: He's really hurting. The next is: Stop this. Get over it. Get your ass up."

"Nothing will get better," her friend said of what she had learned. "Nothing will be as it was before. Nothing will be the way I want it to be. So I have to come up with reasonable expectations of what can be."

"The women have to be the ones to adapt. That's the way it is for all of us," Saskia said as her friend nodded, and now she is beginning another day of trying to do just that as the neighbor's dogs howl and Adam climbs into the passenger seat. For whatever reason, her irritation keeps growing, and the fact that she realizes it and can't stop it makes it worse. She drives a few blocks and abruptly pulls into a convenience store.

"Need gas?" Adam asks.

"Unless you want to push," she says.

"Need anything from inside?"

She doesn't answer.

"Doughnut?" he asks.

"No."

He fills the car and goes inside to pay, and when he comes out he's holding a Mountain Dew and a handful of lottery tickets.

"Are you *kidding* me?" she says as he starts scratching off the first of the tickets. She hates that he wastes money on lottery tickets, much less on Mountain Dew. "Keep dreaming," she says as he tries the second one. She drives through town and follows a minivan onto a ramp to the interstate. "Why are they braking? *Why are they braking? WHY ARE THEY BRAKING?*" she yells.

She hits the gas and flies around an old woman, alone at the wheel, as Adam tries the third one.

"Last night, I passed by that bridge by Walmart, and there was a bum sitting under it surrounded by a huge pile of scratch-off tickets," he tells her. "Somebody gave him some money, I guess, and he used it to buy scratch-offs."

"That would be you," she says.

He tries the fourth one as she accelerates to eighty. They are on their way to the VA hospital in Topeka, sixty miles to the east, for a doctor's appointment. The war left him with PTSD, depression, nightmares, headaches, tinnitus, and mild traumatic brain injury, the result of a mortar round that dropped without warning out of a blue sky and exploded close enough to momentarily knock him silly. Between his government disability check of eight hundred dollars a month and his $36,000-a-year salary from a job he managed to find, he is pulling in about two thirds of what he made in the army, which is why Saskia hates when he wastes money on lottery tickets.

He tries the fifth one and announces, "I won ten bucks."

Saskia looks at him. "You spent five," she says. "You made five. What are you going to do with five?"

"Buy a pack of cigarettes."

She hates that he smokes. She hates that he wants to be alone so much now, either fishing or hunting or out on the front porch having a cigarette in the dark. She hates that her patience didn't turn out to be bottomless after all. A truck swerves in front of her. "You *asshole*," she shouts.

It has been eight years since they met. This was in Minot, North Dakota. She was just out of high school, a girl who never missed curfew and was now on her own in a cheap basement apartment, and one day she emerged from the basement to the sight of a local boy with a rough reputation sitting in the sun without a shirt. What Adam saw was a girl staring at him whose beauty seemed a counterpoint to everything in his life so far, and that was that, for both of them. Soon came marriage and his SASKIA tattoo, and now here they are, her hitting the gas again and him reaching over to tickle her, break the tension, make her laugh. She flinches, as if his fingers have blades on them, and she accelerates until she's only a few feet from another slow-moving car. *"Get out of the way!"* He moves his hand to the back of her head and caresses it, and this calms her enough to slow down to seventy-eight.

Sometimes after they fight, she counts his pills to make sure he hasn't swallowed too many and checks on the guns to make sure they're all there. The thought that he might not recover, that this is how it will be, makes her sick with dread sometimes, and the thought that he might kill himself leaves her feeling like her insides are being twisted until she can't breathe.

The truth is that he has been thinking about killing himself, more and more. But he hasn't said anything to her, or to anyone, not lately, because what would be the point? How many psychiatrists and therapists has he talked to? How many times has he mentioned it, and where has it gotten him?

". . . daily thoughts of SI [suicidal ideation] running through his mind," the psychiatrist who ordered his medical evacuation from the war noted just before he was sent home. "States it is alarming for him to think this way, and while he's had suicidal thoughts in the past, this has been unremitting for him over the last few months."

"Having much less suicidal thinking, but the thoughts come to him quickly," a different psychiatrist noted a few months later, after he had come home.

"His thoughts come and go in phases. He has had thoughts twice this month," another psychiatrist noted a few months after that.

"He acknowledges occasional suicidal ideation, that he would be better off dead, but he has never had a serious plan and never made an attempt. He does have guns but his wife keeps them away from them unless he needs to go hunting" was the next report, a few months later.

"You have suicidal thoughts: you reported daily thoughts of suicide with a plan and a means. However, you repeatedly denied intent to harm yourself due to care for your family" was the next one, which went on to note: "You have the ability to maintain minimum personal hygiene."

Well, at least there's that, Adam thought when he came across that report. Crazy, but clean. He found it when he was down in the furnace room going through papers to see what he might need to bring with him to the VA. His medical file is thick and repetitive and soon bored him, and he turned his attention to several boxes filled with letters that he and Saskia had written to each other while he was overseas, love letters all. They wrote to each other just about every day. That's how they were. He read a few, and when they started making him a little sad over what had been lost between them, he moved on to other boxes, pausing when he came across a single piece of paper with a title on it that said "Places I Have Been."

It was an old piece of paper from his grandfather, the other great soldier in the family, a list he had once made.

Atlantic Ocean.
Naples, Italy—filthy.
Pompeii, Italy—Interesting.
Rome, Italy—Beautiful.
Grosseto—We fought a tough battle there.
Vatican City—Very Beautiful.
Nice, France—girls. wow.

And that was it, one soldier's World War Two. When he came home, he never talked about what he had been through in Grosseto, or Nice, or even crossing the Atlantic, when he would have been filled with the naive optimism of a soldier who hasn't yet reached the war. Instead, he turned into an angry drunk who stayed that way for years. He fought in Korea and stayed that way, and then in Vietnam, and only after twenty-five years of serving his country and being abusive to his family did he get himself under control.

Adam was nine when he got to know his grandfather, and it's hard to say who was more in need at that point. No longer drinking, his grandfather had lapsed into a life lived mostly in silence. Adam, meanwhile, had arrived at the crucial point of a ruinous childhood. When he was very young, he was sexually molested by an older neighborhood boy who was babysitting him. When he was six, he remembers, his father one day started hitting him and kept at it until Adam's mother picked up a chair and charged her husband with it. When he was nine, his mother said one day, "Your father's gone. He's not coming back," and it was true. Adam had been doing well enough until that point—honor-roll grades, no shortage of friends—but his mother had no money, and soon they were evicted from their house, sleeping at a relative's and living out of a car, and then they were moving in with this strange old soldier, who as far as Adam was concerned was just one more man who was going to let him down.

Instead of ignoring him, though, or abusing him, the old man would pile his bruised grandson into his Cadillac and take him for long drives. Just the two of them, keeping each other company. He never said a word, except to swear at other drivers. "You fucking bastard," he would scream, and then keep driving in silence, smoking incessantly. At home, he didn't talk, either. If he was reading the newspaper and wanted to show someone something, he would point to it with his middle finger, always his middle finger, and slide it across the table.

That someone was usually Adam. His grandfather was his first experience with war wounds, and Adam grew to love him, and soon after the old soldier died, he joined the army and became a great soldier and now has his own list of places he has been.

United States—born, molested, beaten, abandoned, girls. wow.

Iraq—We fought a tough battle there.

Interstate 70 in Kansas—"Hi. This is Adam Schumann," he says on the phone now, Topeka nearing, calling to confirm his appointment at the VA. He listens for a moment and hangs up.

"The appointment's not till tomorrow," he says to Saskia.

She shoots him a look, starts to say something, doesn't.

So he says it for her.

"Goddamn it."

They ride in silence for a few miles.

"Fuck," he says. "Fuck."

"Well it's not my fault," she says. "Maybe you should write shit down." She gets off the interstate at the exit for the hospital. Maybe they can worm their way in somehow. "Why didn't you call this morning?"

"I was sure it was today," Adam says. He rubs his forehead. He slaps his head. He drums his fingers on his leg.

There's the hospital in the distance. Saskia slams on the brakes at an intersection in order to avoid a woman crossing the street against the light. "*Dumb bitch*," she explodes.

"God, I can't believe I messed everything up," Adam says.

At the hospital now:

They pass through an entranceway lined with survivors of previous wars in wheelchairs and "Proud to Be an American" T-shirts. "It just stinks like old people and smoke," Saskia says. They walk down a hallway behind a woman who is giving a tour to two men. "The guys from Vietnam are so expressive, but the new ones, from Iraq and Afghanistan, go straight to violence and suicide," the woman says. "Mm-hmm," one of the men says. One of the worst things about Adam's war, the thing that got to everyone, was not having a defined front line. It was a war in 360 degrees, no front to advance toward, no enemy in uniform, no predictable patterns, no relief, and it helped drive some of them crazy. Here, though, in this new war of Adam's, there is a front line: this hospital. This old, underfunded, understaffed hospital, which nevertheless includes a compassionate receptionist who says she will see what she can do and a doctor who is underpaid and overwhelmed and says that of course he can squeeze Adam in. So in Adam goes, preceded by all of the previous histories dictated about him over these two years, rendered as only doctors and interpreting bureaucrats can:

> Topeka VAMC reports you were clean and appropriately and casually dressed. Your psychomotor activity was unremarkable. Your speech was clear and unremarkable. Your attitude toward the examiner was cooperative, friendly and attentive. Your affect was expressive. Your mood was depressed and irritated. Your attention was intact. You were fully oriented to person, place and time. Your thought process was unremarkable, but your thought content was distressed, and irritated with others. You do not have delusions. As to judgment: you understand the outcome of behavior. Your intelligence was average. As to insight: you understand that you have a problem . . .

Saskia waits outside. Sometimes she goes in with him, sometimes not. She wonders if this doctor will be able to speak understandable English, unlike the last one. She wonders if he will look Adam in the eye as he asks his questions or keep his back turned as he types Adam's responses into a computer. She is sure she knows what the doctor will say: Adam is wounded. Adam is ill. Adam needs to stay on his medications. Adam deserves the thanks of a grateful nation. She is seated near a sign for a suicide hotline that says, "It takes the courage and strength of a warrior to ask for help," but she has her own saying at this point: "How much can you pity a person who cannot help himself?"

And then, just like that, as Adam emerges and she sees how lost he appears, even scared, her mood breaks, and she is once again allowing in possibility and all the hurt that comes with it.

On the way home, they pass the little airport where Adam returned from the war.

There were ceremonies when the others came home, raucous celebrations in a Fort Riley gym filled with spangly women, flag-waving children, and signs. "Welcome home, Daddy." "Welcome home, heroes." Straight from the war, the soldiers would march into the gym, in formation, and when they were dismissed a few minutes later, there would be a great rush as the order of the place dissolved into screams and embraces. It happened every time, again and again, as all of the Fort Riley soldiers returned, and at one of the ceremonies, everyone spilled out of the gym and into a perfect Kansas day: blue sky, buttercups in the summer grass, a gentle breeze, and then an unexpected puff of wind. It blew the caps off of men and lifted the flowery skirt of one of the young wives, exposing the thong she had chosen for this day and the new butterfly tattoo she had gotten, and instead of smoothing her skirt back into place, she laughed as she felt it rise like a kite above her shoulders, and the soldier she was with couldn't stop staring and grinning, and everyone around them laughed, knowing what would be coming next, the sex, the desire, the relief that he was home safely, the poetry in the plains, and could there have been a moment further from the one that Adam had when he arrived?

No ceremony, no signs, no spangly dress—just Saskia pressed against a window of the terminal, watching him get off a plane. He descended the steps with the other passengers onto the tarmac, and Saskia thought: *He's a skeleton.* She had been hoping so hard. Now she knew.

As for Adam, as he walked across the tarmac, he wished he were on crutches and covered in bandages. The great soldier, returning from war. He felt ashamed. He walked into the terminal. He dreaded what Saskia would think of him. Now he saw her. She was smiling her beautiful smile. All of a sudden, he wanted to run to her. Here was his moment of welcome, his chance at absolution, and that was when he noticed the woman standing next to Saskia. He had never seen her before, but she seemed to know him because she was rushing toward him, on the verge of tears.

"Can you tell me what happened to my husband?" she was saying. "Can you tell me what happened?"

That was how he came home. Those were his welcoming words.

2

The woman was Amanda Doster, who on that day was one of the war's newest widows.

Now, no longer new at it, she is at home waiting for the door-bell to ring, a ding-dongy chime that to her will always sound like a life coming to an end.

When it rang on the day her husband died, she had her two young daughters in the bathtub and cookies baking in the oven. She opened the door and saw who was standing there, and before they could say anything she had finished the quick calculations. An injury would be a phone call. A serious injury would be a visit from soldiers in regular uniforms. Death would be dressier soldiers, in their Class As. These two, asking if they might come in, were in their Class As. "There are a few things I have to get done before you say it," she answered. She wanted to remain in control. That was important to her. She went into the kitchen and turned off the oven, knowing that she was about to forget about the cookies. She made a list. She phoned some neighbors and asked them to come over and get the girls. She phoned her mother and asked her to get on the first plane. She made sure the door to the bathroom was shut. Finally, she sat on a couch in the living room, and they stood in front of her and said it.

Ding-dong.

This day, it is six moving men who are standing there.

"Good morning!" she says to them, once again trying to sound under control. She has a kind, round face and long curly hair and except for her widow's eyes looks very much the same as the woman her husband last saw.

Amanda Doster

"We got lost," one of the movers says, apologizing for being late, and when they're all inside, she leads them through the house and gives them a few instructions.

"Don't touch that jacket."

"Not that flag case. I will transport that."

"I'll take his uniforms."

"I'll take that phone. It still has his voice on it."

"I'll do the black footlockers. I'll do those."

"Okay," the foreman says, and as he and the others get to work pack-ing, she and her best friend, Sally, who has come over to help, go down into the house's tornado shelter, a windowless concrete room in the basement. She flips on the light. There, against a wall, stands a gun safe almost as big as a refrigerator, and after spinning the combination and swinging open the door, she begins removing what's inside.

First the long guns, nine in all.

Three handguns.

A sword.

Some knives.

The ammo.

And lastly a sealed wood box, inscribed: "James D. Doster, SFC, 19 November 1969, 29 September 2007."

"There's James," Sally says, as Amanda smiles at the box.

"Hi, James," Amanda says.

For a while, she was taking him everywhere. She took him to his parents' house for Christmas, strapping him in with a seatbelt all the way to Arkansas. She took him to Sally's one day when a bad storm was threat-ening, transporting him that time in a laundry basket.

For a long while, she kept him on the bedroom dresser, the dresser they got together, front and center. One day, she put a framed poem about grief and faith there and eased him toward the edge, and another day she got new bedroom furniture and moved the dresser to the guest room and carried him down to the tornado shelter. He was on top of the gun safe initially, but eventually she put him inside, reasoning that it was fireproof in there and giving no thought to the fact that what she was protecting from fire were cremated remains. She closed the door. She spun the lock. She turned off the light. She went upstairs and began adjusting to him being in the safe, behind the door, in the dark. And now she is leaving the house where she last saw him and promised she would be when he came back.

She had been adamant about that, too. As she told the casualty assistance office assigned to her in those first days, "I am staying here forever. I am never leaving." She told her friends that as well, and while at first they sympathized, as the months went by, and then a year, and then another year, most of them began to lose patience with her inability to stop being so relentlessly heartbroken. "There comes a point," one of them said. "You just have to get on with it." So maybe this day, this move, is the coming of a point, she is thinking, even as she suspects that it isn't, that she is still very much the woman she had cemented into by the time James's commander called her from Iraq, just after his death, and said upon hanging up, "That's probably the saddest woman I've talked to yet."

How do some people move on? Why isn't she one of those people? She has asked this of friends, counselors, and other widows. Now she asks no one anymore except God and Sally, of whom she can ask anything, even whether James is really dead. Because the thing is, she is still seeing him alive. Just the other day she was driving and spotted him at a stoplight, behind the wheel of a truck for a pest control company, and it was so clear to her what had happened. He had become bored with the war. He had left it. He was back in Kansas, lying low, waiting till the coast was clear, working pest control, saving money, and soon would be home, ringing the doorbell. *Ding-dong.* There have been plenty of versions of this over the years, going back to when she saw him in the coffin and wondered if it was him. She wanted evidence. She knew his wedding ring had been removed, but she also knew it fit so tightly it left an indentation in his finger that never went away. She needed to see the indentation. She discreetly tried to remove the glove he had been dressed in for his viewing, but to her horror, as she pulled on the glove, she realized that it had been taped into place. He's alive, she began thinking, he's gone covert, this is a wax figure, that's why the glove is taped, it's all a ruse, she would prove it, and so she stood at the coffin, running her fingers back and forth over the glove, trying to feel the dent.

Sally is the one who gets to hear this. She listens to Amanda with the endless patience of someone who spent a few years teaching emotionally disturbed children, three of whom left bite marks in the fleshy part of her right hand, and one with a mother whose tooth fell out in the midst of a parent-teacher conference. "Do you have any Super Glue?" the embarrassed woman asked, holding the tooth, and so Sally understands that life has its complications and sadnesses, including in Kansas. She is also a cheerful person, which Amanda needs, and someone who likes to hum as she goes about her day, which Amanda doesn't mind at all, not from Sally, except for the time she was absentmindedly humming "Taps," giving it a peppy bounce.

Humming away now, she and Amanda are packing up the master bathroom when she suddenly falls silent. She is looking at the contents of a drawer she pulled out. Men's deodorant. Men's shaving cream. A half-empty tube of toothpaste. A toothbrush with hardened bristles, unused for years.

"I'll move that drawer, Sally," Amanda says.

"What?" Sally says, still looking.

"I'll move that drawer," Amanda says.

Sally never met James, who had already deployed by the time she and Amanda became close. She knew him only from what Amanda described: twelve years older than her, the love of her life, her rescuer. Now Sally is the rescuer, and has been since she stood with Amanda as Amanda faced her children to tell them what had happened. Grace, who looks so much like her father, was three, and Kathryn was six, old enough to always be haunted by what her mother was about to say. Don't use euphemisms, Amanda had been advised. Don't say, Daddy went to sleep. Don't say, Daddy went away. Be truthful. Be direct. "Daddy got hurt," she began, and the next sound in the room came from Kathryn, a sharp intake of breath.

"Here's his nail file," Amanda says now, standing next to Sally, cleaning out the drawer. She picks up his nail file and then a blue plastic case with a dental mold in it.

"What's that for?" Sally asks. "His sleep apnea?"

"No. Grinding his teeth," Amanda says, and for a moment, he is alive and grinding his teeth and she can hear it.

In those first hours after James died, the doorbell kept ringing as word spread. In came the casualty assistance officer. In came a pastor. In came neighbors with Swedish meatballs. In came a friend with her little boy, who fell down some stairs and cried and cried. More neighbors came, and more kids, and now into the commotion came Saskia Schumann, who had been called by one of those neighbors saying that James had been hurt.

"Is he going to be okay?" she asked Amanda, not knowing, and as Amanda began crying, she did, too, because she was certain that Adam was dead as well.

She and Amanda had met for the first time just a week before, but they had been e-mailing for a month, since James, at his own request, had transferred out of a desk job he hated at the brigade level and taken over Adam's platoon. All of his new soldiers had been leery at first, especially Adam. Doster had never been in combat. Before his desk job, he had spent ten years as a recruiter. But he was so clearly happy to be among this group of soldiers that his enthusiasm rubbed off on them, and before long Adam and James were hanging out and Adam was thinking he might survive this war after all. As for what James thought: "They're the most amazing group," he told Amanda, sounding so happy that she got teary. "There's one guy in particular," he went on. "His name is Schumann, and he impressed me as soon as I met him."

So Amanda called the wife of the impressive Schumann, asking to get together. She told James how excited she was, and nervous, too, like butterflies before a date. Saskia wanted to meet her as well, because of how much better Adam was sounding. "Not at all what I pictured her to be," she would say after she and Amanda met at a restaurant. "We were the same age, and she looked to be thirty-five." But Amanda would say,

"We just clicked. We just talked about everything," and that's what she told James when he called in the early hours of September 29.

In Kansas, it was still September 28, late in the afternoon. Amanda was in the minivan with Kathryn and Grace when her cell phone rang, and she parked and stayed there for the next hour as the sun set on the last full day of her marriage. At one point, Grace climbed onto her lap as she was telling James that if the doorbell ever rang, she wouldn't answer it. It wasn't a premonition that caused her to say this, it was just the way conversations between a person in a war and a person in a minivan tended to go. Of course you would answer it, James said, all serious. They were supposed to talk again later in the day, this time through a video linkup that soldiers could sign up for from time to time. September 29 was to be James's turn. But he was going to be home on leave in a few weeks, he told Amanda, and talking by video would mean staying on base and missing a mission, so he had given his slot to Schumann, who seemed in need of it.

"Talk to you later," he said.

And that was how Adam, who always found the hidden bombs, stayed behind on September 29. Instead of going out, he talked by video to Saskia and remained on the base afterward while James went out and got blown into pieces by a bomb that no one saw. "None of this shit would have happened if you were there," Adam got to hear soon after from a soldier who had watched James dying, and meanwhile Saskia was at Amanda's, hugging her and thinking the same thought over and over: Adam was with James. Adam is dead, too. "Come home," she begged him the next time they spoke, and a month later he did.

"Can you tell me what happened?" Amanda said at the airport.

"How did it happen?"

"Did he suffer?"

"Were you there?"

"It took Adam so long to put that together," she says now to Sally, looking out at an elaborate wooden play set in the backyard. "On the instructions, it said it would take two moderately skilled adults sixty hours," she says, and remembers how Adam did it by himself while she and Saskia drank mojitos and margaritas.

So much for those days: for whatever reason, she and the Schumanns drifted apart, the play set has been sold to some neighbors who would be coming over soon with a truck, and everything else is being boxed. "Fifteen thousand pounds," the foreman guesses at how much it will all weigh, which, if he's right, would be almost double the poundage they had been expecting. "Maybe sixteen thousand."

Maybe so. The gun safe alone is six hundred pounds, the new bedroom furniture is solid wood, the entertainment center is so big and heavy that it will take four movers to get it off the ground, and then there are all of the other things that Amanda is sorting through.

There is the box labeled "James had on him when he died," and inside the box are the things found in the uniform that was stripped from him so the doctors and nurses could better pound on his chest: three photographs of the girls, his USAA credit card, a card with Arabic phrases, his knife, and a lighter.

There is the gray T-shirt he was wearing his last night home, which reminds her of the beginning of their marriage, when she was eighteen years old and he told her that he liked his T-shirts folded a certain way, and she would practice whenever he left the house.

There is a piece of wood with four hooks in it: "He built that. Gotta take that. I painted it. He was pissed off. I over-sprayed, and it got on the sidewalk. I didn't account for the wind," she says.

There's a bag with cheap tin dog tags that someone sent to her along with a note that said "Please accept these identification tags on behalf of a grateful nation," which infuriated her then and makes her wonder now why she has saved them. There are the three handmade wooden boxes sent by someone from Canada who read of James in the paper, each made of walnut because he read that James liked walnut. Why would an article in Canada mention that a dead American soldier liked walnut, she wonders, but the boxes are beautiful and she'll be taking those.

There's his Purple Heart, his Bronze Star certificate, the condolence letter from President Bush that says "We will forever honor his memory," the flag she was flying outside the house when he died, the flag that was flown in his honor over the Arkansas capitol, and the condolence book in which his first wife, who couldn't have known that his dying words were "I'm hit," wrote "I'm sure his last thoughts were of his family."

There's the autopsy report that begins, "The body is that of a well-developed, well-nourished male," and goes into detail about what happened to that body for six pages, and a copy of the initial army investigation into his death, with the sworn statement of a soldier who wrote, "myself and Golembe started cutting off all his gear and trying to talk to SFC Doster, he was still breathing but was unconscious."

Into his tool room now. The rider mower will go to the new house, she tells the movers. The four hammers. The three saws. The old boom box up on that shelf. The two chainsaws. The workbenches. The steel wool. The rusty nails. All of it, actually, every bit of it, even an old peanut butter jar filled with sawdust.

On to the bookshelves. Yes to the brochure titled "101 Reasons to Own a Chainsaw," yes to *The Complete Book of Composting*, yes to *Military Widow: A Survival Guide*, yes to *Single Parenting That Works*, yes to the rest.

Into her kitchen, where the boxes of aluminum foil and plastic wrap have been lined up in a drawer so that the lettering faces the same way, and more than anything else in the house, the precise arrangement of these boxes explains why Amanda had to turn off the oven and make a list before she could hear that her husband was dead. If they're not lined up that way, she feels off balance. It's the same with her spice jars, and with her shoes, which are categorized by color, subcategorized by material, and sub-subcategorized by style. She is the daughter of a man she describes as an ill-tempered drinker who married and divorced her mother five times, and the daughter of a woman who five times married that man. She had an older brother who left home when he was fourteen and died in a car crash, and then when she was adrift and in need of order in her life, she met James, who was all about order and self-sufficiency. After the military, he wanted a life off the grid, as he put it, just him and Amanda and whatever children they had. They would grow their own food, dig their own well, be powered by solar. But he was also willing to compromise when Amanda said she wanted to be near a hospital for those children, and the compromise was three acres on a street called Liberty Circle and a house where at least the aluminum foil is under control.

Outside now. She'll need to move the flag, but will she need to take the bracket? She won't be able to sleep in the new house if there's not a flag flying, but does the new house have a bracket?

Back inside, where James is propped up in one of the chairs. The movers are trained for these situations. Under contract to the army, they have their own perspective on the consequences of war. Just recently, they moved a soldier from Kansas to a rehab hospital in Texas, and as the soldier watched them pack his things, he kept crying because he had lost his legs in the war and was unable to help. That was bad enough, but they've come to learn that war widows are the hardest by far. Ask nothing about the dead, they are instructed, and so they don't ask what happened to James or why he is in a chair. Instead, one of them asks, "Ma'am, do you want us to pack your mops?"

Yes to the mops. No to the firewood. No to the jacket that James hung on a hook when he came in from splitting the firewood and has been on that hook as long as that dental mold has been in that drawer. She'll move the jacket, and not that they're asking, but she'll move him.

They bought this house for $280,000. She sold it for $375,000. The new one cost $555,000, but money wasn't really an issue because of life insurance policies and the army's tax-free payment of $100,000, which it calls a "death gratuity."

"Blood money," she calls it on her bad days.

"Oops money," she calls it on her better days.

Whatever it's called, it is allowing her to make this giant leap to a new life in a new house that is 2.8 miles away.

To get there takes all of six minutes. After one last night on Liberty Circle that James spends in the living room, she drives along some dirt roads, turns onto a path that seems to be leading into the woods, and arrives at a brand-new house that dazzles even the well-trained movers.

"Sweet, sweet, sweet," one says.

"House has like twelve bedrooms," another says.

It has six, actually, plus an exercise room that in a pinch could be a seventh. "This is my kind of kitchen, if I ever become a chef," another says, all dreamy for a moment as he sees the marble counters and two dishwashers, and then he and the others return to their regular lives of unloading what turned out to be just under sixteen thousand pounds.

"Ma'am, where do you want this?" one asks, carrying in a fan from the first of the trucks.

"Exercise room," she says.

"Ma'am, this room here. This is what you're calling the dining room?" another one asks, and when Amanda looks at him quizzically, he says, "I got confused because it's so big."

"Ma'am, which one was the storage room again?"

"It's . . . it's . . . I'll just go down and show you."

"Ma'am, where do you want your doghouse?"

"Ma'am, where do you want your camcorder?"

"Ma'am, where are the girls' rooms at?"

"Okay," she says, leading him upstairs.

"Ma'am, where's the safe go?"

"The safe goes . . . in the safe room," she says, and after going back downstairs and showing him the safe room, she ducks into one of the bedrooms and says, "Ma'am, ma'am, ma'am, ma'am. I don't like being a ma'am. At twenty-eight, you should be a miss. Or a Mrs." She closes her eyes. She takes deep breaths. She stands in the soft carpet. She is teary. She wishes Sally were here, but Sally had to go home to be with her husband and kids. She wants so much to remain in control. There's a knock at the door.

"Ma'am, can I use your restroom?"

She shows him to one of the four bathrooms and then says to no one in particular, "I don't know what to do."

"What do you *want* to do?" Grace says, who is sitting there eating a biscuit, and Amanda continues to stand where she is, wishing she had an answer. What does she want to do? Why doesn't she know yet? Why isn't he here to help her figure it out? Why is she still talking to him? Why is she still seeing him alive?

What *happened* to him?

Two years later, she is still asking the question she asked Adam at the airport. She had heard initially that James had lost all of his limbs except for his right arm, then that it was only his left leg, that he died immediately, then that he didn't, that he was unconscious, then that he wasn't. She had asked for the autopsy report, waited months for it, and, with Sally sitting next to her, read it from beginning to end. Shrapnel wounds to the pelvis. Left leg amputation, below the knee. Massive bleeding. Protruding viscera. Six pages of details. And still she wonders: What *happened*? Did he feel it? Did he really say, "I'm hit?" Did he say anything else? Were his last thoughts of his family? Did he understand that he was dying? So she went to the airport with Saskia, and instead of seeing a skeleton walking toward her, she saw her chance for answers.

"Did he suffer?" she asked.

"Were you there?" she asked.

And Adam's answer was to take out his wallet and hand her something he had been keeping since the day that James died, when he had picked up James's body armor, taken it into a latrine, and tried to scrub it clean with some body wash and a toothbrush. It took him an hour because there was so much blood. The smell made him sick, but he kept at it, couldn't stop, didn't want to, he had loved James Doster, and at one point as he bore down, he felt something nick his hand. "What the fuck?" he'd said, and that was when he had found the sliver of metal that he handed to Amanda at the airport, and every so often since then she has taken this piece of the bomb that killed her husband and placed it in her palm and tightened her hand around it and kept squeezing until she bled.

This house then: it is sixteen thousand pounds of shrapnel that is continuing to explode, and late at night, after the movers have gone, the furniture has been arranged, the kitchen has been organized, the beds have been made, and the house seems presentable, Amanda goes back to Liberty Circle.

"James," she says.

There he is, on a counter. He is the last thing left.

She places him in the car, buckles him in, leaves their house forever, and drives him to her new home.

3

I don't know if everyone knows your story, but you all are fortunate—because this is a hero," a woman is saying about Tausolo Aieti, who, back in the war, was in the same unit as Adam Schumann and James Doster. The woman, a psychologist, is standing with Tausolo in front of a few dozen people, all on folding chairs that have been set up in a little, out-of-the-way room at the Topeka VA hospital. She is smiling, and when she turns to Tausolo and says, "You define what a hero is," he resists the urge to turn away. This is progress. He knows it. When he was admitted seven weeks ago to Topeka's inpatient PTSD program, he couldn't look anyone in the eye. Now, on his graduation day, the only one he can't look in the eye is himself.

Three other men are graduating with him, all of them old Vietnam guys still trying to recover forty years later. One has the collapsed face of a drunk used to sleeping it off in the sun, and another has the posture of a man who lived for a time under a bridge. "Thank you ever so much," one of them says to the hospital workers, family members, and the program's twenty other patients gathered in this room. "I look at myself in the mirror each morning and tell myself, 'You're worth something.'" Another stands with his wife, who says they've been married forty years and for thirty of them he's been ill, so she'll see.

Tausolo is the youngest by far, the only one of the four still in the army, and the one whose wife has decided not to come. He is twenty-six and from American Samoa, and the stunned look on his face this day is the same as it was on the sunny afternoon that he was covered in soot

Tausolo Aieti, moments after the explosion

and blood and he asked another soldier if Pfc. James Jacob Harrelson was okay.

"And a hero isn't someone who doesn't feel fear, they're someone who in spite of their fear does the right thing and really risks their own safety," the psychologist continues. "You did that."

The theory of this program: Return to the traumatizing event. Remember it in detail. Think about it through therapy and by writing about it. Keep at it until you are thinking about what you did do instead of what you didn't. Learn that truth is relative, and that there is the moment of trauma, and then the moment following the trauma of your first reaction, when shame and guilt can take hold. Healing is an act of persuasion—this is what Tausolo has been trying to learn for seven weeks. "As we were going down the route, I saw some palm trees," he wrote. "Harrelson was playing a nice, relaxing country music song. I looked at those palm trees, and it reminded me of back home in American Samoa. It reminded me of the coconut trees back home and when I was a little kid playing and picking the coconuts that fell off. Everything was right and boom it happened so fast."

"And I hope you hold on to that as you leave here, because you have an opportunity to go back and to your family be a hero every day," the psychologist continues. "To feel fear but do the right thing anyway. We've seen you do that here."

Here is Building Two, second floor, mental health. Here is where no one knows he is. Or almost no one. His wife, Theresa, knows, and so does Adam Schumann, though in his case it's only by accident. There had been another fight with Saskia. He had hit the swinging door between the dining room and the kitchen so hard it had flown off its hinges and crashed to the floor. He had gone into the bedroom and punched the headboard and begun to cry. He had calmed down, come out to the living room, held Jaxson, given him a bottle, nuzzled his baby hair, watched Zoe in her PJs eating grapes, and put the door back on its hinges. The next morning, he had quietly said "I love you" to Saskia, who was folding laundry and whose face was still puffy, and had driven without her to a doctor's appointment in Topeka. "Hey, there's Aieti," he'd said, getting out of the car and looking across the parking lot. He hadn't seen Tausolo since the day he'd left the war, but he recognized his slow, limping walk in an instant. He waved, but Tausolo was too far away to see him, and as Tausolo went across the lawn into Building Two, Adam headed left toward the main hospital, wishing that he could go into Building Two with him.

Lucky Aieti. Getting help.

"Keep doing that as you leave here," the psychologist says. "Congratulations."

She hands Tausolo a certificate for completing the program, and after mumbling a few thank-yous, away he goes with his certificate and fifty-three pages of writing about what happened after the boom. The Humvee rising in the air. The concussion of the bomb. Opening the door and trying to run. Collapsing with a broken leg. Limping back to the Humvee and pulling out a bloody soldier. Pulling out a second one who was moaning and even bloodier as the Humvee sparked and burst into flames. Collapsing again, relieved that everyone was out, and then hearing someone yelling Harrelson's name. "And it hit me ohh shit Harrelson. I forgot all about him," he had written. "I looked over and all I could see was flames and the outline of a body where he was at in the driver's seat." Over and over he had written about it all, except for one thing that he has told no one, a dream he has been having ever since:

Harrelson, on fire, asking him, "Why didn't you save me?"

The dream comes every few nights. He never dreams about the soldiers he did save, only about Harrelson, and only in that way. For a while, he could handle it, and then one day he couldn't.

Home now, and it's just as he had left it seven weeks before. The walls are gouged from him throwing whatever he could get his hands on. The bedroom door has a fist-shaped hole all the way through it. At least Theresa is no longer cowering, but she is looking at him with her own version of a stunned expression, one that tells Tausolo she is wondering what will happen next.

The place they live is Grandview Plaza, a speck of American landscape along the interstate between Junction City and Fort Riley. It's a town of low houses and tall pickup trucks, a towering billboard that says "Obama is a Fraud. Demand Resignation Now. God Bless America!" and Geary Estates, a 372-unit apartment complex that is filled with military families and where there have been two recent suicides. One was a soldier who had just returned from the war. One had yet to go. One very courteously tried not to make a mess, placing a folded sheet on his mattress and his army jacket on top of the sheet and then lying down on top of the jacket before shooting himself. The other shot himself, too, but abruptly against a wall. "I call it Bloody November," says the apartment manager who scrubbed down the walls with bleach and primed them for repainting with a stain-blocking product called KILZ and used office scissors to cut out the sections of ruined carpet and wished the whole time that the county required that such things be done by a HAZMAT team.

Two weeks after the second suicide, Tausolo and Theresa moved in. It wasn't one of those units, but it was only a few doors away from one of them. They didn't have much: a mattress and box spring in the bedroom, a dining room table, a couple of couches in the living room. Their extravagances were a big TV and some framed family photographs on the walls, and the photographs were what Tausolo reached for first when he once again woke up from seeing Harrelson, finally broke down, and began throwing whatever he could get his hands on. He spent a week locked down in a hospital, then tried an outpatient program in Junction City he didn't like, and then was admitted to Topeka.

For the seven weeks he was there, Theresa was on her own in the apartment, just her, the gouged walls, and the punched-in door. Like Tausolo, she had grown up in American Samoa. She had come to Kansas uncertainly, helped a little by the fact that her sister, who was also married to a soldier, had ended up here, too. Now, four months pregnant, she began going to her sister's more often, sitting for hours outside in the sunshine and hoping the summer heat would burn away her growing doubts.

"Deep down, he's scared of something. But he doesn't want to talk about it, so he does stuff," she said on the day before his return, trying to imagine how he would be when he came home by remembering how he had once been. "When I first met him, he was never like that," she said, but then he deployed, and one day he called and mentioned that he had hurt his leg, and then he was back home, waking up every few nights from a dream he would only say was about the war.

He began to take sleeping pills to fall asleep and another kind of pill to get back to sleep when he woke up. He took other pills, too, some for pain, others for anxiety. He began to drink so much vodka that his skin smelled of it, and then he started mentioning suicide.

Maybe this is what happens to soldiers, she had been thinking. Growing up, she'd been aware that a lot of Samoans joined the military, including in her own family, all of whom seemed the same as ever when they came home. But now she was learning otherwise. A few months before, a Samoan she knew a little bit, one tour in Iraq, diagnosed with PTSD, had hanged himself in his barracks in Hawaii. And according to her sister, her brother-in-law was having difficulties recovering from his tour in Iraq, which had caught her off guard because as far as she could tell he seemed as happy as ever.

Still—suicide? Tausolo? "I don't know if he's serious because before this he was never serious. My husband, he would joke about everything. Yeah. So. Suicide," she said, holding her stomach as the baby growing inside her kicked. She stayed in the sun until it was time to go back to Geary Estates, and now, the next day, here he is, home, the hero, showing her his certificate.

He goes to see his company sergeant, Jay Howell, to tell him he's back from Topeka. He hasn't seen anyone from his unit in a couple of months, and as he walks through the building, wondering what everyone is thinking, feeling their eyes on him, Howell, watching him, says, "He thinks they'll look at him for being weak. That's why he's kind of shy when he's out there right now. But there's not one guy who'll look at him that way. Maybe some of the new privates, because they don't know him. The older guys? No.

"There are mental issues, and there are bullshit mental issues. You've got to look at the person. Everybody has a breaking point," Howell goes on. "You cannot overlook the fact that the guy should have got a Bronze

Star or Silver Star. There is no coward in this guy. The guy's never failed at anything."

In this one regard, Tausolo is fortunate. Jay Howell has a reputation of looking after his soldiers. But a nurse case manager is now looking after Tausolo, too. She wants him to transfer into another unit called a Warrior Transition Unit. It's for soldiers who are injured, some physically, most mentally, a unit where a soldier is excused from the daily duties of a healthy soldier and is treated instead as a long-term, recovering patient.

Tausolo comes into Howell's office and pulls up a chair. "I talked to my case manager," he says softly. The door is open. Guys are right outside. "She called me today, and she asked me to ask you if you could send in a packet on me for the WTU."

"The WTU?" Howell asks, surprised.

"Yeah," Tausolo says.

"I can do that," Howell says slowly, thinking, seeing the paperwork that will be involved, "but she's gotta have more involvement than telling us to do shit. The medical guys are the ones who initiate that. It's not on us. We sign off on it."

"Yeah," Tausolo says, and after some silence, Howell asks him what he wants to do after the WTU.

"I want to see if I can come back here," Tausolo says.

"Well, I would recommend you try somewhere else," Howell says. "The reason is that part of your memories is always going to be with this unit. You know what I'm saying?"

Tausolo knows what he's saying.

"When you come here, you'll always remember the guys that you were with," Howell says. "I had Cajimat, I had those guys, to this day, I walk over to that old office of mine and I just start thinking back to the days of that stuff."

He pauses, thinking about the stuff. Cajimat burned to death, too, strapped in his seat, just like Harrelson. "You need to get away from that stuff," he says after a moment.

"Yeah," Tausolo says.

"It'd be a fresh start," Howell says. "Plus, are you from Kansas?"

"No," Tausolo says.

"Where are you from?"

"American Samoa."

"Where?"

"Sa-mo-a," Tausolo says slowly.

"I know Samoa," Howell says, "but have you ever lived in the United States, other than Samoa?"

"Uh, no," Tausolo says. He's not sure where this is going. But this is the army. In the army, you answer the questions.

"Okay. I mean, have you ever thought of trying to do something else?" Howell asks. "I'm not talking about army-wise. I'm talking about what do you like to do?"

"I took some college classes . . ."

"I'm talking about recreation. Get your frustrations out. What do you like to do? Do you like to swim? You like the beach? You like that kind of thing?" And before Tausolo can answer, Howell knows what Tausolo should do. "Hawaii! You would love life. Plus there's a lot of Samoans there."

He laughs.

Tausolo laughs.

Problem solved.

"Also, Mama might be happier, too. Because Kansas is not for everybody."

"Yeah, she wants to go somewhere," Tausolo says. "Germany. Or something like that."

"Yeah, Germany probably wouldn't be the best," Howell says. "Okay, I'll see what we can do about getting that thing started. You go to the WTU, and it really doesn't hurt your career at all. Nowadays, mental health stuff doesn't. You got the back history. That's why I say, time for you to take a knee for a little while, see what's up. Okay?"

"All right," Tausolo says.

"All right," Howell says. "Welcome back."

Tausolo gets up, goes out, feels those crawling eyes. How much do they know? It doesn't matter. He's not one of them anymore.

He goes to see the WTU, which turns out to have a new name: the WTB. The war grinds on. The unit has grown into a battalion.

It had been created as a unit a few years before, in year four of Iraq and year six of Afghanistan, when the army had twenty thousand wounded soldiers on its hands and realized that its system of rehabilitating them had become overwhelmed. With a billion dollars, it began building thirty-two such units across the country, where care would be streamlined and there would be dedicated medical workers, social workers, and sergeants. "A Triad of Support" is how it was phrased in a press release. "Soldiers have one mission—to heal."

At Fort Riley, that healing took place initially in a couple of temporary buildings that a weak Kansas tornado could have sent spinning sky-high. Adam Schumann was there then, blurry days that he would recall afterward as "Let's give you this medication, this medication, this medication." Even as he cycled through the program, though, a stone-solid, $54 million, four-building complex was being built, and although he had left the program by the time it was finished, he thought enough of the idea to show up and sit in the audience for its dedication. "Fucking nice is what it is" was his pronouncement. "But you can gift wrap a piece of shit and it's still a piece of shit."

It was him, an assortment of wounded soldiers, officers making speeches about how these newest buildings in the U.S. Army were "a victory for our entire army and for all warriors and their families," a red ribbon that said "Warrior Transition Battalion Complex," and a giant pair of scissors snipping that ribbon right through the "o" in "transition." Thus did the sad work of war recovery officially become a billion-dollar industry, with promise in the air, new buildings, new furnishings, shined hallways, mowed grass, flowers in bloom, and wounded soldiers who soon began moving in.

The WTB had space for a couple of hundred of them. The unmarried ones would live in barracks, the married ones could live in places such as Geary Estates, and they would stay in the WTB until recovering to the point at which they could return to the regular army or, more likely, be released into the civilian world. To help them, in addition to the staff, was a commander who would sometimes shut the door to his office, call his priest in tears, and ask for advice on how not to become calloused against the pain around him.

"Irritation. Hypervigilance. Anger. A lot of depression. And personally, from what I've noticed, a lot of lethargy, a lot of I-don't-give-a-shit attitude" was the commander's list of the symptoms most common to the soldiers filling the place to capacity, and it got more complicated from there. Inspections revealed that one soldier was decorating his barracks room with snakes; another was stockpiling cats; another was selling his pain meds, which was quite a feat considering that just about every soldier had his own legally prescribed stash. Just like the other soldiers, the WTB soldiers wore uniforms, and just like the other soldiers they began and ended the day with formation. But the truth was that they had little in common with the other soldiers, including the soldiers they had once been themselves. Formation wasn't an exercise in discipline as much as taking attendance to see if everyone survived the previous twelve hours. "Before I forget, there's a breakfast tomorrow, right here, for all you warriors," a sergeant might announce to the crooked lines of softening bodies and darting eyes, and then dismiss them into another day of doctors, nurses, social workers, and therapists, all to prepare them for their eventual place among the country's five hundred thousand glowing dots.

This is the world Tausolo is being pushed toward, and he wonders: How much will the WTB be able to help someone like him get ready for life after the army? He wants to work on improving his memory, which has been getting worse since the explosion. He might enroll in college courses to learn a skill other than the singular infantry skill of closing in on an enemy and killing him, which he suspects has limited applications outside of war. And he wants to bring his dreaming under control. Despite Topeka, Harrelson continues to visit him, asking that same question. "There's no way of stopping dreams," Tausolo had said one morning, looking exhausted, sounding resigned. But maybe, with the help of the WTB, he can.

Entry isn't automatic, however. So many soldiers are trying to get into the WTB—most with legitimate injuries, some willing to fake it for an easy paycheck—that there is an application process, and an interview of some sort that Tausolo hears can be difficult. "Get your hair cut," one of his old sergeants advises as the day of the interview arrives, and he knows that's a good idea and means to write it down so he won't forget it, but he has become distracted by family news from Samoa. His oldest brother has died. The first word, which came in a brief phone call the night before, was that he might have killed himself. Then came an update: someone shot him. Then another update: it's unclear what happened, but Tausolo's large, sprawling family would like him to come home.

So on the day of the interview, instead of preparing, he runs all over Fort Riley, trying to arrange for a plane ticket back to the impoverished island in the South Pacific where he grew up, a place of no job options other than the tuna cannery he worked at until, sick of the work and wanting more out of life, he went to see the army recruiter on the island who always made his numbers.

He goes first to his old unit, the 2-16, for the official Red Cross message confirming a death, which he will need to get a plane reservation, only to find out that the message was sent mistakenly to another unit, the 1-16. He sorts that out and drives to another building he's been directed to, where he waits to talk to a man who is busy on his computer looking at a website for mail-order meat. Wrong office, the man finally says, barely glancing up from a photograph of raw steaks, and directs Tausolo to another building. "Building 212," he says.

"Building 212," Tausolo repeats.

Two entrances, the man continues. Go to the one on the far left.

"The far left," Tausolo repeats.

He goes outside, reaches to put on his beret, and realizes he has forgotten it. He goes back inside, finds it on a table, and heads back out down the wrong hallway. He wanders around until he finds the right one, gets to his car, discovers that he forgot his keys in the ignition, is relieved to see that he forgot to lock the doors. He sighs. He wasn't like this before. Before, everything was easy.

He runs his hand across his head. "Still have to get my haircut," he reminds himself.

He drives toward Building 212 and the entrance on the far left when his phone rings: Building 212 is wrong; go to the S-1 shop and ask for someone named Estramada.

"Estramada," he repeats.

He hangs up and realizes they didn't tell him which S-1 shop. The battalion's? The brigade's? He tries to call back but no one answers. He goes to the battalion S-1 shop, asks for Estramada, and is told there's no Estramada there. He turns to leave. This time he remembers his beret. "Um, we have an Estremera," someone mentions then, as he is almost out the door. Estremera? Did he get the name wrong? He goes in search of Estremera. "Don't you have a board today?" she asks when he locates her. How in the world does she know that? he wonders, but instead of asking, he tells her about his brother, and she in turn picks up a phone and calls Transportation, which refers her to Casualties, which refers her to Soldier Actions, where she finds someone who says that yes, Tausolo can get on a plane. She apologizes for how long this is taking. "I don't know why I didn't figure it out," she says, rolling her eyes and pretending to shoot herself in the head. She tells him which building to go to for the ticket, which building to go to for the control number, and which building to go to for an antiterrorism briefing a soldier is required to have before he can travel. "Too easy!" she says, and sends him on his way to the briefing, except once he gets there he is told he has to take an online test first, and no, they don't have a computer for him to use.

It's 1:30 p.m. now. He has to report for his WTB interview at 2:45. There's still plenty of time for a haircut. At least that will work out. He goes to the barber, gets in line, checks his paperwork, and realizes 2:45 is wrong. He's supposed to report at 1:45. "Ah God," he says, and with his hair still too long, he flees the barbershop and makes it a minute early.

Theresa is there waiting for him with some lunch, suspecting he'll be a while. Eleven other soldiers trying to get into the WTB are there, too, and so are two of Tausolo's sergeants who were with him in Iraq and have shown up in case he needs people to speak on his behalf.

One of them—Sherfield—tells Tausolo what to do when he's called in. Present to the general. Sit between the general and the command sergeant major. The general will go first, then the command sergeant major, and then everyone else. Doctors. Psychiatrists. The WTB commander. There could be forty people in all.

The other—Davison—knows as well as anyone what Tausolo has been through. He was in the convoy that day. He didn't reach Harrelson, either. He got banged around during the deployment, too, and gets headaches so severe now that sometimes he throws up and sometimes his wife has to cover the windows with blankets and sometimes he stands under a shower until the water goes cold and—

"Nobody cares, brother," Sherfield says tenderly.

"This shit is intense shit," Davison says. But Tausolo, he goes on, is in a different category. "He's coped and dealt with some of the most *extreme* shit."

He looks across the room at Tausolo, who is sitting with Theresa. "When you have a soldier of that caliber, you know when he's broken, and when he's broken, he's gotta be fixed," he says. "To go from what he was to what he is? Something *had* to have broke. He needs help, and he needs to keep getting help."

He thinks back to another time he escorted Tausolo to an interview. That time it was a promotions board, long before the explosion. "He was like an M&M in a cardboard box. Nervous as shit. I said, 'You gotta calm down, killer.'" This time, though, it isn't nervousness he is seeing, it's bewilderment, so he walks over to Tausolo, reminds him of that day, and then tells him: "This is different. They're not asking you what you know. They're asking you how you feel. Just be honest. The straight-up shit."

Tausolo watches as the first soldier is called into the room. Ten minutes later he is out, and a woman is approaching him with the decision. She shakes her head. He's a no.

In goes the second soldier. He's limping and wearing a cast.

He's a no, too.

In goes the third.

A yes.

In goes the fourth.

No.

Tausolo is the ninth.

His turn now.

"Okay. Take a deep breath," he tells himself.

In he goes.

Is it forty people in there? He won't remember. Did he salute the right officer, sit in the right place? He won't remember that, either, or the first questions, which couldn't have been more accommodating.

"What do you hope to gain by coming into the WTB?" someone whose name he won't remember asks. "In your understanding of things, what can we do to help facilitate your healing process?"

Everyone in the room has a packet of papers to help them make sense of this soldier who has suddenly appeared before them, number nine, who followed number eight, who precedes number ten, who is saying something about how he hopes the WTB will prepare him for what might come next in his life. Which is what every soldier says. There's his military record for them to consider, his record of mental health appointments, details even of a bar fight he got in one night when he was drunk, and how many times have they seen versions of that? There's also something called a "Warrior Screening Matrix" that scores a soldier's need for help. Anything above a score of 1,000 is supposed to be a shoo-in, or as it says on the form, "Failure to assign or attach Soldier to WTU likely to decrement the medical plan of care." Tausolo's score is 1,400. A formality, then, it would seem. Except the questions become more probing and the way they are asked shifts, too.

"You were put in the hospital?" someone asks. "Okay, tough one to answer, but I gotta ask you: Have you thought about hurting yourself since then? Have you thought about suicide?"

"Uh, negative," Tausolo says.

So much for the straight-up shit.

"Talk to me about alcohol," someone else says.

"I'm . . . I'm not drinking anymore. I stopped at Topeka."

"Is your family here at Fort Riley?"

"My wife is here, and, um, I just found out last week that my brother passed so I'm going home on emergency leave."

"I'm sorry—"

"And home is American Samoa."

"Where was that?"

"American Samoa."

"Is your wife going home on emergency leave with you?"

"Yes sir."

"Is she also from American Samoa?"

"Yes sir."

"Okay, with the alcohol use, what are you doing to keep from using it? Other than just sheer willpower? Are you involved in AA? Are you using any of the support channels?"

"Just my wife."

"Everybody has to have a whole bunch of tools in their toolkit, and if you only have one or two tools, you don't have a lot to choose from," someone now lectures Tausolo, and instead of offering the assurance that he has plenty of tools, that he came home from Topeka with a folder of information titled "Self Esteem," and a folder titled "Relationship," and folders titled "Healthy Living" and "Core Issues" and "Stress Management" and "Seeking Safety," sixteen folders in all of tools, and more tools in the form of therapy, and more tools in the form of medications, he just listens with that look he has had since the explosion.

Sometimes Tausolo sees Harrelson in the daytime, too, just for an instant. Sometimes he sees him from a distance. Sometimes he sees him close up. "Why didn't you save me?" Harrelson is always asking as he burns. Sometimes Tausolo understands that the person really asking the question is Tausolo himself.

The interview is nearly over.

"Three deployments?" an officer asks.

"Yes," Tausolo says.

"At your young age?"

Tausolo shrugs.

"Thank you. That's all I need," the officer says, and a few minutes later, Tausolo is out in the hallway watching the woman approaching with the decision.

"All right," she says. "You were accepted."

Davison hits Tausolo on the chest. "All *right*!" he says. "That's it! Here we go! Get it fixed!"

He hugs Tausolo while Theresa, wary, tired, takes it all in from a distance. "I just hope. I just hope," she had said the day before Tausolo came home from Topeka, and she wonders now: Is this how hope feels?

"I don't know," Tausolo says. He is driving back to Geary Estates. He needs to pack for Samoa. He needs to patch the living room walls. He needs to fix the bedroom door. He needs to look at himself in the mirror each morning and tell himself he's worth something, like the Vietnam guy learned to do. He's a hero, after all.

He drives past a sign announcing that it's Suicide Awareness Month at Fort Riley.

"I don't know," he says again. "But right now, I feel better."

4

The way it worked was that they joined the army because they were patriotic or starry-eyed or heartbroken or maybe just out of work, and then they were assigned to be in the infantry rather than something with better odds like finance or public affairs, and then by chance they were assigned to an infantry division that was about to rotate into the war, and then they were randomly assigned to a combat brigade that included two infantry battalions, one of which was going to a bad place and the other of which was going to a worse place, and then as luck would have it they were assigned to the battalion going to the worse place, and then they were assigned to the company in that battalion that went to the worst place of all. If you listen to the eulogies, so much of war is said to be accidental. Poor Harrelson. Wrong place. Poor Cajimat. Wrong time. But to a member of Bravo Company, which spent fifteen months in a sorry, bomb-filled neighborhood called Kamaliyah, the war felt eventually like the wrong everything. Adam Schumann and James Doster were in 1st platoon. Tausolo Aieti was in 2nd platoon. And Nic DeNinno was in 3rd platoon, where he thought of himself not as starry-eyed but as a patriot, a true patriot, and then he punched his first civilian in the face, and then he pushed his first civilian down some stairs, and now he is back in the United States, crying and saying to his wife, Sascha, "I feel like a monster."

He is in Pueblo, Colorado, in a twenty-three-bed psychiatric facility called Haven Behavioral War Heroes Hospital. It's on the top floor of a six-story building, where the exit doors are bolted and the windows are screwed shut to keep patients from jumping out. This is day seventeen

Nic DeNinno

for Nic. He was sent here from the Fort Riley WTB because his mood swings and talk of suicide had become so alarming, and he has eleven more days here before he's supposed to go back.

Twenty-eight days, then, total, to get it fixed, as Sergeant Davison would say, and if war is accidental, so is what happens afterward. Tausolo got Topeka when he needed critical treatment. Nic is getting Pueblo. Both programs claim to be successful and use similar treatment models. But they are different in basic ways, and with more than two hundred programs across the country at this particular moment claiming to help soldiers, the army has yet to figure out which ones are more effective. Topeka is a seven-week program. Pueblo is four weeks. Topeka is part of the VA system. Pueblo is private and for-profit. Topeka mixes Iraq and Afghanistan soldiers with Vietnam veterans. Pueblo is entirely Iraq and Afghanistan. Topeka's program has been running for years and is settled in. Pueblo's is new, one of a wave of programs begun when the extent of psychological damage being caused by Iraq and Afghanistan was becoming apparent. Is one program better than the other? Is seven weeks better than four weeks? Is mixing up soldiers and veterans from different wars better than isolating them? Is a program established before Iraq and Afghanistan better than one started as a direct reaction to them?

The answer, in Nic's case: Topeka was full. Pueblo had a spot.

"The following items are provided," read the instructions Nic was sent before leaving Fort Riley. "Shampoo & Body wash. Deodorant & Body lotion. Toothbrush & Toothpaste . . ."

He saw the theme here.

"Contraband items:" the instructions continued. "Weapons or any object which could be used as a weapon. Razors. Hangers. Neckties, scarves, belts, shoe laces, strings in sweatpants. Any ropes, strings, or chains. Neck chains longer than 24 inches. Panty hose or long stockings. Glass of any kind. Any electrical appliance using an electrical cord. Any sharp object. Plastic bags—any and all . . ."

He saw the theme here, too.

Sascha drove him to the airport, and as she stood at the terminal window watching him walk toward the plane, she might as well have been Saskia watching Adam or Theresa watching Tausolo. She felt her heart sinking. They had met a week after Nic got home from the war, when she heard that some soldiers were back and went online to see who they were. She had a soft spot for soldiers. Her father had been one. Her grandfather had been one. Most of her uncles were either army or National Guard. When she met Nic, she liked that he was big and muscled and spoke thoughtfully and had a tattoo on his back that said "Unity and Peace." He had gotten it when he was growing up, he told her, before he ever thought of becoming a soldier, and she liked that about him, too. As for the dark circles under his eyes, she found them intriguing. "You do know that something's wrong with him," a friend told her at one point. He didn't like crowds. He had nightmares. Yes, she did know, she said, and she was concerned. She was coming out of a failed marriage to a soldier who had returned from Iraq angry and abusive. She had two young daughters to worry about. But there was something about Nic that made her want to stick with him, and so she did, through his flashbacks, and drinking binges, and a drug overdose that was his first suicide attempt, and then she married him, and now she was six months pregnant and hoping that Pueblo would make him realize he could tell her anything about the war, anything at all. That she wanted to hear it. That she could take it.

"Report to the East Entrance by the flag pole and statue of Mary," continued the instructions Nic had gotten, which he carried with him to Pueblo. "Go to the elevator, 6th floor, left out of elevator and pick up phone dial '0.'" He dialed "0." A door swung open and was bolted behind him, and before long someone was explaining how the program worked. For the first three days he would be monitored day and night and could have no contact with anyone outside of the program. After that, he would gain privileges through good behavior, or lose privileges through bad behavior, up to what was called Level III, which included the privileges of computer use, cell phone use, trips to the Loaf 'N Jug convenience store on the far side of the parking lot, unsupervised shaving, wearing shoes with laces, and having visitors. Days would begin at 6:30 with physical therapy and end at 11:00 with lights-out. There would be group sessions with the other twenty-two people in the program on dealing with anger, setting goals, and, most essential of all, talking about what had happened, over and over. Finally, Nic would be expected to keep a journal—and out of profound need, or just the desire to again wear shoes with laces, he begins doing that right away.

He writes about his anger:

I feel myself slowly losing my cool. I try so hard to be polite to everyone but I don't know how much longer I can do it. I am trying to let this anger out bit by bit but it's like holding up a dam with my mind, letting bit by bit out to keep it from going over the edge or breaking all together. Have I gone past that point where there is a safe way to get all this out without losing control? I am beginning to feel not. I feel it's gonna happen soon. It's just a matter of who says the wrong thing at the right time.

He writes about a mission:

We were supposed to hit the house around 0300 hours. Our trucks dropped us off about 3 blocks from the target house and they proceeded to set up an outer cordon . . . I told the team to stay tight we are gonna move fast. I went straight to the door and hit the door with my boot right on the sweet spot. The door flew open without much noise. My team moved into the house. Not much furniture. Just rugs, a cabinet or two, a kitchen and one bedroom on the first floor. We stacked on the door. The other team started up the stairs to the second floor. My SAW gunner kicked the cheap wooden door half cracking the wood and me and one other soldier moved inside. The door flying open woke the man, his infant and wife all sleeping in the bed. His wife started screaming. I shoved my barrel in the man's mouth and turned on my SureFire. His hands shot straight up. I had the other soldier get the wife and baby out of the room. I grabbed the man by the throat and dragged him into the courtyard making sure his head met every wall or doorway. We then zipcuffed him and tied a blindfold on him. He was wearing nothing but boxers and a t-shirt. We then threw him in the back of a humvee head first, not a fun way to land when your hand-cuffed behind your back.

He writes about a nightmare:

The anti-nightmare meds are not working. I was on a patrol last night and we entered a school, same as one from our deployment, but as we were clearing the school I went into an all girls class and in real life they just screamed but in my dream they screamed and I opened fire killing the whole class. What that is about I do not know. I am angry I have these dreams, I am angry they don't stop. I miss my pleasant dreams of my past.

He writes about the night Cajimat burned to death:

Then I saw the fifth soldier who wasn't pulled out. I was so preoccu-pied with my close call earlier I hadn't put 2 and 2 together when the call came over the radio, "4 casualties medevac'd." What was left of his skeleton was hanging out of the driver side door, his helmet a different color possibly fused to his skull and his IBA and plates which made up his torso, or what was left of it. That image still haunts me, it changed me. I don't know how many others saw that as we turned our trucks around but all I wanted was death and violence from then on. To me this is where I lost my old self.

He writes about another nightmare, or starts to, but doesn't finish because it is day sixteen now, and he has made it past Level I, past Level II, and arrived at Level III. He can wear shoes with laces. He can shave unsupervised, and go to the Loaf 'N Jug. He'll finish writing later when he's alone again, but soon he'll be getting his first visitor, Sascha.
What he has written so far:

What the fuck is going on in my mind. Last night I was sitting in bed and looked across the room to a chair in my room and there was a young girl covered in blood. What happened after that I don't remember. I was told a full scale panic attack. This is not the first time I have seen dead bodies. For awhile I used to find dead Iraqis floating in my bathtub. Why they were in the bathtub I will never know.

I FEEL SO FUCKING VIOLENT RIGHT NOW.

It was an eight-hour drive from Fort Riley to Pueblo, and for a pregnant woman in a compact car Topeka would have been easier. But Sascha made the drive without hesitation. She needed to see if this program she knew nothing about was helping. In Kansas, he'd been taking forty-three pills a day for pain, for anxiety, for depression, for nightmares—were there fewer pills now? Was he still having flashbacks? Thrashing around in his sleep? Sleepwalking into closets, looking for his rifle? Could he now start telling her what had happened during the war? And could she tell him about what was happening to her? She'd had a dream the other night that was the worst dream she'd ever had. She'd given birth, and for some reason she had taken the baby and put it in a pressure cooker, and then she had woken up from the dream, terrified and alone. Could she tell him that soldiers aren't the only people who have nightmares? Was he ready to hear that?

She gets to Pueblo, checks into a hotel, and waits for visiting hours to begin. Nic, meanwhile, is being given his medications. Antidepressants. Mood stabilizers. Pill, water, swallow, pill, water, swallow, all under the observation of a nurse who after the last pill checks Nic's mouth to make sure he swallowed them all. The pills are kept in a locked room behind the main desk along with cigarettes, which are doled out on breaks. When Nic is done, he is replaced by another soldier, and then another, twenty-three PTSD cases in all, including one who was blinded in an explosion and is being guided by a dog. So many soldiers with psychological injuries envy soldiers with physical injuries because those soldiers can see evidence that something is really wrong with them, but what to make of this poor eyeless soldier who doesn't even get that benefit? The soldiers are especially tender with him. So is a nurse who walks over to him, not with pills, but with some donated items. "You hit the jackpot," she says, placing them in his hands. There is a tube of shaving cream.

There is a small bottle of body wash and a small bottle of shampoo. He runs his fingers over the labels.

"Suave," she says.

"Fantastic," the soldier says, smiling like he's the luckiest blind man in the world.

"Smoke break," one of the other soldiers hollers now. "Smoke break."

"Level III smoke break," a nurse calls out, checking the time. The smokers with Level III privileges are led out by an escort who has a key to unlock the door, and soon after they return, all of the soldiers go into a conference room for a session that their daily schedule lists as CPT Group.

It's a therapy session scheduled to last an hour, and the model for it, much like Topeka's, is to get the soldiers to think about what happened to them by reading from their journals and talking with one another until they are no longer avoiding the subject. Of all the treatment protocols being used for PTSD, this form, called Cognitive Processing Therapy, is regarded as one of the more effective, but that doesn't mean the hour will be easy. Doors have been punched after these sessions, furniture has been tossed, and walls have needed to be patched because at one time or another every one of the soldiers in this place has felt fucking violent.

"All right. Everybody pay attention, and don't talk when others are talking," says the staff member leading the session, seated at the head of a long table. He thinks for a moment. "Also, don't fart," he pleads, and with that out of the way, the first soldier starts reading.

He is a soldier who spent his war looking for hidden roadside bombs. "This is just something that's been on my mind for quite a while," he says. "It's entitled Bombs Bombs Everywhere." He sits at the head of the table with his journal, reading slowly, and if this were happening anywhere else guys would be laughing at him, or throwing beer bottles, or doing whatever it would take to get him to be quiet, cut it out, shut the fuck up, but they're all here, in this place, in this room, and when his voice cracks as he says, "I still see the bombs, I see bombs all the time," a few of them duck their heads because of what they're seeing, too. "Make it stop," he reads. "Make the bombs go away. I don't want to see them anymore. How do I become normal? How can I stop seeing bombs?"

He looks up from his journal and sees who is listening to him. Heads hang. One guy is in sunglasses. Feet are tapping. Legs are twitching. Another guy presses his hands between his knees and then stands up from the table, too nervous to sit. Nic is standing, too, at the far end, and he asks the guy who has been reading, "What kind of vehicle were you driving?"

"I was the Husky guy."

"The Husky's the big one?" Nic asks.

"It's the vehicle that goes in front of the convoy."

"You were in Iraq, right?" another guy asks.

"Yes."

"Were you hit?"

"Yeah."

"It's hard being the first one," someone else says, another Husky driver, an Afghanistan guy, "because, I mean, you have the whole convoy coming behind you, and if someone behind you gets hit, you feel bad because you're supposed to be the one to find it."

"Yeah."

"Let's talk about habituation," the session leader says. "Think about when you guys go see a scary movie. The first time you see a scary movie, at least for me, it sucks. I get home, and I have nightmares, and I'm frustrated, and I don't sleep well, and just whatever because I'm a wuss at scary movies. If I go see the same scary movie the next day, and I go see it a third day, the third day, it's still a little bit scary, but it's not getting to me as bad. The fourth and fifth day is when I'm starting to sit there and I'm actually starting to get a little bit bored. The tenth time I see that scary movie, I'm like, okay, cue Freddy Krueger, here's the cheerleader who gets her neck cut off, here's the blood, and now the chain saw, and I'm getting bored. It's the same principle with explosions for you guys. If you guys can go to a place and have the experience repeatedly and stay with it until it starts to dissipate, that's when the explosion starts to be less and less impactful. It's called habituation. To habituate. Make sense?"

And it does make sense until the next soldier starts reading what he has written. "Here goes," he begins. "I personally never shot a round into somebody but goddamn if I didn't see my fair share of deaths, charred bodies, and dismembered—" He pauses for a moment, and when he resumes he describes the thing he is trying to habituate, a day in which he discovered a pile of skulls. He had no idea what to do, he says. He didn't know who they were. Insurgents? Victims? Men? Women? He decided that taking them back to the base was the right thing, so he picked them up, skull by skull, loaded them into his vehicle, began driving, and then, near the base, pulled over. "What the fuck was I doing?" he reads. "I kicked them off. I booted the skulls into the ditch next to the road, and drove through the gate thinking, 'Fucking ragheads.'"

"That story right there," Nic says. "Would you tell your wife that story?"

"The first time I ever told my wife about an Iraq incident was two weeks ago," he says.

"How'd she take it?" Nic asks.

"She started crying," he says. "She said, 'I'm so sorry.' She didn't know."

"I think the fact that she took it like that? That shows right there how much she cares about you," Nic says.

"If you told her that story and she started crying, be grateful," someone else says. "I told my wife some of my stories about my experiences, and her response to me was 'You knew what you were getting into when you signed on the dotted line and I don't feel sorry for you.' And you know what? That fucking killed me. She didn't give a shit about me. When she said that to me, I turned to the bottle, and I never shared another fucking word with her."

He is crying. Three guys are standing up now, moving around, unable to sit still.

"Anything else for this gentleman?" the session leader asks, and when there isn't anything else, a third soldier takes his place at the head of the table and begins reading a story about a day his unit came upon a burlap bag and opened it to see what was inside. "It was an Iraqi chopped up into pieces," the soldier reads. "So they called me over to police it up. I said, cool. Fuck it. I'm a medic. Oh well. I did it. Don't get me wrong. It's not like I picked up a fucking Dumpster full of dead bodies. It was kind of fascinating to me, really interesting seeing a dead human, especially in pieces. To see the lifeless eyes, and the end of life, was amazing. Even with all the war wounds I've seen in my lifetime," he says, and goes on about being a medic, and seeing bodies chewed on by dogs, and "the smell, the fucking smell," and what he did one day to an Iraqi as a result of all that. "There were times as I would render aid to soldiers, the platoon leader said, 'What about the Iraqis?' I said, 'Sure,' as I took my time to get to them, and it was a long time. As a medic I should take care of people, but I was pissed. So I would just take my time. To make it short, I gave this one guy a needle decompression for the hell of it. I know it hurt. But fuck it. As far as I knew, he had helped emplace a fucking IED. Did I care? No. Do I care now? No. Was that right? Fuck it."

Silence.

Everyone's twitching now.

"I know what you mean," another soldier finally says. "We never had any remorse for anybody we saw dead. Because fuck it."

"I guess I'm trying to learn compassion again," the medic says.

"We used to occupy an Iraqi police station," Nic says, "and every once in a while, the Iraqi police would bring in dead bodies, a couple of dead bodies, they'd throw 'em in the back of a truck, bring 'em in, shit like that, and at the time, this was the beginning of my deployment, we'd all run down there and go take pictures. You know? And one guy his head was chopped off, his body was all bloated and shit because it had been sitting in raw sewage, you know? And now I can't get those images out of my mind. At the time, though, it was: Yeah, this is so cool. This is so cool. I mean, what were we thinking? Why did we even want to go look at that shit? You know?"

"Yeah, I just remember this one time, I don't talk about it, I got a picture of it," another soldier says, describing a day he found a skeleton, mostly bone, still some skin, and he picked up a piece of it. "The femur or something like that. I got pictures of me looking like I'm taking a bite out of it," he says. "What was I thinking?"

"Exactly," Nic says. "I had a hard drive that I destroyed. Pictures and stuff like that, next to dead bodies, shit like that. Horrible, horrible stuff. Horrible stuff. Us hanging out with dead bodies. At the time, I mean we were rockin' and rollin', we were mean mean killing machines. Now I look back and I'm like, God, what were we doing? What were we thinking?"

Everyone is talking now except for one sweet-faced soldier who looks to be the youngest of all and is suddenly shaking. His eyes flutter and roll back in his head, and he blinks them back into place. He holds up his right hand, watches it tremble, and grabs it with his left hand until whatever is happening passes through him. He takes a sip of soda. He is steady again. But not for long, because as the medic starts talking about the next thing that happened to him, he tears up, grabs some tissues, and covers his face.

"And it really hit me when I saw my first baby come in burned" is what the medic is saying. He is no longer reading, just talking, surely a step toward habituation. "Dipped in boiling water and skin sloughing off," he says. "And you know what? I got to the point where I started carrying extra fucking medical supplies. I got to the point where I started feeling kind of sorry for them. I started feeling sorry that we're sitting there fucking beating these people and it's just like that fucking baby. We're just using them, like they're fucking nothing. Like they're not even human. And you get to a point . . ."

And now he is the one shaking and sobbing in an otherwise silent room until one of the other soldiers comes to his rescue.

"I thank you for fucking being there," the soldier says, putting his arm around him. "Secondly, I would like to applaud you for your usage of fuck."

Laughter. Tears. Smoke break.

She goes to the east entrance by the flagpole and statue of Mary, takes the elevator to the sixth floor, dials "0," waits for the door to be unlocked, is escorted in. There's Nic, by the nursing station.

"Hi, sweetie," he says.

He walks over and kisses her. They'd had only a few awkward moments last night, before visiting hours ended.

"How'd you sleep?" he asks her. "Was the baby kicking?"

She slept terribly is the answer, though she doesn't tell him that. Nic hasn't slept well, either. She can tell. The circles under his eyes look like bruises. He had been up writing, trying to make sense of the hallucination he'd had about the girl in the chair. "Dark hair with light strips of red flowing down to her shoulders," he had written. "She couldn't be more than 7 or 8. She was wearing a flower dress ripped and soaked in blood. Her eyes seemed to stare right through my soul . . ."

It went on for three pages, and as he walks down the hall with Sascha, he has his journal with him, wondering whether to show it to her and wondering whether she'll be the wife who says "I'm so sorry."

They duck into a visitation room stocked with some worn books and board games and sit at a table. They begin a game of Scrabble, and at some point Nic decides. He'll tell her. If she really wants to know what the war was like, he'll tell her what the war was like. He slides the journal to her, opened not to the story about the bloody girl but to what he wrote next, about a search for a high-value target.

"Baby," it's titled.

"I loved owning the night," it begins.

She starts to read, and as she does, he looks down at the table and starts rearranging some of the Scrabble pieces.

"I don't remember what time of the year it was but it had to be cold outside," he has written.

As we near the house the only light that is on is the one in the courtyard so we need to move quick into this house for this HVT. The mission, secure all military aged males to be able to identify a certain HVT. The first team kicks the gate clean open. I lead the second team straight through the courtyard to the front door. Using my momentum I kick the stained glass door open sending broken glass into the room and the door against the wall. As we move through the first room glass cracking under our boots we identify only women sleeping in there so we clear the kitchen and bathroom and move upstairs. Just as I come around the staircase a man is running down. I slam him against the wall forcing my rifle into his neck. Just as he starts to scream I push harder crushing his windpipe and muffling the high-pitched yelp. I yell to one of the soldiers downstairs "I got one." He replies "Send him down." I grab the terrified man's arm pulling him down off balance over my left foot sending him tumbling down the stairs. We keep moving up. There are three rooms upstairs. One was already empty, another had a man with his wife and child waiting at their bedroom door and there was another door closed. I told one soldier to take them downstairs as me and my buddy prepared to breach this last door. I had my rifle drawn while my buddy kicked it open, and there sitting on the side of the bed was an older couple just waiting like they have been through this before. I sent the woman downstairs and just stared at the man as he stared back at me, waiting for me to do something. After a few seconds I lost my temper, grabbed him by the throat and walked him out toward the stairs. I don't know if he understood me when I told him you can either walk down or fly down but after about 2 seconds he started to move.

Sascha finishes reading that and turns the page, but there's no more to the story. She doesn't say anything. She just looks at Nic as he continues to rearrange the Scrabble pieces. He lines up five tiles in a row. He takes five more tiles and lines them up in another row. He takes the tile holders and lines them up in between.

He keeps at it with more tiles and holders, and now Sascha can see a grid. What Nic is seeing, though, is Humvees and houses, and now he says that that house right there—he points to one of the tile holders—is where he threw the man down the stairs. He can see it clearly, as clear as he saw the bloody girl, and apparently he can hear it, too, because what he says next to Sascha is the part of the story he has yet to write. That there was a baby crying. That there was a woman screaming. That he got to the bottom of the stairs and saw the screaming woman holding the crying baby and that the baby was wrapped in a blanket and the blanket was covered in shards of stained glass. And it took him a moment, but then he got it, that the baby had been sleeping by the door he had kicked open using his two hundred pounds of momentum, and when he ran in, he had just missed stepping on it, squashing it, crushing it, killing it.

His scary movie, then. Here's the soldier kicking in the door, and cue the sleeping baby, and here's the squish, and here's the blood, and now the screams, and even though he has seen it three times, ten times, many more than ten times, he has yet to get even remotely bored. As for what actually happened, he sees that movie, too, the man he threw down the stairs, the old man he had by the throat, the screaming woman, the crying baby, the blanket covered in glass shards, the soldiers filing out, and then the lieutenant saying to them once they're outside, "This is the wrong fucking house."

"The wrong fucking house," Nic says to Sascha now. "One of the things I want to remember is how many times we hit the wrong house," and then he waits for her to say it. "I don't feel sorry for you."

"But you did get the right house sometimes" is what she says.

And is this how his habituation begins? Right then? With those forgiving words?

"So how has this taken a toll on your marriage?" a counselor asks Nic a few hours later as Sascha sits next to him.

"I'm afraid to tell her stuff," Nic says, wanting to tell her everything, breaking down. "I don't want to tell her about the dreams I have. I don't want to tell her about the nightmares I have. I don't want her to know that her husband, the person she married, has nightmares about killing people. It just makes me feel like a monster."

"The nightmares? Or that she'll look at you like you're not understood?" the counselor asks.

"That she'll hate me," Nic says. "What kind of person has dreams like that?"

"I don't hate you," Sascha says.

"So do you feel like a monster?" the counselor asks.

"I feel like a monster," Nic says, turning to Sascha.

"It's not your fault," the counselor says.

"I know it's not my fault," Nic says, and then when no one says anything, not the counselor or Sascha, he says, crying harder now, "Oh fuck."

Two weeks later, released from Pueblo, Nic gets on a plane and makes one last entry in his journal:

> Taking off during a sunrise in bad turbulence is one of the most beautiful things in the world, the fear that something could go wrong like the wings fly off or the pilot decides to up and quit and jump out compared to the beauty of the sun cresting over the edge of the planet gradually turning the edge of the sky from dark orange to a fading black as night retreats as the chase goes on, and there's that fucking turbulence, like an 8 year old driver at the wheel of a 68 Ford Bronco driving through Walmart, fuck, keep the main sails steady! I'm surprised I can keep my pen straight.

And then he is home with Sascha, who knows now about one day of the war.

Four hundred more to go.

5

At 6:35 in the morning every house on the street is still dark, including the little house with the swinging kitchen door hanging cockeyed on its hinges. Somewhere inside, Adam should be tiptoeing around by now, slipping into a shirt and tie while trying not to wake Saskia, but that's never the way it works out. Every night he sets his alarm for 6:30, hoping to get to work on time, but once again in the middle of the night Jax was howling, and then Zoe wet her bed yet again, and now Saskia is mentioning very loudly that the goddamned alarm has been ringing for five minutes. He gets up, stumbles into the shower, and falls asleep under the spray. He throws on an old shirt and the jeans he was wearing last night when he was out fishing, with traces of fish guts and blood smears on the legs, and by the time he walks out the front door, the sun is coming up. Late again.

Oh well.

He's got his antidepressants in one hand and a sack lunch with a Walmart enchilada and a Mountain Dew in the other. He swallows his pills as he turns onto the highway and passes by Geary Estates. He exits at Fort Riley, clears security, parks outside of an old limestone building, smokes a last cigarette as if he's about to be blindfolded and executed, and heads toward a work cubicle that is just outside the sight lines of his boss, who is hopeful about her new employee: "I hear him on the phone. He sounds very confident. He's really picking up fast." She adds, "If you don't have compassion for people, you probably won't make it in a call center."

That's what this place is—a call-in center for army retirees who need

General Peter Chiarelli, U.S. Army vice chief of staff

help figuring out their benefits, which strikes Adam as comical because if he had gotten better benefits for himself he wouldn't need to be working here. To keep up with bills, he had found a job at the Fort Riley range, but maybe the daily explosions weren't the best thing for someone with war-related PTSD. So here he is at the call center, where sometimes he thinks he should call himself, explain his problems, and see if he can get some answers.

Instead, the first thing he does is what he does every day: turn on his computer, sign on to a website called militaryhire.com, and look for another job. He wants to be a forester. He wants to be a park ranger. He wants to work at a golf course if it will pay enough. He wants to be outside. The ringing in his right ear is particularly loud today, but not loud enough to drown out the woman two cubicles away who is driving him absolutely batty. "Right . . . right . . . right . . . right," she is saying into her headset, like a metronome, like a pile driver, like a car alarm, and Adam fantasizes about picking up his pencil and stabbing her in the neck. Here comes the boss, walking around, and he quickly signs on to e-mail, where the message he happens to open up as the boss walks by is from the guy in the next cubicle. "Gun control isn't about guns, it's about control," it says in big letters. Totally inappropriate. But the boss doesn't notice, and the guy in the cubicle is laughing, and the woman two cubicles away is smiling, and the realization that everyone seems so happy here makes it even worse for Adam because he feels like he is dying. He is an ex-soldier who wishes he still were a soldier, and instead he is sitting in a cubicle and putting on a rubber fingertip so he can more efficiently sort through the papers of someone who is bitching that his benefits don't match up with his annual salary of $137,410.

Galling. All of it. And most galling of all? That would be the attitude of the guy down the hall who told Adam about this job.

His name is Calvin McCloy, and back in the war, during Adam's second deployment, he and Adam were in the same unit together. Poor Calvin, who one day was up in a hatch of a Bradley Fighting Vehicle when a roadside bomb exploded and the Bradley caught on fire. He was thirty-six years old and a platoon sergeant, like Doster had been. He was burned over 40 percent of his body. His back was burned. His backside, too. His stomach. His wrists. Under his arms. His uniform was burnt off, all of it except for part of his T-shirt and boots. He spent four months in a hospital burn unit undergoing skin grafts and another year in compression clothing. He has PTSD and TBI and a limited range of motion and wears hearing aids in both ears. His brain was bruised and he passes out sometimes, without warning, just slumps and goes down, and a few times has awakened on the ground with his head busted wide open. He went through a guilt phase. He went through a pissed-off phase. He went through a why-me phase. He went through a pills phase, and two years of intensive therapy. "There comes a point when you have to make a decision," he has told Adam of the point he finally came to, and so one day he made a decision. "It isn't about what I want to do. It's about what I have to do. I don't want to be sitting behind a damn desk. If I had my say, I'd be a sergeant major, training soldiers. But I can't do that. I'm not going to be able to change the way I think. I'm not going to be able to change my memory. I'm not going to make the brain injury go away. It's not going to happen. So I have to find ways to live with the injuries I have." So that was his decision, to be sitting gratefully behind a damn desk, and every night he not only sets his alarm, he lays out his clothing in a certain way in order not to forget anything when he wakes up in a daze the next morning. He hangs his pants and shirt on the bathroom door. He puts his socks and T-shirt on the nightstand. He puts his shoes at the foot of the nightstand and his rolled-up belt in one of his shoes. He puts his cell phone, wallet, and car keys by the microwave. It's a system for getting by that in his previous life he might have found humiliating but not in this life because here he is, at work, on time, in a shirt and tie and pants free of fish blood, happy to have a job that depends on repetition, which is what he can handle, and happy to have become a man who never gets angry anymore, not even on his birthday when his coworkers decorate his cubicle with a banner while he's at lunch, and Adam wants to put a frozen can of shaving cream in a desk drawer where it will explode, and the coworkers say that's not such a good idea, and Adam instead takes several months' worth of hole punches he's been saving, thousands and thousands of little dots, and dumps them like confetti onto Calvin's desk, his chair, his keyboard, everywhere. "In my drawers, too?" Calvin asks incredulously when he returns, which will be the closest he comes to losing his temper as he starts to clean up.

Why, Adam wonders, can't he be more like Calvin? Why can't he get better? "You gotta face reality," Calvin has told him, and is that all it takes? Making a decision? He sits at his desk. The hours go by. The days go by. The overhead fluorescent lights hum. The copy machine grinds. The water cooler bubbles. The phone lines blink with waiting callers. "Three calls in the queue," the boss announces over the intercom to a roomful of well-dressed workers wearing rubber fingertips. "Oh my God," Adam sighs. He switches his computer screen from his work e-mail to a news site. "Army Releases Report on Suicide Prevention" is one of the headlines. "Can the Army's New Suicide Prevention Plan Really Work?" is another.

He ignores them.

"Montana Bear Attack Survivor Played Dead" is another, and that's the one he reads until he makes a decision to answer his ringing phone.

In Washington, D.C., meanwhile, in conjunction with the release of the suicide report, the army is holding a press conference.

"General, you've been looking at this for a long time now. You've overseen this report. The army today, your bottom-line assessment: How good a job is the service doing at preventing suicides?" a reporter asks. "Are they doing a better job today than they did fifteen months ago when you started this task force?"

"Well, I happen to believe we are," says Peter Chiarelli, the army's vice chief of staff, who has come armed with charts and statistics about the 242 soldiers who killed themselves the previous year.

"Sir, how did the army get so far behind the curve on all of this?" another reporter asks.

"What in simple language does the army need to do?" another asks.

"So everybody understands this is a priority now?" another asks.

"That's exactly right," Chiarelli replies, and of all the answers he gives, this is the most wishful by far.

The fact is that suicide prevention, and the wider issue of mental health, has never been the most urgent of priorities in the army, and if there's any single person who knows this, it is Chiarelli. Before becoming the vice chief of staff, he was in charge of all the ground forces in Iraq during a time when fighting was nearing its worst. That was the priority, the fighting, and if there was a medical priority, it was getting injured soldiers back into the fight. Only after he came home and was promoted to vice chief of staff did he begin paying close attention to mental health issues when he was assigned to look into the rising suicide numbers. He had other assignments, too. Force modernization. Dealing with the budget. He understood that mental health was a back-burner issue. But soon he was spending half of his time on it as he realized how strained and ineffective the system had become.

Soldiers were breaking apart but were reluctant to ask for help because of the stigma, and in some cases the consequences, of doing so. For those who did ask, there was a shortage of therapists and an over-reliance on medication that led to secondary issues of addiction. As the number of military suicides for the first time rose above the rate for civilians, Chiarelli would say to anyone who would listen, "I've got to try to change the *culture*," and to that end he began traveling to army posts around the country, including, one summer day, Fort Riley for the dedication of the WTB.

There, after the ribbon cutting, where the guests included Adam, who had never seen a four-star general before, Chiarelli was asked by an interviewer about the significance of the day. "I think a facility such as the one behind me shows our total commitment to our wounded warriors and our willingness to do everything we possibly can," he said, and his earnestness made an overly rosy answer seem entirely believable, at least momentarily.

That earnestness is what always has separated Chiarelli from the other generals who have been running these wars. The pleading in his voice as he practically begs soldiers about to deploy to "please, please, *please*" ask him any questions they might have, the emotion he makes no attempt to hide as he tells their commanders, "If you do anything, help me eliminate the stigma," the furrow lines in his forehead, the way his eyes droop a little at the edges—all of it suggests someone with wounds under his skin. And now there is the way he is throwing himself at this impossible assignment.

His wife, Beth, says this isn't so, that there are no wounds to speak of. Yes, she mentions to people at a dinner party one night, he weirdly leaves cabinets open all the time now, and drawers, and he never did either before going to Iraq, but that's probably because he's gotten used to being followed around by an aide. And yes, he's become a more impatient driver since coming home, even irritated at times, but who doesn't get impatient in Washington traffic?

"What you see is what you get. He's really not that complicated," she says. She taps her forehead. "Like a slab of meat," she says, laughing.

And maybe he is that and that's all there is to it. But there is also the story of his first deployment to Iraq, when he was a division commander who in the course of a year lost 169 soldiers. One by one, he wrote their names and hometowns on index cards that he carried in his pocket until there were too many to fit. He attended all of the memorial services and wrote 169 condolence letters in 365 days. But the worst part may have come later, at home, when it was time to erect a memorial, and he was approached by some of his junior officers who wanted 168 names on the memorial, not 169.

"The greatest regret of my military career was as Commanding General of the 1st Cavalry Division in Iraq in 2004–05," he later wrote of the decision he made. "I lost 169 soldiers during that year-long deployment. However, the monument we erected at Fort Hood, Texas, in memoriam lists 168 names. I approved the request of others not to include the name of the one soldier who committed suicide. I deeply regret my decision."

By the time he wrote that, he had become the vice chief of staff. When he had gone back to Iraq a second time, he had hoped to be put in charge of the entire war—ground, air, the overall strategy—but that wasn't how it worked out. Now, as Vice, he had his war at last. "This is it," Beth says. "This is his contribution." His war would be the after-war, and one of his first acts as its commander was to convene a monthly meeting of a type never before held at the Pentagon, with roots in his regret.

"Joe, I hope you've had coffee," he says now, beginning one of them, talking one afternoon by video linkup with a general in Korea, where it is 4:00 a.m. "Okay. You're on."

"Sir, we have a really unfortunate one here," the general, Joseph Fil, replies. "I'll let Mike Tucker talk us through the details."

"Sir, this is Mike Tucker. Can you hear me?"

"I can, Mike," Chiarelli says.

"Okay," Tucker says. "Sir, he was actually a married soldier, living off post with a professional girl who worked down in the ville. This is a case, sir, where the chain of command thought they knew that he was involved in this type of behavior and counseled him, but they had nothing definitive. So when they first heard of it, they counseled him on it, and yet he continued to pursue this. Another NCO at another unit actually engaged him and told him this was not the right thing to do, you have a wife and a child back in Texas, you shouldn't be doing this type of activity, and on the first of March, when he actually committed the offense, he had, according to her, had sexually assaulted her, and he felt as though she had cheated on him because that was obviously her business, and he told her, quote, unquote, 'You will watch me die.' And so he strung himself up on a door hinge, standing on a table, kicked the table out from under his legs, and as much as she tried to put the table back under his legs, he kept kicking her until he died. A very unfortunate incident, sir, for this young soldier."

"Okay, Mike," Chiarelli says when Mike has finished, and after a brief discussion about what lessons can be learned from such a soldier, with twenty-eight more suicides to get through in two hours, he moves on to a general in Iraq who will tell him about suicide number two.

"Ladies and gentlemen, the Vice."

Another meeting, another month, another twenty-four suicides to review. Chiarelli walks into a conference room where those invited to the meeting rise to their feet as he looks embarrassed and tells them to sit. He takes his own seat at the head of a long conference table with a nice military shine. The curtains are drawn. The SECRET sign is lit. The video screens are linked to army posts around the world, where other officers, surrounded by their own staffs, sit at their own tables, waiting to be called on to talk about a particular suicide that happened under their watch.

The setting for this meeting is the Gardner Room, a Pentagon conference room that was named in honor of a Vietnam War soldier named James Gardner, who died on his twenty-third birthday and was posthumously awarded the Medal of Honor. According to the award citation:

> 1st Lt. Gardner charged through a withering hail of fire across an open rice paddy. On reaching the first bunker he destroyed it with a grenade and without hesitation dashed to the second bunker and eliminated it by tossing a grenade inside. Then, crawling swiftly along the dike of a rice paddy, he reached the third bunker. Before he could arm a grenade, the enemy gunner leaped forth, firing at him. 1st Lt. Gardner instantly returned the fire and killed the enemy gunner at a distance of 6 feet. Following the seizure of the main enemy position, he reorganized the platoon to continue the attack. Advancing to the new assault position, the platoon was pinned down by an enemy machine gun emplaced in a fortified bunker. 1st Lt. Gardner immediately collected several grenades and charged the enemy position, firing his rifle as he advanced to neutralize the defenders. He dropped a grenade into the bunker and vaulted beyond. As the bunker blew up, he came under fire again. Rolling into a ditch to gain cover, he moved toward the new source of fire. Nearing the position, he leaped from the ditch and advanced with a grenade in one hand and firing his rifle with the other. He was gravely wounded just before he reached the bunker, but with a last valiant effort he staggered forward and destroyed the bunker, and its defenders with a grenade.

Left out of the citation, but cited elsewhere, were Gardner's final words. "It's the best I can do," he is supposed to have said after being shot in the chest four times, and the question for the ages, or at least those gathered in the Gardner Room forty-five years later, is why some soldiers become James Gardner and some become the soldier whose final words are "You will watch me die."

They are, by military measures, an impressive group: a few colonels here and there but mostly generals, and not just one-stars, either. Every high-backed leather seat is filled with an army success story. They are the achievers, the ones who got in and rose up and kept rising until they were one day invited by the vice chief of staff of the army to learn about some of the others who didn't rise, who if they were in this room would look at the rows of medals and see their own failures, and the rows of water glasses and see shards of opportunity to slide across their wrists. No one would prefer to be here, not when you get down to it. It is a brutal, depressing meeting. At the end, people always walk out looking stunned. But here they are anyway, ready to go, as Chiarelli starts to talk to them about what they might do.

"I think if you go back, I think you'll see that in the last fourteen or fifteen days, we've had about fifteen suicides," he says. "Now one of the things I think you can do to help your soldiers is not necessarily focus on suicide as much as you need to focus on the high-risk behavior. High-risk behavior is found once an individual enters the phase and starts to go deeper into that phase because that, in most of these cases, is the precursor for a suicide or a suicide attempt. If we were to focus our efforts there, not just when an individual says he or she is going to hurt themselves, but when they notice that they are relying on alcohol too much, that they have a prescription drug dependency, involved in risky behavior of any type, that we take the action necessary. And I'd ask you all to redouble your efforts to do that.

"And with that I'll stop, and let's head into today's cases."

"He was a nineteen-year-old male who hung himself" is the way the first case is described.

"Age twenty-five, he was a previously deployed combat veteran. The soldier just recently moved back in with his mother and subsequently jumped off a three-hundred-foot bridge."

"Age eighteen, suicide by hanging."

"He was twenty years old and committed suicide by automotive exhaust."

"He was twenty-three years old, self-inflicted gunshot wound to the head. This incident occurred in a Dumpster behind a store."

"Twenty-three, non-deployed, generally called happy, upbeat, positive, had just reenlisted on a Thursday, was on a four-day reenlistment pass and killed himself Saturday by gunshot."

"This happened sometime I think between two and four in the morning. Nobody in the house hears anything and his mother actually finds him but not until late morning."

"She committed suicide by hanging herself."

"He committed suicide by hanging himself. It was clear by the documentation he left behind it was a very deliberate effort. He documented in a personal diary and a series of letters exactly what he was doing, to include binding his legs in such a way that if he chickened out at the last minute or had second thoughts he couldn't help himself."

Again and again, Chiarelli reminds people: "We are more interested in the lessons learned from the cases and what you are doing about it than necessarily the details, although they are helpful. Okay?"

But the details keep coming, and vary so widely that it is difficult to learn much at all. Some of the soldiers had been in combat, some had never deployed. Some had been diagnosed with PTSD, some hadn't. Some had never gotten mental health treatment, but just as disturbingly, half of them had. A few things *were* clear. Soldiers with repeated deployments were more likely to commit suicide. Married soldiers were less likely. Guns and liquor were a bad combination. More time at home between deployments helped. A soldier in an explosion who talked about what he experienced before going to sleep did better than a soldier who didn't. But explanations for these things remained as elusive as patterns, and patterns remained as elusive as remedies. What *was* the cause for the high rates—not just of suicide but also of PTSD? Were the rates measurably higher than in previous wars? If so, could the cause have something to do with the military now being an all-volunteer force, and a disproportionate percentage of those volunteering coming from backgrounds that made them predisposed to trauma? Could it have nothing to do with the soldier and everything to do with the type of war now being fought?

Far from ignoring what was going on, the army was trying to make sense of it. Its biggest effort was an ongoing study of the mental health of some fifty-five thousand soldiers to develop profiles of who would become prone to suicide and who would be resilient. But the study, which was being done in partnership with the National Institute of Mental Health, was going to take five years to complete, by which time both the Iraq and Afghanistan wars would be all but finished and, at current suicide rates, another thousand soldiers would be dead.

Not that all of them could be prevented—Chiarelli knew better than that—but the idea that some of them could was why the slow pace would get to him at times. "I come from 'Take a hill by five p.m.' You are 'Take as long as you want,'" he once said in exasperation to a group of doctors and researchers who had gathered at his invitation to talk about traumatic brain injuries (causing one researcher to whisper to another, "He seems very *proactive*"). They had been discussing an autopsy done on a Marine who had killed himself after two combat tours. The autopsy had shown evidence of a degenerative brain disease that has been associated with memory loss, confusion, depression, paranoia, and problems with impulse control, and has been seen in autopsies of athletes such as boxers and football players who have endured constant head trauma. Could this be why people who had been in repeated explosions in combat were killing themselves? Not because of PTSD, but because of a disease that was overtaking their brain and destroying their self-control? One of the scientists mentioned an effort under way to develop a test for biomarkers that could indicate who would be susceptible to the disease. Excited, Chiarelli had asked how long it would take. Those people could be kept out of combat, put in support roles. Two years was the answer, minimum. There would have to be more autopsies. Protocols would have to be developed. Independent review boards would have to scrub the findings. The findings would have to be published in a scholarly journal. "Good science takes time," Chiarelli was told, and suddenly he looked like a man driving in Washington traffic.

Now, as the suicide meeting continues, he says, "This, as I've said so often, is a very imperfect science, as it stands right now. We just don't know why people do the things that they do." But that doesn't mean they can't do some things while waiting for bigger explanations, he goes on, and mentions another possible suicidal indicator, only recently discovered, that people who enter the army in their late twenties are three times more likely to kill themselves than those who enter in their early twenties or late teens. "It's just counterintuitive to a lot of folks," he says, "unless you start to unpack it and you say, okay why does a young man or woman decide to join the army at twenty-eight or twenty-nine years old? They're either a tremendous patriot, or they've lost their job, have a couple of kids, lost their medical care, and are coming in as kind of an opportunity to get their life straight again. They come in with all these stressors, and we say, hey guess what, buddy? You're going downrange in six months."

Around the table and on the video screens, the generals are nodding. Now it makes sense, and as a result they will instruct their brigade commanders, who will instruct their battalion commanders, who will instruct their company commanders, who will instruct their platoon leaders, who will instruct their squad leaders and team leaders, to pay extra attention to their twenty-eight- and twenty-nine-year-olds who are new to the army.

A lesson learned, then, and as the meeting goes from its first hour into its second, Chiarelli keeps asking for more.

"Sir, lessons learned," one general says after telling of a soldier who had covered himself with a blanket and shot himself with his rifle. "Better shakedown procedures are needed for soldiers coming off of a range detail. He had been on a range cleanup detail the day before he committed suicide. An incomplete check for ammo was conducted for soldiers on the detail, and it wasn't done thoroughly enough. After the suicide, the CID conducted an inspection and found significant contraband to include some loose ammunition. So we gotta school our younger officers on procedures for doing that."

Sometimes Chiarelli listens, shakes his head, and says, "We have got to do better."

"Sir, our main lesson learned is that though we have a variety of useful tools—the global assessment tool and our unit risk inventory—we really don't have one that flat-out lets a drill sergeant or a squad leader see that the soldier flat-out has issues," another general says after describing a soldier who had placed plastic over his head and run tubes from a helium tank under the plastic. "The two things that came out during the investigation, one that may or may not have been related to it, he broke up with a girlfriend, but it was two years ago. The other was, remarkably, his father had committed suicide about three years ago in a similar fashion. That came to light when the mother spoke with our investigative officer and was unknown to the chain of command."

Sometimes Chiarelli says, "Yeah, well, this is a sad case."

"A couple of internal lessons learned, which are very important," another general says of a soldier whose diagnoses included PTSD and depression and who overdosed on his twelve medications. "He was assigned a battle buddy who lived in the barracks with him. But of note, his battle buddy was also listed as a high-risk soldier, and that policy has now changed. That when we assign a battle buddy, it needs to be a soldier that's a low-risk soldier."

Sometimes, Chiarelli says, "I don't know what to say."

"Sir, at this time, I've got one good news story that might be worth sharing," a general says.

"Okay," he says. "Go ahead."

"Sir, there's a staff sergeant who recently redeployed, he was having behavioral health problems when he came back. We spotted that in the behavioral health assessment, got him into treatment. His behavioral health specialist, a psychologist, a psychiatrist rather, believed that he was fit to go on leave and signed off on his ability to take leave. Shortly after his departure on leave, a cousin who was also in the military came to us and told us he was very worried about this individual, that he was exhibiting paranoid behavior and acting irrationally. That allowed us to get hold of the soldier's family. It allowed law enforcement to ping his cell phone. Found out in talking to him that he was portraying himself as being in one place when in fact he was in another, he was headed to near Camp Pendleton. In coordination with the Marines, we were able to gain control of him at Pendleton through the chain of command down there. Got him into behavioral health down there. Got an additional assessment, brought him back here, he's back in treatment. He was armed at the time and clearly having problems with his schizophrenia, and we feel like the system worked very well there, the kinds of things we expect people to do. Sir, that completes my presentation pending any questions or comments from you."

Sometimes, Chiarelli looks like he's on the verge of saying, "It's the best I can do."

"That was very uplifting," he says.

Sometimes Chiarelli leaves the Pentagon and drives to Walter Reed Army Medical Center to remind himself what all of this is about.

"So how'd it happen?" he says, walking into a room and sitting down so that he is at eye level.

The soldier starts to answer. He was walking down a trail. There was an explosion. He lost his right arm. He lost most of his left arm. He lost his right leg. He lost his left leg. He . . .

"Oh my goodness," the soldier says. "I forgot my train of thought."

"That's okay," Chiarelli says, reaching over to touch what remains of him.

He goes back to the Pentagon, back to Gardner, back to another suicide meeting, where some months are better than others.

"I have never seen a downturn in the numbers quite like I'm seeing now," he announces one month, smiling. "We could be seeing that all our efforts are starting to pay off in lower numbers."

But then it is another month, a January in fact, the start of another year, and the preliminary numbers for the previous year are in: an increase of fifty-eight over the year before.

"That is, I think it's fair to say, a huge increase, an increase we are trying to understand," he says.

He tells everyone not to get discouraged. He says that without their efforts, the numbers would have been far worse. Not that there's a way to tell, but he's sure of it. He just is. "I want to thank everyone here for their continued support and everything you're doing for our soldiers," he says. "And with that . . ."

"He's a twenty-year-old American Eskimo."

"A twenty-four-year-old Caucasian male, married, three children."

"Seventeen-year-old, single, Caucasian."

"Thirty-six-year-old Caucasian male. The soldier committed suicide by hanging in his barracks room."

"He was found on a boat in the river that runs through his town with a gunshot wound to the head and an empty bottle of vodka."

"She had asked her daughter to shoot her, but the daughter refused so she picked up the gun and shot herself."

"Her stepfather discovered her next to the railroad tracks where she had shot herself with her father's gun."

"Committed suicide by hanging himself in his mother's garage."

"Hung himself with an electrical cord secured over a door."

"Overdosed on lorazepam, which is used to treat anxiety."

"A non-swimmer, jumped from a bridge into a lake, drowned."

"He was found the next morning outside the apartment near the Dumpster with a single gunshot wound to the head. There were really no warning signs, and this is a big mystery."

"This was a shock to us all."

"His chain of command was unaware that he had communicated suicidal ideations to his father at least twenty times and had put a gun to his head five times."

"The unit leadership was totally unaware that he had been diagnosed with bipolar and socio and anxiety disorders by two different off-post providers and was on several medications, including antidepressants."

"So it really came as a big shock."

"Again, nobody expected this."

"So this was a horrific event, I think we can all agree."

They all agree.

And then they are done.

"I thank you very much," Chiarelli says, meaning it, "and I'll see you next month."

6

One day, Adam tries to fix a boat.

It's a little aluminum skiff that he had discovered in some woods, apparently abandoned and being overtaken by leaves. He found it on a hunting trip and left it alone, but when he saw it again on another hunting trip, he decided to drag it home.

He really wanted a boat.

For a brief time after the war, he'd had one, a good one. It was a sixteen-footer that he and Saskia bought the first summer after he came home. It cost $17,000, trailer included, $2,000 down, the rest easily financed for an American warrior, just sign here and thank you for your service, and when Adam and Saskia took it out on the lake, they became for those hours the people they imagined themselves to be. Adam, unbroken. Saskia afloat at last upon the life that was her promise. Zoe, being pulled behind the boat on an inner tube, soaked and laughing. Life was okay. That's how they felt on the boat. They would pull over at a little beach area and barbecue hamburgers on a cheap grill. Adam would fish, Saskia and Zoe would swim, nobody would fight.

Sometimes, after the boat was gone, repossessed seven months after they bought it, they would see it around town, being pulled behind some stranger's pickup truck.

"Hey, that's my old boat," Adam would say, lighting up as if he had spotted one of his old squad members.

"That's depressing," Saskia would say, watching it go by, no doubt on the way to the lake.

But anyway, it was gone, and now Adam is the common-law owner

Adam Schumann, Michael Emory, Saskia Schumann

of a skiff. It has no engine, but he has a trolling motor that will do the trick. The back of the boat, where he will hang the motor, feels flimsy, but he can shore that up with some plywood. The bottom has some gaps in the seams, but he can take care of that with some caulk. He drives to the hardware store and forty-four dollars later is hard at it, filling the street with the screech of his circular saw.

Hours go by. The sun is hot and he works up a sweat. He goes through half a pack of cigarettes and a six-pack of Mountain Dew. Across the street, a neighbor comes out onto his front porch.

"What are you building? The Love Boat?" he yells.

This is Dave, who owns a couple of tow trucks, and when Adam doesn't answer, he comes over to watch.

"Noah's Ark?" he asks.

He watches for a while more.

"Ugliest boat ever," he says.

Not to Adam, who is finishing up. The seams are caulked, and the caulk is drying. The motor is in place, attached to a perfectly cut piece of plywood and connected to an old boat battery Adam had in the garage. It was his father who taught him about boats and about fixing them. He'd had a skiff, too, much like this one, and just before he left, he and Adam had spent the afternoon on it. Now, twenty years later, Adam tests the motor and the little propeller spins to life. With some satisfaction, he steps back to look at what he has done.

"I believe I may have a boat," he says.

Saskia emerges from the house to look.

"You don't like it?" he asks her.

"I do like it," she says with that same smile he has been seeing since she first spotted him sunbathing in North Dakota without a shirt. "I'm just never getting in it."

She goes back inside. Dave goes back across the street.

"My boat," Adam christens it.

He heaves it into the back of his pickup and heads toward the city limits, past the used car lots and Chinese takeouts, past the trailer parks and strip clubs, until, past everything, he gets to a boat ramp at a spot where the Republican River is thin.

No one's around. The wind is still. The water is smooth. He eases the boat in. A little bit of the river dribbles into the bottom along one of the seams, but not enough to be a concern. He pushes off with a paddle and feels the grab of the current. Instead of using the motor, he lets the water take over. It spins him so he is pointed downriver and moves him along faster than he thought it would. It feels good, this. The boat is floating. The boat is fixed. He drifts for a while longer and then hits the switch on the trolling motor so he can come back upriver to the ramp, get his fishing pole, make an afternoon of it.

"Uh-oh," he says when nothing happens.

He hits the switch again.

It's the battery, he realizes.

He checks the wires, and tries the switch again. Nothing. He tries again. But the battery is dead. It must have been down to its last juice when he tested it. He tries again. The current keeps moving him along. Again. Nothing. No way he can afford a new battery. Again. Again.

So that's that.

He reaches for the paddle. It takes him some time, but eventually he is back home.

He had really wanted a boat.

It is such a lonely life, this life afterward. During the war, it wasn't that way, even in the loneliest moments, when somewhere in the big night sky was a mortar that was on its way down and there was nothing to do but wait for it. Over time, the war came to mean less and less until it meant nothing at all, and meanwhile the other soldiers meant more and more until they came to mean everything. "None of this shit would have happened if you were there," the soldier had said to Adam the day James Doster died, and it wasn't only the possibility that had stung Adam so much, it was the friendship he and the soldier had. His name was Christopher Golembe, and in that soldier's way, just as Adam had loved Doster, he had loved Golembe, too. To be a soldier in combat was to fall in love constantly, and then Doster was dead and Golembe was saying what he said, and what did Adam do next? He fell apart alone and flew away alone and came home alone, and even with Saskia and Zoe and Jax, he has felt alone at times ever since.

In Peter Chiarelli's suicide meetings, they talk often about the importance of camaraderie, and how many times has Adam wished for that very thing? "Well, I'll walk you as far as the shitters, because I have to go to the bathroom" were the last words he heard in combat from the soldiers he was with, and since then he has exchanged e-mails with some of them from time to time, but that's been about the extent of it. He has yet to talk to Golembe, who didn't say goodbye, but maybe that's just the way it goes. Love hurts and all that.

Whatever, Adam's closest friend now is a guy named Stephen, with whom Adam had served during his first deployment, and part of his second, until a bomb blast sent Stephen home with a traumatic brain injury and PTSD. They met again a few years later, when Adam was home, too, and both were trying to recover in the Fort Riley WTU. They decided to introduce their wives to each other, and at a first dinner, things were rolling along just fine, right up until Stephen pitched forward and began trembling. Saskia watched, horrified. Worse, Stephen's wife, Christina, who was in the middle of telling a story, kept on with it until she saw the look on Saskia's face. "He'll get up," she said with the calmness of someone who had seen this before. "He's fine."

And she was right. Eventually he did get up, and he was fine, if fine can mean TBI and PTSD and headaches and a cyst on his brain the size of a baseball and a lack of focus and an inability to work and a total disability rating from the VA.

"You're my best friend," Stephen declares from time to time.

"Um, you, too, man," Adam says reluctantly.

As for Christina, she isn't so fine at times, which Saskia finds reassuring. Misery loves company and all that.

"I'm supposed to be grieving right now," Christina tells Saskia one day when Saskia stops by her house. They had been pushing each other for months to start counseling, and Christina, the braver of the two, has just come back from her first appointment.

"Grieving?" Saskia says.

"For the loss of my husband. For the man he was," Christina says.

She rolls her eyes. "Yeah, technically, I'm supposed to be grieving. I don't know exactly how I'm supposed to be grieving or what exactly I'm supposed to be doing. But I'm grieving."

She looks away. She reaches into a diaper bag to get some wipes to clean one of her children's dirty bottoms. She looks up at Saskia and is crying.

"It's just too much," she says.

She gets up and leaves the room to compose herself, but there is nowhere to go because every room in the house is a reminder in some way of Stephen's condition. The kitchen sink is filled with dishes that he seems incapable some days of helping with. The deep freeze is filled on one side with popsicles for the kids and on the other side with packages of dead rats, hundreds of them, which Stephen thaws and feeds to his eighty snakes, including boa constrictors named Coco and Chanel that he likes to wear around his neck. The more hobbies he has, the better, he has been told, so he builds rockets, too, all over the house, and he is putting together a little museum of war-related items for whoever might wander into his basement. He has a few things from Vietnam and World War Two, but the focus so far is on himself. There's his helmet, in a glass display case. There's his uniform, on a mannequin. There's the hat he wore on all of his sniper missions. There are his boots. There are his guns, his many, many guns, more even than James Doster had.

"I had a guy trade me a rifle for a shovel one time," he boasts to Adam and Saskia one night.

"You gave him a shovel and he gave you a gun?" Adam asks.

Stephen nods and tells them about another deal. "I traded a flashlight for a World War Two pistol. It's almost like I could trade a quarter for a thousand dollars."

"Rub some of that luck on us," Saskia says.

"Think lucky and you'll *be* lucky," Stephen says.

"Oh God," Saskia says.

So it goes with Adam's closest friend, and maybe only friend, whose wife calls Saskia one day to tell her that when they checked their bank account that morning, there was an unexpected deposit from the government. That they didn't know if it was back pay or an adjustment to Stephen's disability rating or what it was, only that it was eleven thousand dollars.

"Eleven thousand dollars," Adam says now to Saskia. They are in Saskia's car. Adam is driving.

"We have officially become those people," Saskia says.

"The jealous people," Adam says.

"I don't hate them," Saskia says. "I just hate——"

"The system," Adam says.

"Yeah," Saskia says. "Like every time they struggle, they get something. 'A sign from God.' That's what Stephen said."

"And he's not even religious," Adam says.

"'Their time of need,' he said," Saskia goes on. "Well, *we* need."

They drive in silence, thinking in their own ways about eleven thousand dollars. Adam takes out his cigarettes. He always buys the cheap ones, the ones that taste bitter and stale. He lights one and inhales.

"What'd I ask you?" Saskia says sharply.

Adam looks over at her, confused.

"What'd I ask you?" she repeats and starts spitting out sentences as prompts. "When you drive my car? To have the decency? Not to?"

"Not to smoke," he says.

"Put it out," she says. "Put. It. Out."

He puts it out.

They are on their way to Whiskey Lake Raceway, a third-rate dirt oval on the far side of Fort Riley. It was Dave's idea, from across the street. He supplies the tow truck at the races, in case of accidents, and he also has a car to race, an off-white thing he's been working on with a number 4 on the side fashioned from duct tape. If Adam and Saskia wanted a night out, he offered, his wife would watch Zoe and Jax while they handled the tow truck.

Now, as they near the racetrack, Adam's cell phone rings. It is Stephen. "Guess what I'm doing right now?" he is hollering. "I'm lying naked on my bed. I'm lying on a pile of money."

Now they are at the racetrack, walking toward Dave's tow truck through a field thick with summer grasshoppers and watching a car even rattier than Dave's passing by with the words "Livin' the dream" painted on the back of it. "Aren't we all," Adam says.

Now they spot a soldier from Adam's old unit here with his wife, and the four of them talk for a while amid the grasshoppers.

"You seen Sherfield lately?" the soldier, whose name is Tim, asks at one point.

"No, last time I talked to him he was getting surgery and he was getting re-classed to finance or some shit like that," Adam says.

"Yeah, I don't know about that," Tim says.

"Remember the time he was running around with a vibrator on a string at the PX?" Adam says. "Remember that shit?"

"Yeah, he didn't know what it was," Tim says, laughing.

"Helicopter. Helicopter," Adam says, laughing, too, as he remembers what Sherfield was yelling when he picked up the vibrator and swung it around his head, and meanwhile, Tim's wife, Sondra, not so interested in Sherfield, is saying to Saskia, "Tim bought a new car."

"Really?" Saskia says.

"Uh-huh. He traded in his GTO," Sondra says. "Got an '06 Mustang GT."

"Awww," Saskia says.

"Really pretty," Sondra says.

Meanwhile, Tim is telling Adam that he stayed in the unit that Adam left and, after a year home, was with them when they went back to a completely different war. "All the new guys I got were so disappointed they didn't see any action," he says.

"Oh well," Adam says.

"What color is it?" Saskia says.

"Red with white stripes," Sondra says.

"Yum," Saskia says.

"You know my dog got killed," Tim says.

"What?" Adam says.

"He got hit by a car," Tim says. "While I was in Iraq. My wife took him to Missouri. He got hit by a car."

"No shit," Adam says. "Jesus. I remember we had two dogs in Iraq the first time. I still think about them, you know? They were like our patrol dogs. These dogs didn't have nothing. They just liked us. They'd follow us to the chow hall and wait outside, and we'd come out and feed them and they'd get in the back of the Bradley and go out on missions."

Now Adam and Saskia are driving home after the races, and Saskia asks how he's doing.

"Good," Adam says, sounding distracted.

"Good," Saskia says.

"Gotta take a heartburn pill and my medication," Adam says.

Now they are home, and they have carried the kids across the street and put them to bed, and Saskia is inside waiting for Adam, who is outside on the porch, by himself in the dark and thinking about the dogs in Iraq some more—about how he loved them, too, in that soldier's way, and how the soldiers had given them names, and how they slept with the soldiers sometimes, and how one day one of them wouldn't stop barking and growling at an Iraqi policeman who took out a knife and grabbed the dog and held it down and before anyone could stop him sliced its Achilles tendon, and how some soldiers boasted later that they had held the Iraqi down and done the same to him.

He lights another cigarette. He stays on the porch a little longer.

Such is the depth of his lonely life, into which one day arrives an e-mail from another soldier, Michael Emory, saying he had been thinking about Adam and would like to come visit sometime.

The last time Adam saw Michael Emory was years before, when Emory was just about dead and draped across Adam's back, and the blood coming from a bullet hole in Emory's head kept going into Adam's mouth.

"Your friend" is how Emory signs the e-mail.

"I'm looking forward to it," Adam writes back. "You got a place to stay while you're here?"

The life afterward: Michael Emory's has taken place in hospitals, rehabilitation facilities, and lately, a double-wide trailer south of Atlanta. He was supposed to die and didn't, was supposed to not walk and does, was supposed to not talk and does that, too. "He's a walking miracle," his chief doctor says, and then revises that. "He's an absolute walking phenomenon to those who don't know differently."

He was shot in the head and the bullet ruined the part of his brain that regulates such things as emotions and impulse control. It also left him partially paralyzed. "Hemiparesis," he says, proud that he can say such a word. He has no sensation on his left side. He can't easily stand. He can't move his left foot or toes. He can't straighten his left arm. He can't wiggle his left fingers. He can't wink his left eye.

He is divorced now from Maria, the woman he was married to when he was in the hospital and who didn't leave his bedside. "I love you, baby," she would say over and over to him in those first days, when he couldn't talk and could barely move. "Her and her damn mouth" is what he says about what happened after that. "If we weren't sleeping or fucking, we were arguing."

He has a young daughter who was in the family truck one day when he all of a sudden went haywire, punched the rearview mirror, shattered the windshield, grabbed Maria by the top of her head, shook her back and forth, and screamed, "I'm gonna fucking kill you." Now the daughter is gone to Texas with her mother and he is grateful that she doesn't have to grow up around such a man as himself. Before he was shot, he was never angry. Now he can't control it. Now he telephones his daughter every day from a safe distance. "My little giraffe," he calls her.

He walks with a cane that he used once to smash his mother's curio cabinet. He had gone to live with her after the rehab center. "Get me breakfast," she would say on occasion, as if she were the one who couldn't walk very well. "You don't love me. You don't care," she would say when he didn't bring her breakfast. One day she came home from having her blood drawn, sat next to him, and said it hurt so much she couldn't move her arm. "Are you fucking kidding me?" he said. One day she came home with a bumper sticker on her car that said "Proud Mother of a Soldier." "Mom, take that shit off," he said. He lived with her for five months, and then he smashed the curio cabinet and pushed over the dining room table and moved to the double-wide.

He has two teenage sons from a first marriage who live nearby and sometimes visit him, but he wishes they would visit more.

He has an aide, paid for by the VA, who helps him with his leg brace, his arm brace, his hand brace, his clothing, his shoes that she double-knots, his medications, and his food. Sometimes, when she takes him to lunch in the nearby town, he asks her to dress him in a T-shirt that says "What Have You Done for Your Country?" on the front and "I Took a Bullet in the Head for Mine" on the back, so people who stare at him won't think they're looking at the results of some drunk in a car wreck. She takes him to Subway or Chick-fil-A and brings him back to the double-wide and then leaves him alone for the rest of the day while she goes on to her other client, a ninety-one-year-old ex-Marine who likes to tell her about the time he was shot in the shoulder in World War Two and the medic told him to bite down on something as he heated a knife and cut out the bullet. "Same time tomorrow?" she always says when she leaves.

He puts his wallet in the same place every night so he'll know where it is in the morning.

He owns a giant TV and likes to watch a show about Vietnam vets who join gangs and get in trouble as he thinks, *Is that why I was shot? So I wouldn't become that?*

He has a computer he uses to introduce himself to women on dating sites. He is always honest, saying he got injured in the war, and in six months, there's been one response, from someone who wrote back, "Thank you for serving our country."

He calls women he grew up with who promise they'll come to see him and never do. The one call he can count on receiving is from a woman he met in one of the hospitals, who always calls him on the anniversary of the day he was shot. "Happy birthday," she said on the most recent call, his third anniversary. "You're three now."

He still has the helmet he was wearing when he was shot, which has the hole where the bullet went in and the hole where the bullet went out, and which he uses every Halloween as a candy bowl.

He wishes he had his dog tags, but Maria took them when she left. "I want them back," he said on the phone. "I don't have them," she said.

"What'd you do with them?" he said. "I threw them out," she said. "Why the hell'd you do that?" he said, and added for good measure, unable to stop himself, "Bitch."

He was suicidal for a while, but isn't so much anymore. One time, when he wasn't yet walking, he tried to tip over his wheelchair, hoping he would bang his head hard enough on the floor to die. One time, when Maria was still taking care of him, he asked her to bring him a pencil so he could stab himself in the neck. One time—his last attempt—he tried to bite through his right wrist.

He's not as angry anymore, either, he says, although sometimes he is, and he's not as depressed anymore, although sometimes he is that, too. Mostly, he is alone, just alone, and sometimes he thinks about how he joined the army to become a mechanic, and if he hadn't switched jobs, none of this would have happened, so it's no one's fault but his own. "Everybody tells me it's not my fault. 'It's not your fault. It's not your fault.' Yes, it *is*," he says. "It's always in my head. I'll sit here for hours. If I hadn't done this. If I hadn't done that. I'll drive myself crazy."

He has a psychologist to help him with this. Her name is Andrea Elkon, and she knows, like everyone knows, that everything he is going through—the paralysis, the depression, the suicidal impulses, the mood swings, the outbursts, the fury—is the result of what the bullet did to his brain. It *isn't* his fault. "He's such a success story in so many ways," Elkon says, but getting him to understand that has been difficult because his self-awareness was affected as well. "Really, the crux of our therapy has been making good choices. It's that basic," she says. There was the choice to get divorced. There was the choice to leave his mother's house and live on his own. There was the choice to get an aide and accept her help. And now comes his newest choice, to go see Adam Schumann. "I think Emory is incredibly indebted to Schumann. I mean he tears up when he speaks of how grateful he is," she says. However, she goes on, "He has some guilt about Schumann's condition, that Schumann is like he is from having to carry Emory down the stairs and have blood in his mouth." And so she has mixed feelings about the visit. The benefit: "Being able to say thank you." But: "He can't ever predict how he's going to relate to someone. If the environment gets emotional or volatile,

Emory doesn't have the impulse control to walk away. He could get emotional, angry, agitated. He's unpredictable, through no fault of his own. When you put somebody with a brain injury in an unpredictable situation, there's no telling how he'll react."

And that's who goes to see Adam, who pulls up to the airport terminal in Kansas City a few minutes after Michael arrives. "Let me get up," Michael says to the attendant wheeling him through the airport when he sees Adam through the terminal window getting out of his car. "Stay in the chair," the attendant tells him as he tries to stand up. "Stay in the chair. Stay in the chair."

The next morning, Adam knocks on Michael's hotel door to take him to breakfast. He can hear Michael moving around inside. He knocks again. Eventually the door opens, and there's Michael, dressed only in shorts.

"Hungry?" Adam asks him.

"Yeah. I gotta get dressed first," Michael says, and it takes a moment for Adam to realize he needs help. "If you don't mind?"

"Nope," Adam says. "How's it work?"

He comes into the hotel room, and Michael shows him one of his braces, next to his cane. It is the one to hold his useless left arm in place, like a sling of sorts. Michael sits in a chair. His hair is buzzed short, and chunks of it are missing where he is scarred. He has another scar on his neck from the tracheotomy and a rectangular lump on his back, inside of which is a pump that pushes out doses of a drug to help reduce his spasticity. Tentatively, Adam slides the brace up Michael's arm and tightens its straps across his back, just under his shoulder blades. "Like that?"

"Yeah," Michael says.

"How tight do you want it?"

"Snug."

Adam tightens the straps more. "Goddamn, that's gotta be uncomfortable all day."

"Yeah it is," Michael says. "Make it a little tighter."

"Okay," Adam says.

Next, he kneels and straps the second brace around Michael's lower leg. "Snug," Michael says again, and Adam tightens that, too.

He helps Michael into a T-shirt.

He ties Michael's shoes.

He helps with the third brace, which has been designed to keep Michael's fingers from curling into a claw. "Can you move your fingers?" he asks.

"No," Michael says, and then, reconsidering the mystery of who he has become, says, "If I yawn, they'll move a bit. So that gives me hope. And when I ejaculate, my foot twitches."

Adam looks at that foot now, which he is glad to see is as steady as can be. Bit by bit, he is getting used to this man whose blood he still can taste. He straightens up. "Does one side of your dick not work?" he asks.

"No, it works fine," Michael says, laughing. He is getting used to Adam, too.

The ride home from the airport had started awkwardly. "Well, the weather's supposed to be pretty good this weekend," Adam said once he got Michael in the car. "You hot? Cold?"

"I'm all right," Michael said.

"This drive takes forever, it seems like," Adam said after some silence. Ten minutes down at that point. Two hours to go until Junction City.

But Michael hadn't come all this way not to talk about what had happened, and soon he was saying, "My first deployment, I didn't get a scratch on me. My second more than made up for it." And Adam, who talks to no one—not Saskia, according to Saskia, not therapists, according to therapists—also wanted to talk.

"Yeah, my first two were good. The third one broke me mentally," he said.

"I went through a suicidal stage," Michael said. "At one point I tried to bite through my wrists."

"I heard about that. It made me sick. It made me sick. I feel like I'm responsible for that," Adam said.

"But you're not."

"I know."

And it was at that point that Michael told Adam what he remembered of that day, that he kept saying, "My head hurts," and Adam kept saying, "You'll be all right," and that once Adam got him down three flights of stairs and he had been placed on a litter, Adam tripped over something and nearly dropped him.

Adam remembered that, too. He remembered all of it. He remembered that the gunshot seemed the loudest he had ever heard in his three deployments and thousand days of combat. He remembered running with his eighty pounds of gear up to the roof of the building. He remembered grabbing a corner of the litter Michael had been put on and that Michael kept rolling off of it as he went into and out of consciousness, making it impossible to maneuver him down the stairs. He remembered putting the litter down, stripping off his gear, and telling some other soldiers to hoist Michael onto his back. He remembered the sudden dead weight of this dying man. He remembered his mouth filling with blood and gulping for air as he moved down the stairs and his mouth filling again. He remembered the taste of the blood, the smell of the blood, the heat of the blood, and the wet of the blood as it spilled down his chin and onto his uniform and through his uniform and onto his skin. He remembered helping to lay Michael back on the litter at the bottom of the stairs and saying, "You'll be all right." He remembered picking up the end with Michael's head, which was the slippery end, and his legs turning to jelly as he stepped through the door, and he remembered the rest of it, too: tripping over something unseen, Michael falling, the floor a few inches away, the coming crack, the coming thud, the coming death blow, the coming blame, and somehow he lunged and caught Michael in time and spent the rest of the day feeling ashamed.

None of which he said to Michael. Just: "You were a big motherfucker, man. How much did you weigh? Two thirty?"

"Two twenty-five," Michael said.

"Yeah, I almost didn't recognize you. From then to now," Adam said.

"A lot has changed," Michael said.

Now, the next morning, after helping Michael get dressed, holding doors open for him, closing doors for him, getting him into and out of a car and into a restaurant booth, Adam listens as Michael makes a confession.

"When I got out of my coma, I began having all these nightmares about your dropping me," he says.

Adam looks at him, stricken.

"I'm fucking with you, man," Michael says, laughing, and tells him the real dream he had. "I don't know if it was your hand, DeLay's hand, or Stern's hand, but I had all these nightmares about a hand drenched in blood, and I would wake up screaming."

"I was covered in blood head-to-toe that day," Adam says.

"My psychologist said this might be good for both of us because the last time you saw me, you saw me at my worst," Michael says.

"All day, my guys kept asking me: 'You think he's gonna be all right?'" Adam says.

"I look at it as shit happens. It wasn't my time," Michael says, and gives Adam some advice. "Don't ever try to bite your wrist. That shit hurts."

He laughs again and digs into his breakfast. Lots of eggs. Lots of potatoes. Lots of ketchup on those potatoes.

Adam watches. He's not hungry. "Let's go fishing, man," he says after a while.

In the car now, Michael holds out his right hand, the one he bit, toward Adam. He wishes he could have tried it on his left hand, he says, because he wouldn't have felt his teeth and might have been able to finish, but the right one was the one he could lift to his mouth.

Adam takes Michael's hand.

"I appreciate it," Michael says.

Adam's eyes redden and fill with tears.

"Somebody had to do it," he says.

The following morning, Adam is once again at Michael's hotel room door.

"Another damn day," Michael says.

"You got some shaving cream on your ear," Adam says, coming into the room. Before Michael can ask, Adam cleans him and starts helping with his braces, and this time there isn't a tentativeness to anything he is doing. Instead, there's a tenderness that had begun when they were fishing the afternoon before.

They had pulled up as close to the big lake as Adam could get his truck, but there was still a distance of ten yards or so to the water's edge. Adam held on to Michael and guided him over the rocks and ran back to the truck for a folding chair. He helped Michael into the chair, baited a fishing pole, cast it, and put the pole into Michael's right hand. "Want to reel it in?" he asked when nothing was happening. He held the pole while Michael worked the reel. He netted some baby shad and used one of them to re-bait the hook. "Want me to send it back out?" he asked, and then he stood next to Michael attentively, as if watching another man fish was the most interesting thing in the world.

Saskia was there, too, watching from the front seat of the truck and trying to get her head around the way Adam was behaving. Was this the same man who smokes in her car? Who was too distracted last night to notice her suffering from a migraine? Who can't even bring her a cheap chocolate bar from Walmart as a surprise? Who knew she was coming along and packed only one chair? She had no idea that he was still capable of such devotion. She wanted to like him better because of what she was seeing, but she couldn't help it. Part of her felt hurt, and the other part felt petty for feeling hurt, and she wished there was a part left over for grieving but that didn't seem to be the case. As for Michael, and his scarred head, and his slow way of moving, and his "I Took a Bullet in the Head for Mine" T-shirt, she couldn't take her eyes off of him, except at one point when she typed a message to Christina on her cell phone.

"This is so sad," she wrote. "Makes you realize our husbands really need to suck it up. They have it pretty good."

She stayed in the truck until she heard Adam's excited voice drift through the open window. "Ohh, I think you got one," he was saying to Michael, and at that, she got out of the truck and balanced her way across the rocks. Michael tried to reel in the fish on his own by propping the pole between his legs and clamping it with his thighs, but Adam saw it wasn't working and reached over to steady the pole. It was a nice-sized bass. Adam took it off the hook, handed it to Michael, took a photo, baited the line, recast, and handed the pole back to Michael, who immediately got another fish.

"I can hold it up," Saskia said when she saw the pole bend, hurrying over, and this time she was the one who helped.

And so went an afternoon. At some point, Saskia took a seat on the rocks, ignoring the old beer cans and fish skeletons in the crevices. That night, they cooked some of the fish for dinner, and now, as Adam picks up Michael's suitcase and helps him out of the hotel, Saskia is waiting in the car.

Michael sits up front. Saskia sits behind Adam and can't see him as he discreetly tucks some chewing tobacco in his mouth, but she can hear it when he quietly spits into a water bottle he's holding, and that's all it takes.

"Do you have chew in your mouth?" she asks.

"No," he says.

"Then why are you spitting in a bottle?"

"I have a bad taste in my mouth."

"That's disgusting," she says. "Your teeth will fall out and you'll get lung cancer."

"That's what I'm going for," he says, trying to not lose his temper.

The first night Michael arrived, when it was just Michael and Adam at dinner, one of the things Adam had asked was what it was like to be divorced.

"I kick myself every day. She's the best woman I've ever been with. I'd run back to her in a second if I could," Michael had answered, and suspecting the reason for the question, said, "Don't give up on your wife."

So Adam takes the chew out of his mouth and says to Saskia, "I love you."

"I love you," he says again.

"Nothing?" he asks.

"Not today," she says.

"Tomorrow?" he asks.

"We'll see," she says.

They are on the highway now, a carful of wounds with a long way to go till the airport. "You all be good to each other," Michael will say when they get to the airport. "We will," Saskia will say. "Be easy on him," Michael will say to her. "Yeah, I'm broke," Adam will say, laughing.

For now, though, everyone in the car is silent, uncomfortably so, until Adam sees a truck pulling a boat on a trailer.

"That's like my old boat," he says, more to himself than anyone in the car, but Michael, who hears him, and who knows better than anyone what a man sounds like when he is so lonely that he could bite his own wrist, tries to swivel to see it without losing his balance.

"Where?" he asks.

Eleven days later. Another fight. This one begins on the drive home from the VA hospital, when Adam mentions the PTSD program, the one that Tausolo Aieti had gone through. Maybe it would help, he says. Maybe it would, Saskia agrees, but it would mean seven weeks of no work and no pay. That's two missed house payments. Car payments, too. Electricity. Gas. Phone. Groceries. She reminds him that they have no savings. She imagines the graduation speech: "Congratulations for conquering PTSD. And now you're fucked." And it escalates from there until they are home and she is telling Adam to move out and his mind is whirling and his thoughts are out of control and he is throwing some things in a duffel bag and she is digging through the duffel bag to see what he has packed.

Some clothing.

His helmet.

His dog tags.

Doster's dog tags.

Their handgun.

"What the hell do you need that for?" she says, holding up the gun.

"If I need money, I can sell it," he says.

She stands with the gun, shaking her head no. It is the middle of the afternoon. Jaxson is a few feet away, in his room, napping. Zoe is at a friend's. Adam disappears into the master bedroom, and when he comes out he is holding a loaded shotgun against his forehead.

"Pull the fucking trigger," he says, walking toward her, thrusting the butt of the gun at her, now pushing it into her stomach, trying to goad her. "*Pull the fucking trigger,*" he yells, and what surprises her is how much she wants to do it. She wants to pull the fucking trigger and end his life and end her misery and clean the walls afterward and be done with it, all of it. The years have caught up at last. "*Pull the fucking trigger,*" he says, and she wants to pull it, reload if she has to and pull it again, but instead she spins and walks away from him. "Be a man" is all she can think of to say, and then she goes onto the front porch, slams the door behind her, and stands with her back to him so he can't see her shaking and trying to catch her breath.

She remains outside.

He remains inside.

They were fighting more and more now, every day it seemed, at home, in the car, in front of the kids, even in text messages when Adam was at work. "Look at our life! Not only have we had to start completely over but our marriage is failing in the process. We have nothing and cant even count on each other 4 support," she had texted him a few weeks before. "If you honestly see this workin I stay, if not I go."

"Well what would u like to do, i'll try anything at this point, so tell me what u want and i'll do it," he had written back.

"I just wish u would show me some emotion and that you really do love me and think bout how I feel," she had written.

"Well, u know I love u, if not then maybe we do need to split . . ."

That fight was bad, but as Saskia stands on the porch shaking, she knows that this one feels different. Scarier. Worse. She gathers herself and goes back inside.

Adam is nowhere in sight. The duffel bag is still there. So is the handgun. The shotgun is gone. She looks in the bedroom. He's not there. He's not in the living room, the dining room, the kitchen, the bathroom, or Jax's room. He's not in the backyard. She opens the door leading to the basement and starts down the stairs.

She hates it down there. Twelve creaking steps, and at the bottom is a hallway that leads to the laundry room, a bathroom, and finally Zoe's room, a little room with a low doorway and a couple of small basement

windows that allow in smudges of daylight. For her next birthday, Zoe
wants to paint one half of the room pink and the other half black and
arrange everything in the room accordingly. Her pink toys will go on the
pink side and her black toys will go on the black side. The bed she has
been wetting now for three weeks in a row will go on the pink side and
the spiders she finds sometimes will go on the black side. The space
heater that keeps the room warm in the winter will go on the pink side
and the TV that accompanies her to sleep will go on the black side. Still
to be figured out is what she will do with the flimsy wall made of lou-
vered doors that Adam put up to separate her room from the rest of
the furnace room it had originally been part of. That room, the furnace
room, is the worst room in the house, and Saskia goes there now.

It's a room of dimness and shadows. The bare lightbulb hanging from
the ceiling is unlit, and what little light is leaking into the room feels
gray and dirty. Adam is in the middle of the room, seated on a folding
chair. He is faced away from her and holding the shotgun against the
underside of his chin. His thumb is on the trigger. The safety is off. To
his right is the furnace. To his left are shelves filled with old appliances
and the letters he and Saskia wrote to each other when he was in Iraq. In
front of him is a taxidermy stand with a faded fish skin on it, onto which
he recently had glued a realistic-looking rubber eye.

So this is where he will die, then. Not in a Humvee like James Doster.
Not in the war, but here in the furnace room, next to the room his daughter wants him to paint, under the room where his son is asleep, and a
few inches from his terrified wife.

She asks him to put the gun down.

He doesn't.

She approaches him, leans over and gets a hand on the gun, but before she can pull it away he takes his free hand and pinches her arm until
she lets go.

He moves the barrel of the gun from his chin to his forehead.

His thumb is still on the trigger.

He moves the barrel back underneath his chin and starts crying so
hard that the barrel becomes wet.

Later, Saskia will say that she has no idea how long this went on.

Fifteen minutes? A half hour? She will remember the minutes as motionless as she pleaded with Adam to give her the gun. She will remember that as much as she had wanted to pull the trigger a few minutes before, now she wanted no such thing.

She will remember saying, "Zoe's going to be home soon."

He says something now, something about wishing he had died in Iraq. More things come out. About guilt. About being a bad husband, a bad father, a disappointment; about being twenty-nine and feeling ninety; about being a disgrace. His mind is roaring, and meanwhile his thumb is still on the trigger, the safety is off, the gun remains loaded, and Saskia stands next to him begging and waiting for the sound of the gun and for him to explode.

And what saves him is another sound, that of Jaxson. His crying comes through the floorboards, sudden and insistent, like it was when he rolled off Adam and fell to the floor. That time Adam had awakened when Saskia crawled across him; this time he does it on his own. Like coming up from underwater, he will say later. It's a faraway sound he hears, familiar enough to jolt him out of wherever he is, and then it is louder, and then he is breaking through the surface and hearing everything: Jaxson crying, Saskia saying she needs him and the kids need him, him crying.

She gets her hands back on the gun, pulls it away, leans it against a wall.

He stands. Saskia wraps her arms around him, and he doesn't resist.

Jaxson is in full wail now, and his needs take over the house. They walk out of the furnace room, toward the stairs. "You go first," Saskia says.

By coincidence, at the very same time they have been in the furnace room, Peter Chiarelli has been in another meeting, this one framed by the unfortunate news of four fresh suicides at Fort Hood, Texas.

On the video screen is the general in command of Fort Hood, who is telling Chiarelli that every one of his 46,500 soldiers is being reviewed to see who might be high risk. "We stand prepared to lead them through this difficult period," the general says with a general's determination.

But he also says what is rarely heard at these meetings, that "ninety-nine percent of the soldiers, as you know, tens of thousands of soldiers, every day, at Fort Hood, Texas, and throughout the army . . . are doing fine. They're working through the issues, they're dealing with the stressors, they're using the programs, and they're moving on throughout their careers learning, growing, maturing, developing more resilience, and succeeding."

That's the question, then, always the question, the why of it, why most are okay and others are not, and of all the answers offered this day, the simplest one, given by another general explaining another suicide, seems the truest. "His pressing guilt. That's the only way I can put it," the general says, and meanwhile Adam is feeling better with every step up the stairs.

He unpacks. The dog tags and helmet go back on display in the dining room, and the guns go back in the bedroom. For the rest of the day, he and Saskia are too raw to fight, or even to talk very much, but after a week of no arguments, and then, amazingly, two weeks, Saskia tells Christina that their marriage is the best it's been since Adam got home. "The tension's gone," she says. "I have no idea why. I wish I knew."

Even in the basement things are better, at least in Zoe's room, where she now has company at night, a new puppy named Eddie that Adam and Saskia brought home for her when they decided she wasn't getting enough attention. That makes for three dogs and four people jammed into the little house, but somehow it's working better than it ever has, right up until the moment when the biggest dog in the house sits on the puppy and breaks its leg.

In the parlance of a Pentagon suicide meeting, this would be a stressor. Or an issue.

In Kansas, though, it is a veterinarian saying it will cost $1,100 to fix the leg, and Adam and Saskia realizing that if they had $1,100 they would have used it toward the mortgage and car payments so Adam could go to the Topeka VA's PTSD program.

But Zoe loves the puppy.

But they don't have $1,100, and they've only had the dog a week.

But since his arrival, Zoe hasn't wet her bed even once.

But they don't have $1,100.

But just before the dog arrived, they were at a birthday party for one of Stephen and Christina's children and Zoe ran around a playground singing at the top of her lungs, "My daddy almost killed himself."

But they don't have $1,100, and they don't have a boat to sell, and Adam has already sold two of his three hunting bows, and Saskia has already sold the Coach purse she bought when she first got to Fort Riley and saw that all of the wives seemed to have them, and it's not like anyone would want the aluminum skiff.

But years after, Adam still thinks sometimes about what an Iraqi policeman did to a dog's Achilles tendon, and so he tells Saskia what he thinks they ought to do about Eddie.

"Just do the pistol," Saskia says.

"No. I've used the shotgun three times in three years," Adam says.

Almost four times, Saskia keeps from saying.

It's decided then. They call Dave, across the street, who says he can help.

"How r things goin?" Saskia texts Adam later in the day.

"Good," he writes back. "Vet called and said eddie looks good. U sell the guns?"

"Don't know," Saskia writes back. "Havent talked to dave since he took them."

A little later, she writes to him again.

"Got the money. When u gonna b home?"

"Bout 10 min."

She waits for him in a house that two weeks before had a handgun hidden in a duffel bag and a shotgun with a trigger that she wanted to pull. "They're both gone," she says, astonished at how this has turned out. "Thank God."

With her nervous blessing, he goes hunting. It's archery season, she is thinking, and in all of the suicides she's ever heard of, none involved a bow and arrow.

He puts his bow in the back of his truck and heads for the most isolated reaches of Fort Riley. Four lanes become two lanes, and after a while he is the only one on the road. He passes a tree split by lightning and a charred log covered with crows. He passes fields of prairie grasses lined with long patches of smooth sumac that have turned bright crimson for autumn, and from one angle they look like red leaves and from another they look like bleeding gashes cut into the grasses. He keeps going, past a spot where they trained for the war once—a plywood replica of a village, a fake mosque, a few burned-up cars—and it appears so abruptly and is gone so quickly it might be a mirage. He turns onto an even thinner road, and then a dirt road, and when that road ends, he gets out and starts walking into the woods. He selects a tree and climbs it until he is hidden in the leaves, and then he begins to wait. The wind is gusting. Leaves are dropping. Clouds are skidding. Bushes are bending. Birds are cartwheeling. Everything seems in crazy motion, spinning and swirling, and so it is again with his thoughts. Saskia. Zoe. Jaxson. Emory. Doster. All of them are running together. His life is once again feeling out of control, and he knows now to be worried when such thinking comes tiptoeing back. He needs to steady himself. The deer is coming. He is sure of it. All he has to do is wait for it. Wait for it. Wait for it.

There. He is still. He is ready. He feels so alive suddenly. If only the moment could last.

7

Since moving, Amanda has driven by the old house only once.

The grass needed mowing.

What's with that birdbath?

The mailbox was different.

"Who changes the mailbox?"

She couldn't get out of there fast enough. Not that she was settled into the new house, either.

"No, the tree has to be done *tomorrow*," she is saying into the phone. She is talking to the owner of a nursery who dug up a baby maple tree at the old house that had been planted in honor of James. For months, it has been at the nursery, surviving on a drip line. He had promised to replant it at the new house on the third anniversary of James's death, and now is saying he might not be able to get a crew. "It's a big deal," Amanda says, near tears, and Kathryn, who has been half listening, asks, "Is tomorrow your anniversary?" She has her eyes on a dozen red velvet cupcakes that have been overnighted from a cupcake store in Washington, D.C., and some flowers, sent by a friend, who wrote on the card, "I know James is proud of you."

"No," Amanda begins to answer, and then says, "All right. Let's go for a walk and track down Larry."

Kathryn gets her scooter. Grace gets her bicycle. Amanda leads them up their long, unfinished driveway toward Larry's, who designed and built the house, and who Amanda phones, texts, e-mails, or goes in search of when anything goes wrong. Surely he can help with the tree, which

Grace, Amanda, and Kathryn Doster

has to be planted tomorrow, has to be, but as Amanda nears his house she can see he's not home.

So it'll be that kind of day, lousy through and through.

There are so many of them now. His birthday. Thanksgiving. Christmas. New Year's. Their wedding anniversary. The day they met. Father's Day. Valentine's Day. She knows it's out of hand. But the day he died is the worst of them, so bad that she begins feeling its arrival weeks before. As she wrote in a letter to a friend, "Things, all manner of crazy things, stupid things, mean things, have been happening lately, and it seems as if September is out to get me."

She has been writing a lot lately. Get it down on paper, she has been told. It'll help. Might as well try.

"This morning was a beautiful taste of what autumn is going to feel like and my deepest desire was to take a walk with James, hold his hand, and catch up on the past three years," she wrote one day. "It hit me that this loneliness, this overwhelming feeling that a part of me is missing, will never really go away. Sometimes it's a dull ache that I can push aside and just keep going. Today my heart actually hurts from missing him."

She wrote that, read it back to herself, felt no better at all.

"This morning was the Ceremony of Remembrance for the Fallen at Ft. Riley, followed by the 9/11 Commemoration Ceremony," she wrote on September 11.

The girls were each presented with medals from Ft Riley, as well as a memory box and dog tag with James' name engraved on it. I was a mess before we even arrived and I think the receiving line after the medal ceremony was the last straw for me. Can I just say that those things are meant for happy events, such as weddings or perhaps a birthday party. Whoever had the idea that a grieving family should stand for 40 minutes with Toby Keith singing "American Soldier" in the background and be forced to shake hands with and hug strangers who say the STUPIDEST things like "Congratulations" to you and your children needs to go a round in the ring with me.

She felt a little better after that one.

"I am melancholy. Again. Still. Whatever," she wrote a few days after that.

I'm alone. I feel helpless. Many days I feel hopeless. I'm anxious about the future and even terrified to imagine or plan for what might be right around the corner. I'm still waiting for the other shoe to drop. I'm again asking, "What next?" I feel ill equipped to protect my children. That is terrifying. I always assumed that James would be the one constant in my world. No matter where we moved, we had each other. I could go anywhere and be happy as long as I had him. If anything, God forbid, ever happened to one of our babies, or one of our parents, we had each other. I knew he knew me inside and out. He knew how to handle me and knew what I needed from him. Now? I'm so alone. And I don't know what I'm doing. I don't look to the future. I look about as far as bedtime. And then I'm alone again. I'm carrying so much all by myself. Losing James rocked my world to the core. I don't know that there's one thing in my life I haven't doubted since then. I long to feel safe, protected, sheltered and loved again. I long to have someone to lean on again, but only if it's him. I'm shocked that after nearly 3 years, I haven't hit rock bottom yet. You think you are there only to find yourself deeper in despair and surprised by it. This is what being a widow looks like.

Not every day was that bad. Eleven days before the anniversary, she wrote, "As sad as I am, it's such a beautiful season here. The sorghum is beginning to change and the soybeans are turning golden. The sunflowers are going strong and take my breath away. Mornings are crisp and the apples are nearly ready so pies can be made. This is what I love about Kansas." But such days were rare for her in September.

"I worry that I'm forgetting him. I can't remember the certain way he dried off after his shower anymore. It sounds silly, I'm sure. But I've lost that piece of him forever now and I can't ask him to show me again. It's simply gone," she wrote, and then, with a week to go, it was, "What went wrong? Why us? Why me?" and now it's the day before and where is Larry and what is she going to do about the tree?

She decides to keep walking around the neighborhood with the girls. It is a neighborhood so new that it isn't yet on maps. No one could find this place accidentally. The streets all dead end. The neighbors all wave. Surely, a safer place to take a walk doesn't exist, but as Kathryn and Grace get ahead of her, Amanda calls sharply to them to wait for her by the side of the road until she catches up.

"Okay," she says when she does. "Now you can go."

"To where?" Kathryn asks.

Amanda scans the empty road. "We're going slow until we get to the straight spot," she says, pointing to a spot not even twenty yards away, just past a slight curve.

They take off, get to the straight spot, and wait.

"To the driveway," Amanda says, picking out the next landmark.

They get to the driveway and wait.

"To the corner . . ."

To the corner. They wait.

"Okay, black-and-white mailbox . . ."

"Okay, around the circle to the orange bucket . . ."

Three years ago right now, we were eating pizza, Amanda is thinking. We were about to go to some yard sales. James was about to call. "Talk to you later. I love you," he was going to say before hanging up. "I love you," she was going to say back. So she had the last words in their last conversation. But wait. Did she? Maybe she said, "I love you" first and then he said, "Talk to you later. I love you." Or maybe he said, "I love you" first and then he said, "Talk to you later." Did he have the last words? What were those words?

"Mommy!" Kathryn suddenly screams from ahead, interrupting. "Car!"

Amanda looks up and sees it.

"Grace!" she screams. "*Stop*."

Grace freezes. Kathryn does, too. Amanda starts toward them but can't get there in time.

Here comes the car. The driver is a waving neighbor. He's going maybe five miles an hour.

———

It's not that she sees herself as beyond repair. A person doesn't get through the chaotic upbringing she had without developing some spine. In most ways, she believes herself more sufficient than needy. She almost never breaks down in front of the children. She's begun taking boxing lessons and is proud of her bruises.

Still, even as she insists she wants no one other than James to lean on, she has found them anyway, including a succession of people with one thing in common: James himself.

Adam was the first and, along with Saskia, ultimately the most painful to her. In those first days, Amanda wanted to have the wife of her husband's favorite soldier around as much as possible, and so Saskia was with her as the army explained about headstones and urns, and Saskia was with her when she picked out a casket, and Saskia was with her when she signed the insurance papers. She *needed* Saskia, she would say later, and not long after the funeral, when Saskia asked her about borrowing some money to fix up the house for Adam's homecoming, she didn't hesitate. She dipped into her survivor's benefits and pulled out several thousand dollars, and three years later, the friendship fizzled, the reasons still unclear, she is realizing that the Schumanns won't be paying her back, and neither will they be returning the glass dish in which she made seven-layer bean dip on the day that they watched the Super Bowl.

After Adam and Saskia came Alex Boland, who was the lieutenant in charge of the platoon. Along with Adam, he had delivered one of the eulogies at James's memorial service in Iraq, and nine months later, home now, James on his brain, he telephoned Amanda to introduce himself and wondered if she might want to talk. They met at a restaurant, and it was Adam at the airport all over again. *How did it happen? Did he suffer? Were you there?* From the restaurant they went to Amanda's porch, where they spent much of an afternoon, and soon he was staying for dinner and the girls were calling him Uncle Alex. She texted him, and he always texted back. She telephoned him, and he always tried to answer. "My voice of reason" is how she began thinking of him, and then he had to leave Kansas for another assignment, and Kathryn was back to having nightmares again, and that was when Amanda drew ever closer to another platoon member named Matthew Stern, which has turned into the most complicated relationship of all.

"Poor Matt, being one of the ones who tried to save him and now being my friend," Amanda says of him. "It can get very bad. The blame. The guilt."

"We've all got our little quirks from that deployment" is what Matt says.

He was the medic in the platoon, and on the day that he didn't save James, he was twenty years old. Usually he and James rode in the same Humvee in their convoys, James front right, him back left, but for whatever reason they switched things up on that trip. There were seven vehicles in all, strung out over a hundred yards. James was in number two. Matt was in number six. They had said goodbye to Schumann, who was staying back, and were traveling at about the same speed a waving neighbor might go through a Kansas subdivision when the explosion came from the right. The roar faded. The dirt settled. Someone was on the radio: *Hold your positions.* "Fuck it," Matt remembers saying. "I'm going." He ran forward. People were shooting now. He dove to the ground, and as some of the soldiers fired back, he got to James's Humvee, opened his door, felt for a pulse, grabbed him, and pulled him out. "And that's when I saw the full extent of what happened. The one leg missing. Half his pelvic area was missing. Like three quarters of the other leg." Years later, a therapist would tell Matt how James was like a father figure to him, and maybe so, but what Matt had on his mind was that leg, the left one. It was hanging by a piece of skin, nothing else, and Matt couldn't bring himself to cut it. It wouldn't have made a difference, but he thinks about it anyway. Some medic, is what he thinks. So the leg hung there while Matt went to work on the rest of James, trying to control the bleeding. "I think I stuffed thirty-three rolls of Kerlix in him," he says, and then James was dead, and then everyone came home from the war, and then he was taking antidepressants for night terrors and depression, and then, as Adam had done, and Alex Boland had done, he was meeting James's widow. "I was really scared. I didn't know how she was going to react to me. I didn't know if she was going to blame me. I said, 'Mrs. Doster, I'm Specialist Stern. I was your husband's medic.'"

And?

"I remember she shook my hand."

And:

He became Uncle Matt.

He's over at the house a lot now, which he much prefers to another night in the barracks with the new, young soldiers who have come into his unit, all of them the stupid age he once was and eager to go to a place where they might get to dive for cover. He has told Amanda everything he has to tell about what happened, and for that alone she is glad to have him with her. He is her best link, the one person on earth who stuffed thirty-three rolls of Kerlix into the torn-open insides of her dying husband. He comes over and hangs out, and sometimes if it's late he'll sleep over, which has happened enough times for her to get used to seeing his uniform hanging in the closet where James's ought to be. There's never been anything romantic, just two people keeping each other company and a connection that at times seems too complicated to make sense.

She remembers picking him up at the airport one time. She rushed toward him and he rushed toward her and people started clapping as they embraced.

"I think we just got married!" she said.

"I know!" he said.

It's weird. They realize this. Doesn't matter. There's happiness in being around each other.

Sometimes, though less often now, he wonders whether she blames him, and sometimes she wonders when he will stop blaming himself.

"I hate you," she texts him one day, and he is pretty sure he knows what she is saying.

"You can't leave it," he says. He means the war. "You just end up carrying it."

Night now. Thirteen hours to go.

"Mommy, can I watch the TV?" Grace asks.

"Bring me the remote," Amanda says.

"Mommy, where's the remote?" Grace asks.

"In the drawer," Amanda says.

"Mommy . . ."

Ding-dong.

"Sally!" Kathryn says, looking toward the door.

The new doorbell is like the old doorbell, but the tone is different, softer, a little higher on the scale, and that makes all the difference. Amanda doesn't flinch.

In comes Sally. "How are you?" she says to everyone, putting her things on a table near the cupcakes that came from Washington, D.C. Fifty-five dollars Amanda paid for those cupcakes—twenty-nine for the cupcakes, twenty-six for shipping. Well, whatever. There's a jewelry box, too, with a necklace inside, something else that Amanda got for herself for the anniversary. Sally opens the box. The necklace has three stones, a sapphire and two diamonds.

"Mommy's going to wear that tomorrow," Kathryn says, and runs off to watch TV with Grace. By now they are used to Sally, who is here so often that she has taken over one of the drawers in the bathroom. She was with them for anniversary number two and anniversary number one and would have been with them the day James died except she didn't know. She and her husband, Brandon, were away in the little town they grew up in on the other side of the lake. It was a big day there, the annual fall festival, with a parade around the town square and past the grain silo that featured among other things a strutting girl in a red spangly top who could twirl three batons at once. There was a wedding that night, too, and what Sally remembers about that, other than missing the calls about James, is a woman with one eye who kept popping it in and out. So she wasn't around for James's dying, but she has been around since and is now the person Amanda leans on most of all, whose very life is Amanda's wish, and not only because it includes a husband who is alive. The note that Amanda wrote mentioning sunflowers and pies— that was written while she was at Sally's, about the life that Sally and Brandon get to have.

Crisp mornings.

Golden soybeans.

It's more imagined than true, of course. There may be mums on Sally's porch and bluebirds in the big tree, but those bite marks in Sally's hand are part of Kansas, too, and the soybeans that Amanda saw not even two weeks ago are already turning brittle and brown. In Sally's life, a house costs $95,000, not $555,000, and when something goes wrong it is fixed by her and Brandon, not Larry down the street. In the kitchen, the boxes of aluminum foil are anything but lined up. In the bathroom, on top of a stack of diapers, is a credit card that one of their three children nearly flushed down the toilet. It's a good house, loud and disorganized, especially now, at the end of September, when the harvest is beginning and Brandon will spend the next few weeks taking off from work and helping his parents with their hundreds of acres of soybeans. The work is dirty. The combine will break down at one point. They will all gather around a part that bent in the wrong direction as it scraped over the uneven ground and worry that they don't have time for this, that the first frosts are coming and the beans have to get out of the pods and into the trucks and onto the scales while the going rate is still ten dollars a bushel. Their life of rhapsody is in truth a practical one, with only so much room for luxuries such as melancholy. The sorghum that Amanda noticed? If she were to walk into one particular field behind Brandon's parents' new house and dig down into the dirt, she would come across a nail. And then more nails. And then eventually pieces of shingle and some charred pieces of wood. Once, Brandon's family home stood in that field. Then it was time for a new house for his aging parents, so a trench was dug, the old house was pushed into it without ceremony and set on fire, and now from a grave of memories that no one mourns over grows beautiful sorghum while the family gathers in a new prefab to pray for a safe and bountiful day. That's who they are, Christians above all, get-it-done Christians, and when Amanda came into their lives with such grief and force they turned to their Bible for guidance. "Religion that God our Father accepts as pure and faultless is this: to look after orphans and widows in their distress," it said in James. "Give proper recognition to those widows who are really in need," it said in Timothy, and when it didn't go on to make an exception for widows living in $555,000 houses on oops money, they had their answer.

"I think I was put in this place and this time to meet her and go through this experience with her. I don't think anything is random," Sally explains one day, and so she will forever show up at Amanda's house on James's anniversary without Amanda even asking.

She settles onto a chair. She'll stay the night. She starts humming some George Jones as she watches Amanda, a little frantic, clean up the kitchen, wipe down the stove that won't ever get clean enough, rearrange the dishwasher that the kids once again loaded incorrectly, get frustrated that the new paper towels she bought won't fit on her old holder.

"Can I just go to your room?" Grace asks at one point, and she heads off to Amanda's bedroom, where she sleeps almost every night now, either because she will come in on her own or because if she doesn't Amanda will go get her and carry her in. "So it's not only her issue," Amanda says about that.

Twelve hours now. Her phone chimes with a text message. Larry, she hopes, with news about the tree, even though she knows deep down that it's already too late, but the message is from her mother.

"What are your plans for tomorrow?"

Amanda knows her plans down to the minute.

She will put up a new flag. She will take Sally and the girls out to breakfast and give the girls new necklaces. They will get their nails done and eat cupcakes. She will drop the girls off at school and go with Sally to a movie, and by the time the movie ends James will be dead and there will be nothing she can do about it except to start feeling better.

She also knows what she won't do, which includes talking to her mother. Or her father. She won't talk to James's family, either. She will want to talk to Matt and Alex, and Sally of course, but that's it. No one else.

"What's tomorrow? Is tomorrow something important?" she writes back to her mother, and a few minutes later, when her phone chimes again, she sighs.

"The tree will be planted tomorrow morning."

It's from Larry.

Amanda bursts into tears. She hates crying in front of people. But she can't stop herself.

Sally puts her arm around her and reminds her of the day when the tree was first planted at the old house. It was in early November, two months after James died, and Sally got a call from someone saying that Amanda was having a hard time and it would be good if Sally could go to her right away. Sally hung up and ran out the door. She hadn't showered. She was still in her pajamas. But a widow was in distress.

"And you didn't have your bra on," Amanda says, remembering, laughing really hard all of a sudden, and is there a better friend to have than Sally?

Bedtime now.

Sally takes one side of the bed, and Amanda takes the other. Sally falls asleep right away, and Amanda doesn't. "It's going to happen," she lies awake thinking, and there are nine hours to go until she is on her way to writing the sentence, "This is what being a widow looks like."

A few days later, Sally gone, Matt gone, Alex gone, the cupcakes gone, with one thing left to do, Amanda tells the girls to get their jackets.

"Which one?"

"The Columbia."

"The light blue one?"

She grabs some flowers she has bought, and soon they are on the road in the SUV that Amanda got after James's death, which gets such terrible mileage that she is glad sometimes that James doesn't know. "I told you so," she hears him say sometimes. "I told you to stay practical."

"Mommy, try some of your pumpkin seeds," Kathryn says.

"I am on a very winding road right now. I'll try some when I get on the interstate," she says a little too sharply, and when her next sentence comes out no better, she reaches into the console next to her seat and pulls out a Bible.

"Philippians. Chapter Four. Verse Six," she says, handing it back to Kathryn to read to her. It's the verse someone gave to her when James deployed. Pray and be thankful and everything will work out, it says, and how many times has she read it? And how many times has it helped? "Do not be anxious about anything," she waits to hear Kathryn read, but what Kathryn says after a moment is, "Mommy, what's this?"

She has discovered a folded-up piece of paper tucked behind the cover. "The Perfect Man," it is titled, and it's in Amanda's handwriting.

1) kind

2) considerate

3) patient

4) considers my children assets not liabilities

5) understanding of my undying love for James and isn't threatened

The list covers both sides of the paper and goes up to number thirty-seven: *knows marriage is forever.*

Amanda says nothing. She wrote it one day as one of those exercises in hope and placed it in her Bible for whatever reasons a person would choose such a hiding place. She waits for Kathryn to read the Bible verse. Kathryn keeps looking at the list. A mile goes by. The car is quiet. Finally, Kathryn turns to the verse and reads it out loud and Amanda explains what it means. "God is in control," she says anxiously. She turns on the radio and tunes it to a Christian station, and when Kathryn complains, Amanda says, "That's one dollar." Kathryn keeps complaining. "Two dollars."

"But . . ."

"Three."

"But . . ."

"Four."

"I don't have four," Kathryn says.

"Five."

"Six."

"Seven."

Kathryn begins to cry, and Amanda wonders about her own behavior. Why isn't she feeling better yet? The anniversary is over, and except for the thirty paralyzed minutes she spent in the car outside of Bed Bath & Beyond not knowing where to go or what to do next, it went according to plan. And the plan included feeling better.

The miles go by.

"Are we almost there?" Kathryn asks.

"Yes, and we will be there when we get there, and if you'd like to whine about it I can start charging you again," Amanda says.

What is *wrong* with me, she keeps thinking.

At last, after two hours, they drive through the entrance to Fort Leavenworth and toward the thousands of white tablet headstones in the cemetery.

"How did they get so many?" Kathryn asks, looking out the window. "How do they put them in the ground?" And then: "I see Daddy!"

They have come to a small section of the cemetery marked by a sign that says, "The markers in this memorial area honor veterans whose remains have not been recovered or identified, were buried at sea, donated to science, or cremated and their ashes scattered."

Or are currently in a gun safe, it doesn't say, but close enough.

This is the last thing to do: the yearly visit to a headstone with James's name on it, the date of his birth, the date of his death, the name of his war, and, Amanda sees as she gets closer, some dried droppings from the birds perched overhead in an oak tree. She grabs a package of disposable baby wipes from the car and starts cleaning as Grace spreads her arms like airplane wings and takes off serpentining through the neighboring headstones. "Grace. Not appropriate," she calls out, trying not to holler, which would be inappropriate, too. The hush of the place is like air pressure here, and that's what Amanda was hoping for when she made her request for a headstone—a place for the girls and her to visit that would feel a little more formal and permanent than visiting a box of remains.

It's a moody day, made more so by an iron sky and strong gusts of a chilly wind. Acorns are dropping and bouncing all over the cemetery. Kathryn, off by herself, kicks at a few of them, and now one must have conked Grace on the head because she is suddenly teary. Amanda goes to her, and as Grace latches on to her legs she realizes it is the sadness of this place at work, so she tries to distract her by pointing to the first thing she notices, an acorn that has just dropped next to James's headstone. "Look. It's a perfect acorn," she says, and Grace apparently thinks so, too, because she takes it from Amanda and places it in her pocket. On the drive back, she keeps taking it out and looking at it every so often, and Amanda, noticing this, gets an idea.

Home now, she goes to her drawer of aluminum foil and plastic bags. She'll also need sawdust, according to the instructions she has found on a website, and as she thinks about all of the things she moved from the old house, she remembers the jar down in the tool room. It's a peanut butter jar that James cleaned out and filled with sawdust one day when he was building the doghouse. Or was it when he was building the rack to hold the firewood? Or the rack to hold the coats? Well, it makes no difference. The point is that before he died, he was thoughtful enough to save some sawdust, and now she scoops some of it into a plastic bag, dampens it, drops in the acorn, places it in the refrigerator, and begins to feel better at last.

"So if all goes well, come spring, we will plant an oak tree," she tells the girls with a sense of anticipation, and she loves her dead man right now for making this moment possible, her perfect, kind, considerate, patient dead man who wasn't threatened by her undying love for him and knew that marriage is forever.

8

The suggestion for the pheasant hunt comes from Patti Walker, whose suggestions usually work out better. Her job is to work with wounded soldiers and ex-soldiers at Fort Riley, one of whom is Adam Schumann. She helped him find the job at the artillery range, and when that didn't work helped him find the job at the benefits center. She found an organization willing to pay for his car repairs, has gotten him free turkeys at Thanksgiving, and meets with him every so often to see what else she might do. "Likes to hunt and fish; that's his therapy," she wrote about him once in her field notes, and so when she hears about an all-expenses-paid pheasant hunt that is being organized in western Kansas for combat-wounded soldiers, she thinks of him right away.

"Healing Heroes, Healing Families!" the flyer promoting the hunt says. "3 nights of lodging and 2 days of hunting." "Spouse Downtown Pampering Excursion." "Children Fun-a-thon."

"Advised on pheasant hunt," Patti writes in her notes after telling Adam about it, and a week later Adam, Saskia, Zoe, and Jaxson are in the car, headed west. It's a 250-mile drive, and thirty minutes into it, as they're passing through Abilene, home of Dwight D. Eisenhower, president and war hero, Adam turns on the radio. Saskia reaches forward and changes the station. Adam looks at her and changes it back. Saskia shoots him a look and changes it back.

And that's all it takes. The fight gets so bad, so quickly, that Adam pulls a U-turn and guns it back to Junction City, and as Saskia and the kids get out of the car, she is screaming at him to get help or get out of her life forever.

Hunting in Kansas

He drives off. He doesn't know where else to go, so he gets back on the highway.

Four hours later, checked into the hotel, thoughts creeping back into his mind of wanting his life to be over, he gathers with the other wounded soldiers and their families in a conference room for welcoming speeches and receives his first gift of the weekend.

A shotgun? he thinks as he sees the box. *Really?*

Back in his room, he removes it from the box and assembles it so he'll be ready to go in the morning, and things slide downhill from there. He sets his alarm. He asks someone to wake him up just in case. He doesn't hear his alarm. No one knocks on his door. He gets to the hunt two hours late and sees more people than he expected. Who are they? he wonders, his mood darkening even more. Volunteers? Sponsors? Those people who drive around with "We Support the Troops" signs on their cars, as if a sign on a car makes any difference? The ones who have never been to war and will never go to war and say to soldiers, "Thank you for your service," with their gooey eyes and orthodontist smiles? They're certainly not hunters, not the way they're wandering around, and look at them now, fawning over the soldiers with visible injuries, the one with gunshot scars, the amputee. And here come the inevitable thoughts. Those soldiers are injured. He's not. They're wounded warriors, and he's weak, a pussy, a piece of shit. He stands off by himself. He talks to no one. He has lost the capacity to see that his behavior *is* the behavior of the wounded. At some point, a few pheasants rise into the air, and when a dozen guns begin blasting away, he decides he's had enough. He goes back to the hotel, packs in a fury, and leaves, and soon he is back in Junction City.

Home again.

And once again, he has a shotgun.

" 'I can't pay my rent.'

" 'I ran out of meds.'

" 'I haven't gotten my pay.' "

Patti Walker is reading the messages waiting for her at the start of a new day. She sighs. She is a big sigher, although that may come with a job described as "Soldier Family Advocate" on the business cards she hands out to soldiers, which also include the promise "for as long as it takes."

"He's burned," she keeps reading. "He needs clothes for the summertime."

"His wife doesn't speak English. How am I going to get her a job?"

She is a talker, too, and a hugger, and as Saskia once said of Amanda Doster, "She can put on the waterworks like *that*." Unlike Amanda, though, who is defined so much by sorrow, Patti is defined by the stress of dealing with the problems of forty-nine wounded soldiers during the day—forty-nine Adams is one way to think of it—and then going home at night to the fiftieth. This is her husband, Kevin, who was blown up in Iraq, lost an eye, lost some of his brain, lost most of his hearing, lost his sense of smell, has some facial disfiguration, has a long list of diagnoses, including PTSD and TBI, and among his many surgical scars has one on the back of his head that Patti has affectionately suggested looks like a penis, which may be why he prefers to wear a cap. There are two children at home as well, a young son who at one point seemed so confused by the sight of a fake eye that his father decided to stop wearing it, and a teenage daughter who one day announced that she wanted to dye her hair blue. "We're not trash," Patti said. "Why?" "So when we go to Walmart, people will stare at me instead of Daddy," the daughter said. In Patti's life, the wounded are everywhere, awaiting her answers, and her answer in this case was to let her daughter dye a small section of hair as blue as she wanted, and when blue hair didn't merit a second glance at the Junction City Walmart, she let her change it to pink.

So Patti knows things about soldiers and their families and how they get better and don't. "I think they all try, really, really hard," she says, awe in her voice, and she gets to help them by having a job that she despises at the most elemental level—not the work itself but the need for it. "Why does my job have to exist?" she wonders.

It exists not only at Riley, but also across the country. There are, on this day, about eight thousand soldiers in the program Patti works for, called the Army Wounded Warrior Program, or AW2. They are the soldiers who have been diagnosed with the war's severest wounds, and the primary diagnosis for about half of them is PTSD. The diagnosis, in other words, is a psychological wound rather than a physical one, such as amputation (11 percent of them), and to help in their transition to civilian life are a hundred or so advocates like Patti who make up one more layer in a growing army bureaucracy for mental wounds that stretches from a soldier's homecoming, when he is presumed to be okay, to the WTB, where good endings are still expected, to an advocate's office, where good endings are still possible, to the Gardner Room at the Pentagon, where all possibility is gone. The fear of a soldier's killing himself is always there for Patti, and she does what she can to keep that from happening, by telling an employer, for instance, that yes the soldier he hired gets headaches sometimes, but the reason for the headaches is that he got rattled in an explosion fighting a war that most people in the country didn't think about then and don't care about now, and maybe, instead of only being concerned about his business, the employer could be so kind as to set up a room with some dark curtains for the soldier to rest in from time to time until the goddamn headache is better.

"Ya *know?*" she might tack on for emphasis.

She says that a lot, because in all of Fort Riley, no one feels more about wounded soldiers than Patti, or takes it more personally, and sometimes what she feels is irrepressible anger over their raw deal—the high unemployment rate, the high rates of PTSD and TBI, the high suicide numbers, all of it. "I'm really happy that we're so resilient, and I'm really happy that we're doing so good," she is saying one day, the sarcasm full throttle, the waterworks on the verge. As often happens with her, she is about to say something more, but before she can finish the thought, someone is outside her door knocking.

It is one of her forty-nine, a soldier who happens to have been in Adam's battalion. His name is Brandon, and he has come with his wife to tell Patti that he can't find work, none of the leads she was able to scrape together for him are panning out, they are almost out of money and are moving to Arizona, where at least there is family to fall back upon.

"You're killing me," Patti says to him.

"I'm killing *me*," he corrects her.

He is a haunted-looking young man who, like most of the others, didn't know what he was getting into, a good soldier right up until the end, when he was out on a mission to retrieve a blown-up Humvee in which two soldiers had died, and some rocket-propelled grenades landed close by and did him in. He came home and fell apart. His memory is sketchy and his dreams are bad. He knows he needs more counseling, and he has promised Patti he'll get some, but what he wants most of all is a job. A liquor store showed some interest in hiring him, but he suspects he shouldn't be around liquor. An airport shuttle company also seemed interested, but he doesn't want to be driving a van full of people along roads that he sometimes imagines are lined with bombs.

"We just want to get out of Kansas," he says, a soldier defeated.

"How's your marriage doing?" Patti asks.

"We're doing good," he says.

"We're doing good," his wife repeats.

And the way they glance at each other makes Patti see that they are doing good, that it's everything else. They live in one of the shabbier apartment buildings in Junction City, their car has bad tires and broken windows, and they're down to their last eight hundred dollars, which they're going to use to fix the tires, fix the windows, fill up the gas tank, and get out.

One thing Patti has learned is that the only thing left for her to do sometimes is wish people the best of luck and tell them she'll stay in touch.

"As always, I'm proud of you," she says.

Brandon smiles at her.

"Hooray," he says.

Now it is the wife of a soldier who comes to see Patti. He was in the same company as Adam and Tausolo Aieti, and in the same platoon as Nic DeNinno. He had deployed several times, lost three friends, blamed himself for one of them, and left the war for good after being shot in the neck, and some of what happened next is in his wife's statement in a court file.

"As soon as he got home," he "really wasn't the same no more at all," she had written. "He was forgetting constantly even the real easy things like he would put laundry in the washer but then forget about it. He would turn the oven on and forget it was on and a few times he got the food in the oven but forgot about it being in there so I stopped him from using the stove and oven.

"One night we were in bed sleeping," she continued.

I always sleep in my husband's arms with my head on his chest. Well this night he started screaming "HELP" which I assume was from when he was shot . . . He was sweating badly and then he started choking me in his sleep. Finally something in him just released and he stopped choking me. He woke up to hearing my gasping for air and crying. He asked what was wrong and turned the light on. I told him he was choking me. He apologized many times and said he don't remember choking me. But he could see the marks on me and the discoloration of my face and neck . . .

We tried to take a trip over to Topeka one day and we didn't even get to make it all the way there . . . He started sweating profusely. He said to pull over he needs air and that his head was killing him. I pulled over into a gas station for him. He said he was burning up. When I looked over at him it looked like someone poured a big bucket of water all over him but when I touched him he was freezing . . . I said ok let's go back home and as soon as I got back on the interstate he started shaking more and panicking and then passed out on me.

Her statement goes on for five pages. It includes twenty-eight examples of her husband's behavior after he came home, and it is buttressed by other statements from other people also trying to understand what had happened.

"I trust him with my life and couldn't ask for a better leader," wrote the soldier who dragged him to safety after he had been shot. "He always upheld high moral values and made sure we did the same."

"I am one of his soldiers. I served this last deployment with him and he is the most squared away person I have ever met," another soldier wrote. "I know he would never do anything to dishonor his family. He told me once that if everything is lost to always keep your honor. He believed in that very much."

". . . a devoted father and family man," another soldier wrote. "When his son was born, he was beaming for weeks."

". . . he could not have done any of the crimes he has been accused of," another wrote. "It is not in his character and it goes against all of the army values that he holds dear."

A psychologist who examined him and diagnosed him as having PTSD with psychosis, major depression, and dementia wrote that he was "a very ill man who has deteriorated so much that he is now quite dysfunctional."

His defense attorney wrote in a motion asking for no prison sentence: "It was only after these multiple instances of physical and mental trauma that [he] engaged in the conduct for which he stands before the court."

Finally, there was the statement of the victim in the case, who was his thirteen-year-old daughter. "I know that my dad was not himself, like someone had taken over him because he would never done something like this," she told investigators, according to the court file. "He was always the one who protected us from things like this. When he had gotten back from Iraq wounded he has not been the same person."

The charges all had to do with sex with a minor. Counts One and Two: "lewd fondling or touching of." Count Three: "sexual intercourse." The testimony, if the case had gone to trial, would have included what the daughter also told investigators, that while her father was in her bed, he kept calling her by the name of his wife. And the evidence included "a brown blanket and a Spiderman blanket" that were returned to the family after a plea deal was accepted on one charge of aggravated indecent solicitation of a child.

The terms of the deal were counseling, five years probation, and no contact with the family until the daughter's therapist said it would be okay. That permission had come fairly quickly after the plea deal, and now the entire family was back together and the most heartbroken woman in Junction City has come to Patti's office to tell her how things have been going.

"Come in! Give me a hug!" Patti says, and listens as the woman says of her husband, "He's doing good. He knows where he is, who he is, all the time."

"What made the difference?" Patti asks.

"Meds," the woman says, and then starts telling Patti about what a long road it has been, about the choking, about his running red lights, about his stopping in the middle of intersections and not knowing where he was. "He still keeps to himself," she says. "He doesn't go in any stores or anything like that. He keeps himself away from crowds. He doesn't do crowds."

"What was his home unit?" Patti asks, jotting notes.

"Two-sixteen."

"What company?"

"Oh, that's a long-time-ago question," the woman says, almost dreamily. She thinks about it for a moment but can't remember and mentions instead that even though he was shot, he never got any medals or awards.

"I am so so sorry," Patti says.

"Yeah," she says.

"So so sorry."

"Poor guy," she says.

"Regardless of what he did when he came home, he earned what he earned," Patti says.

The woman leans toward Patti. She takes a breath and sighs. "It never happened," she says.

Patti looks at her in confusion, wondering if she just heard what she heard.

"We told them about him trying to kill me in my sleep," she says. "They did nothing. We told them about him getting rough with the kids. They did nothing—"

"So he did not molest your daughter?" Patti interrupts.

"No."

"I thought he did."

"No."

"So you said this—to get help?"

The woman begins crying. Not loudly. Worse. Without sound. "I got the idea from *Law & Order*," she says after a bit, and now Patti can barely hear her as she says that her husband was having constant migraines, his worst ever, and his doctor wouldn't give him an immediate appointment, and she remembered a TV show where some people couldn't get anyone to pay attention to them until they concocted a story about child molestation, so she called the doctor back and said her husband may have touched their daughter. She did it out of desperation, she says, and it all of a sudden got out of control.

The doctor told her to take her daughter to the hospital right away, the hospital took swabs, the police took statements, the blankets were confiscated, her husband was arrested.

And it didn't matter that the blankets were clean, the swabs showed nothing unusual, and the daughter later said none of it was true, she says, because her husband was being told that he might never see his family again unless he took a deal.

So, she says, he took the deal.

Patti is dumbstruck. Could this be right, she is thinking—does this make any sense?—and then she realizes it makes no difference. He pled guilty. It's fact. Just as it's fact that he went to war and came home different, and he has a daughter, now sixteen, who whether she was or wasn't molested is suffering lately from crushing headaches, and he has a wife who when she's at work receives texts from him thirty or forty times a day.

"Do the kids have school today?" he texts. He has already texted this. She has already told him no.

"No," she replies.

He texts about the children, about the weather, about dinner. Now that his medication is helping, she is allowing him to use the oven again, but she has to guide him through every step. Look in the refrigerator, she texts. Take out the box that says Stouffer's. Turn on the oven to four hundred. Remove the covering on top. Put it in the oven.

Fifty-five minutes later: Take it out, and turn off the oven.

A few minutes later: Did you turn off the oven?

Those are her days.

As for her nights, because he needs to hold her to get to sleep and she worries that he will choke her, she has learned to sleep with his arms around her waist and her own arms wrapped around her head.

She demonstrates this.

"Are you getting counseling?" Patti asks.

"I did."

"Now?"

"No."

"Why?"

"Because they'll keep digging," the woman says, "and the more they dig I'll break down, and I don't have time to break down."

They've been talking for more than an hour now.

"Well," Patti says, at a loss.

The woman thanks her for listening.

They're done.

Now it is Patti's husband, Kevin, who comes to see her after he called her and sounded so upset that she told him, "You need to take a breath. You're a mess." She hung up, gave him time to take that breath, called him back. "You still sound pissy," she said. "You sound so incredibly discouraged that you're breaking my heart."

He comes into her office and stands by the window, all fidgety, even though there are two empty chairs. He is tall and solid and handsome, if a little lopsided. Somewhere in his sealed-up eye socket is his eye, a useless raisin of a thing, but enough time has gone by since the explosion for him to have adjusted to that. "Everyone can get better. It's all up to them," he likes to tell people, and as proof he offers his own example: wounded, just about dead, a coma, surgeries, recovering, better. The tremors that move through him from time to time: he deals with them. The pill he needs to take to get to sleep: he takes it. The two miles he used to run for his PT test: he walks them. The guilt he feels about the two soldiers of his who died: he feels it, but not to the point of shame. The images he continues to see of the one who was twenty-two years old and came from a town called Pleasanton and got hit and took two steps forward before falling: he can will those two ghost steps away. The anger he feels coming on sometimes: he takes deep breaths, as many as necessary, until it is gone.

He is the resilient soldier the army likes to talk about. Just not right now.

"I am fucking pissed," he tells Patti. "For him to chew your ass? For something you were asked to do for me?"

The "him" is an army major who wrote something about Kevin for his pending retirement, which in itself is one more accommodation he is making to the war.

He doesn't want to retire. He has been in the army for twenty-three years, the only thing he's ever done. But it has become clear to him that the army doesn't have a lot of use for him anymore, so he will get out with one final hope, that he will receive some award at his retirement ceremony, some acknowledgment of what he has sacrificed, anything official, so that he won't just be the lopsided guy standing up there with the weird eye. To that end, paperwork was submitted, and that's where the army major came in.

In support of the award, the major wrote a narrative testifying to the greatness of Kevin Walker. Not that he knew Kevin. He was a recent arrival to the unit Kevin was now in. But he was assigned to write it anyway, and when Kevin and Patti saw what he had come up with, they asked one of Kevin's previous commanders to write something instead. That commander did know Kevin. He was in charge of the tank unit that Kevin was part of when he got injured, and he had thought so highly of him that he would describe Kevin in the most flattering way possible among tankers, as nothing less than "a tanking motherfucker." The narrative he wrote about Kevin for the award was so moving that it brought Patti to tears. But, as she would soon find out, it also violated army regulation 600-8-22, section 3-19, paragraph r, which she had never heard of until it was rejected and returned. "Narrative should be prepared on 8½-by-11-inch bond paper and is limited to one double-spaced typewritten page," it states, and the new narrative went on for a page and a half. Patti's solution was to take some of what he had written and mix it in with some of what the major had written. One page, typed, double-spaced, bond paper. Perfect. But when the major learned of what had been going on without his approval, he came into her office roaring.

And now Kevin is in her office, trying not to. He is clenching his jaw, grinding his teeth, furious. He takes some breaths. In. Out. In. Out. And meanwhile, Patti is getting more and more upset. "I am so *stressed*," she is saying.

In. Out. In. Out.

"This is so *stupid*," Patti says.

Finally, calmer, Kevin tells Patti what they have to do. They cannot afford to have an officer mad at her. They need the income from her job. He is retiring with no job waiting for him, and there's no way to know whether his TBI will worsen over time, leaving him increasingly incapacitated. So they have to write a letter to the major saying that Kevin is to blame, and it has to be a letter of apology.

He's right. Patti knows it. The thought nauseates her. But as Kevin paces, she sits at her computer and begins typing, knowing what she wants to say:

That her husband was in Iraq, on a mission in a Humvee to find some missing Marines, looking out his window.

That when the bomb exploded, a piece of shrapnel, maybe an inch by an inch, according to the doctors, came straight at his face, sliced into him just on the side of his nose, angled back behind his left eye, and went into his brain.

That in those first seconds, he would remember screaming "Shut the fuck up" to the gunner, who was howling because his eardrums had exploded.

That just before passing out, he heard the code word his medics would use for saying an injury was serious and a guy needed to be undressed and realizing the guy was him.

That when he woke up for the first time several weeks later, a doctor asked him if he knew where he was. "A factory," he said.

That the first time he saw himself in a mirror, he tried to shut the one eye he had left and go back to sleep.

That once he was a tanking motherfucker and now he is a hurting motherfucker, and that he is loved and adored by a son who has learned to look him in the eye socket, a daughter who dyed a patch of hair for him, and a wife who would rather be doing anything other than writing this fucking letter.

Instead:

"Please allow me to apologize," she writes, and when she gets to the end and doesn't know how to wrap up, Kevin tells her.

"Again, I was only doing . . ." he says.

"Again, I was only doing," she types.

"What I was asked," he says.

"What I was asked," she types, "by my husband."

She reads it back. Here come the waterworks. Her phone has been ringing, and she needs to get back to her forty-nine.

"Thank you for your service," she says, hitting the send key on her computer. "Not."

Now it is Adam who comes to see her.

"I had a few calls today that may change the course of everything," he says, after taking a seat.

"What do you mean?" Patti asks.

"Two job offers," Adam says.

"For you?"

"Mm-hmm," he says.

"Where?" she says. She's surprised. When she called him and asked him to stop by, she expected they'd talk about the usual subjects. His job. His marriage. His children. Maybe the pheasant hunt, although she'd already told him about the earful she had gotten when he left without telling anyone. She hadn't expected this.

"One's actually back in Iraq. It's a contractor," he says, and when he sees the look on her face, he quickly adds, "I'm not gonna do that one. Don't worry about it. There's no way in hell I would do that." He takes a breath and tells her about the second one. "And then there was a guy in two-sixteen, he was our company medic, now with a company out of San Antonio, they do private security, and they just get on the ships in the shipping lanes in the Horn of Africa just to provide protection as they go to and from, and it's like three hundred bucks a day."

"Wow," she says.

"You're gone for thirty days, and then you're home for as long as you want and you go again."

"What do you think about that?" she asks.

"It sounds pretty good. Because me and my wife, we got along so much better when I was in the army," Adam says.

"What does *she* think?" Patti asks.

"Oh I don't know. She doesn't really want me—it's not that she doesn't want me to do it, she doesn't think it's legit. Like I would do it and end up just getting fucked somehow. But the company's very reputable. Their website, I checked it out."

"I would hate to see you get screwed, too," Patti says. "But if that's something you want to do—"

"I miss it," Adam says. "Holding a gun, and being with a group of guys. It probably sounds really homosexual, but—"

"You know what? Not really."

"I miss that—"

"Camaraderie."

"Yes. Being a team, and working together."

"My husband has told me that more than once," Patti says.

"Yup. If I just had a group of buddies living around me, even if we could just sit out back and smoke dope or fucking cigarettes, or drink some fucking beers—"

"You'd be content," she says.

"Do that for a couple of years, and everything will be paid off, and—"

"Slow down."

"I know."

"Okay?"

"It's nice to think about, though," Adam says.

"Are you running?" Patti asks.

"Running?"

"Mm-hmm."

"No, I'm not running," Adam says.

"Yes, you're running," Patti says. "You're running."

"I'm not running," Adam says.

"Are you trying to get back what you left?" she asks.

"Trying to get back what I left?"

"Because you left mid-deployment?"

"No. Oh no. No. Because there's no way this would make up for that," Adam says.

"You sure?"

"Maybe if I had gone back to Iraq or something like that. But this? I'll never get that back. Short of a time machine showing up here and actually taking me back to ten minutes before I made my decision, there's nothing that's going to change that."

"Okay."

"Unless there *was* a time machine—" Adam says.

Patti sighs one of her big sighs as his phone rings. It's a special ringtone he downloaded just for Saskia's calls.

Love—it's a motherfucker, it says.

Love—it's a motherfucker, it says again.

Love—

"Hello?"

She watches him sag. She knows things about soldiers and families. That some of them get better and some of them don't.

"Sorry," he says when he hangs up.

"So," she says.

"I'll have to think about it," he says.

"Love you much," she says, standing up and offering him a hug.

"Thank you," he says.

He's not getting better. She knows this. He needs help. A program, she thinks. Topeka. And if Topeka is full, Pueblo. And if Pueblo is full, she'll find somewhere else.

Maybe the pheasant hunt didn't work out. But she's not ready to wish Adam luck yet.

9

A few doors down from Patti Walker's office is the office of Tim Jung, who is in charge of new arrivals at the WTB. The wide-eyed, the nervous-eyed, the closed-eyed, the dead-eyed, they all start out with Tim Jung, a friendly, gum-chewing, boyish-looking sergeant first class who one day, without telling anyone, goes for a drive by himself into the Kansas countryside.

Fifteen miles from the WTB, he pulls into a dirt parking area next to the Big Blue River. It's late afternoon and not many people are around, but just to be sure he won't be interrupted, he decides to go to the far side of the river. He climbs an embankment and starts across a long train trestle. If a train comes, there won't be much he can do, but at this point it hardly matters. He has plenty of sleeping pills with him and blank paper on which to write letters to his children. His plan is simple: write the letters, swallow the pills, wade into the river, and let the water take it from there. It's hard to say what has brought him to this point. Probably, like so many cases he's seen at the WTB, it's not one thing in particular but an accumulation of everything.

On the far side now—no train, he'll have to do it himself—he walks south along the river's edge until he finds a place to sit. The air has that damp, moldy smell of mud and ripe leaves, but he doesn't mind it. He takes out the paper and a pen and wonders in his life's last moments what to write of all that has happened. A life of soldiering. A long marriage that failed. A period of cancer treatments. Any one of them could be its own letter, but what he chooses instead for his final words are the thoughts of a father who is proud of his children and knows absolutely

Train trestle across the Big Blue River

that they will go on to accomplish great things. He writes for a while in the stink of the river until he is sure he has written something okay for his children to read and reread in a lifetime of trying to drown out the noise of what he's about to do, and then he gets the pills ready and takes a look around the spot he has chosen. This is his furnace room, his parking lot next to the Dumpster, his garage behind the house of his mother, his table to stand on and then kick away. He is looking west, into a setting sun, that seems to be lighting the river on fire.

It is beautiful, he allows himself to think, and as he keeps looking he takes notice of the river's current, which strikes him as beautiful, too. He watches some water bugs skimming along the surface and some birds riding the late-afternoon drafts. There are crickets, also, pining away in the grasses and weeds, and whereas a few minutes ago he was hearing and seeing none of this, now he sits, with pills in hand and letters next to him, transfixed. The crickets keep singing. The water keeps moving. The sun keeps dropping. It's beautiful, he keeps thinking, and in that little bit of hesitation something inside of him turns, or recedes, or cracks open, or does whatever happens when someone no longer wants to die, because when he at last stands up it is to go gratefully away from the river, back across the trestle, back home to hide the letters in a desk drawer, and back to the WTB, where the new arrivals keep coming, and coming, and coming, all of them headed to the river, including one day Tausolo Aieti.

He is sitting on a couch outside of Tim Jung's office, holding a folded quilt, because a few minutes ago, a woman passing by noticed him and asked, "Do you want a quilt?"

"Why not?" Tausolo answered, shrugging, which seemed in keeping with what had happened so far in his first day at the WTB. He had shown up early for orientation and been given a list of thirty-nine WTB offices he would have to visit and get signatures from to prove that he had been there. He'd gone first to human resources, where the door was shut and locked and no one answered his knock even though the sign on the door said OPEN. He'd gone to the mailroom, where the guy working there had screamed over the music he was playing, "Are you a fast-tracker?" "A what?" Tausolo said. "A fast-tracker," the guy yelled, and added a little ominously, "You'd know if you was." He'd gone to the chaplain, who wasn't there. He'd gone to the security office to get an ID badge, where the person he handed his orders to said with irritation, "These are your *thirty*-day orders. We need your *ninety*-day orders. You have to go see your S-1." He had gone to see his S-1, who wasn't there. He'd gone to the army career office, where the woman said, "Mondays are *crazy*," handed him a brochure, and asked, "Do you have any aspirations, dreams, desires, or hopes to do college?" "Uh, yeah," he replied. He'd gone to see his military family life consultant, who explained that MFLC may sound like AFLAC but it's really more like behavioral health, except "we keep no records, none whatsoever." "Okay," he said. "Very nice to have met you," she said. "You too," he said. He had paused to look out a window at another soldier in front of the WTB who was on a cell phone and spinning around in agitated circles. He had gone back to the chaplain, whose assistant handed him a brochure. He had gone to see Tim Jung, who would be his new commander, and was directed to wait on the couch, where he was in the midst of counting up the signatures he had collected so far when the woman passed by and asked about the quilt.

"Here you go," she said, returning from somewhere with a lovely quilt that was hand-sewn by a volunteer who wanted to do something for wounded soldiers.

"Okay, thanks," he said, taking it, and now he sits looking at it. "What the hell is this?" he says quietly. He feels like he's been given a baby blanket.

A sergeant passes by, sees him, sees the quilt, and looks at his name tag. "What the hell's going on with you, Aieti?" he asks.

"Good," Tausolo answers.

"Good?" the sergeant says, confused by this answer. "Good?"

Tausolo sighs. He's up to six signatures. He has been given a quilt, a piece of candy, a pen, two brochures, and a certificate for a turkey.

"You!" he hears now.

He looks up. It is Tim Jung, motioning Tausolo into his office. Tausolo knows nothing about him, other than he will be his commander and is looking in puzzlement at a form on his computer screen. "Well, I don't understand," he says as Tausolo sits across from him. "I get this in last week and you are only a moderate. But . . ." He keeps reading. It is an assessment of how much of a risk Tausolo is to himself. "They want to put you on the high-risk tracker. Are you aware of that?"

"No," Tausolo says.

"You're not?"

"No."

Now it is Tim Jung who sighs. He is as aware as anyone of how difficult the army can make things. But he is also aware of the hidden ways of human beings, and so he works down a list of questions in order to assess how Tausolo has been doing.

Nightmares?

"Yeah," Tausolo says.

Recurring?

"Yeah."

Racing thoughts?

"No."

Reliving past events?

"Yeah."

Problems in sleeping?

"Yeah."

"Okay. High risk is not a bad thing," Jung says. "It means we're going to pay particular attention."

He hands Tausolo a form and tells him that he has to sign it and read it aloud. "It is important you remember this is not a punishment," he says.

"Contract for Safety," Tausolo reads aloud. "I, Aieti, Tausolo, know that I am in a difficult state and may look for a way out by harming myself or others. I will not intentionally harm myself or others and if I have thoughts about harming myself or others I will contact my Chain of Command immediately. I agree to take these precautions and stay safe because I know that my life and the lives of those around me are worth holding on to."

He signs it and looks down at his folded hands as Jung explains to him that high risk means he can't drink, can't be around guns or knives, will have to check in with his squad leader every morning and night, and can be given only a week's worth of medications at a time.

"I need to know what meds you're on."

"Zoloft. Trazodone. Lunesta. Abilify. Concerta. And ibuprofen," Tausolo says, listing his medications to treat depression, anxiety, insomnia, attention deficit, and knee pain. "I think that's it."

"PTSD?" Jung asks.

"Yeah."

"Depression?"

"Yeah."

"Adjustment disorder?"

"Yeah."

There is a look that Tausolo gets sometimes. He had it in Iraq when he found out that Harrelson was dead. He had it just this morning when he woke up after dreaming yet again, despite everything, of Harrelson on fire asking him why he didn't save him. And he has it now.

Jung sees it. He puts the paperwork aside. He waits until Tausolo meets his eyes and says with a level of intensity that catches Tausolo by surprise, "The good thing is you've recognized it and want to get some help for it. And we can do that."

A few minutes later, Tausolo is standing outside, holding his quilt and checklist with thirty-three more signatures to go.

High risk.

"Wow," he says, hanging his head.

There are times that he wonders what that day was really about, other than a mission to go from here to there after a mission that had taken him from there to here. Later, others in the convoy would disagree over how high his 12,000-pound Humvee was blown into the air. Ten feet. No, idiot, ten *yards*. No, jackass, thirty feet. No, dumbshit, thirty feet *is* ten yards. Whatever, the rise was violent, the landing hard. He got the door open. He got out with that broken leg and then on that broken leg turned back. He pulled out one guy and helped pull out another as the Humvee burst into flames and rounds began cooking off, and later, some of the guys who were there that day said he deserved the Medal of Honor for what he had done, certainly a Silver Star, or at least a Bronze Star with Valor. He was told once that paperwork had been filled out for something or other and subsequently lost, but he has no idea about that. He did get a Purple Heart out of it, and he'll forever have a bum knee, and PTSD, and TBI, but it is the guilt from that day that he carries most of all, so much so that when he was at Topeka after destroying his apartment, he wrote a shaky letter to a fellow soldier named Drew Edwards, who was the gunner in the Humvee.

"How you dealing with life bro?" he had written. "I'm going through treatment for PTSD at the VA hospital in Topeka. Been struggling with anger at times but getting this treatment has helped me out a lot. I just wanted to ask you if you remember anything from that IED incident in Iraq? I remember helping you out from that truck. What I'm trying to get at is if you remember it like I do, do you hate me for helping you out? You don't have to answer back if this gives you flashbacks. Much luv to you brother and be safe."

Edwards, who was up in the gun turret, did remember it, of course. He remembered having his foot on the radio mount between the seats, his heel shattering and his ankle breaking in half. He remembered all of it, right down to the light flash that has been part of his life since, along with the shrapnel still in his face, another piece still in his eye, bad dreams, anger problems, memory problems, pain meds, sleep meds, and after almost two years of trying so hard in rehab, the decision by doctors to give up and amputate his leg. None of which he mentioned in his reply to Tausolo, just as he didn't mention being back in school and married and starting a family and being grateful to be alive except for the times he isn't grateful and has to be away from everyone and everything in complete isolation. "Not at all man, I have nothing but respect for you guys" is what he wrote back. "To be honest I didn't go into shock at all and remember it vividly. I have some anger issues too. If it was an option I would re-enlist and get back after it. I am living up in KC but will be back down at Riley soon to see you guys. Miss you man. Later."

That was it, all he had to say. "Do you hate me?" Tausolo had asked, opening a vein to a brother in combat, and if the answer he got wasn't quite the exoneration he'd been seeking, it would have to do, because while the truth of war is that it's always about loving the guy next to you, the truth of the after-war is that you're on your own. There were five guys in the Humvee that day, and the only one not trying to figure out what happened in his own way, at his own speed, is Harrelson. For the other four, the individual reckonings continue, and now one of them begins his second day at the WTB by laying his head on a table, closing his eyes, and wondering how many signatures he can get in the next eight hours.

It happens to be a significant day in the army, not at Fort Riley but in Washington, D.C. As Tausolo moves from one office to another with his list, a ceremony gets under way at the White House to present the first Medal of Honor awarded to a living person since the Vietnam War. "It is my privilege to present our nation's highest military decoration, the Medal of Honor, to a soldier as humble as he is heroic: Staff Sergeant Salvatore A. Giunta," President Obama says in remarks directed to a soldier whose nervous eyes bear some resemblance to Tausolo's, and then describes what happened one day in Afghanistan:

"Sal and his platoon were several days into a mission in the Korengal Valley—the most dangerous valley in northeast Afghanistan. The moon was full. The light it cast was enough to travel by without using their night-vision goggles. With heavy gear on their backs, and air support overhead, they made their way single file down a rocky ridge crest, along terrain so steep that sliding was sometimes easier than walking. They hadn't traveled a quarter mile before the silence was shattered. It was an ambush, so close that the cracks of the guns and the whizz of the bullets were simultaneous. Tracer fire hammered the ridge at hundreds of rounds per minute—'more,' Sal said later, 'than the stars in the sky.' The Apache gunships above saw it all, but couldn't engage with the enemy so close to our soldiers. The next platoon heard the shooting, but were too far away to join the fight in time. And the two lead men were hit by enemy fire and knocked down instantly. When the third was struck in the helmet and fell to the ground, Sal charged headlong into the wall of bullets to pull him to safety behind what little cover there was. As he did, Sal was hit twice, one round slamming into his body armor, the other shattering a weapon slung across his back. They were pinned down, and two wounded Americans still lay up ahead. So Sal and his comrades regrouped and counterattacked. They threw grenades, using the explosions as cover to run forward, shooting at the muzzle flashes still erupting from the trees. Then they did it again. And again. Throwing grenades, charging ahead. Finally, they reached one of their men. He'd been shot twice in the leg, but he had kept returning fire until his gun jammed. As another soldier tended to his wounds, Sal sprinted ahead, at every step meeting relentless enemy fire with his own. He crested a hill alone, with no cover but the dust kicked up by the storm of bullets still biting into the ground. There, he saw a chilling sight: the silhouettes of two insurgents carrying the other wounded American away—who happened to be one of Sal's best friends. Sal never broke stride. He leapt forward. He took aim. He killed one of the insurgents and wounded the other, who ran off. Sal found his friend alive, but badly wounded. Sal had saved him from the enemy—now he had to try to save his life. Even as bullets impacted all around him, Sal grabbed his friend by the vest and dragged him to cover. For nearly half an hour, Sal worked to stop the bleeding and help his friend breathe until the MEDEVAC arrived to lift the wounded from the ridge. American gunships worked to clear the enemy from the hills. And with the battle over, First Platoon picked up their gear and resumed their march through the valley. They continued their mission . . ."

Obama goes on from there, talking about one day in one part of one war, and meanwhile, in one part of another war, on that very same day, in those very same hours, Tausolo was hobbling around Iraq on crutches and telling no one about his dreams of Harrelson, all of which goes to show how long it can take for a Medal of Honor to be approved.

". . . our brave servicemen and women and their families have done everything they've been asked to do," Obama is saying now. "They have been everything that we have asked them to be. 'If I am a hero,' Sal has said, 'then every man who stands around me, every woman in the military, every person who defends this country is.' And he's right. This medal today is a testament to his uncommon valor, but also to the parents and the community that raised him; the military that trained him; and all the men and women who served by his side. All of them deserve our enduring thanks and gratitude. They represent a small fraction of the American population, but they and the families who await their safe return carry far more than their fair share of our burden. They fight halfway around the globe, but they do it in hopes that our children and our grandchildren won't have to. They are the very best part of us. They are our friends, our family, our neighbors, our classmates, our coworkers. They are why our banner still waves, our founding principles still shine, and our country, the United States of America, still stands as a force for good all over the world. So please join me in welcoming Staff Sergeant Salvatore A. Giunta for the reading of the citation."

And if only Tausolo could be hearing this part, maybe he would feel better about being a soldier, but instead at this moment, as the president is hanging the Medal of Honor around Sal Giunta's neck, the thing he is feeling good about as he heads toward the pharmacy is being up to twenty-one signatures.

"So I'm Sue, and I'm the pharmacist here. Do you have any questions?"

"No," Tausolo says.

"Okay. You want to just get everything out?"

He has brought all of his prescriptions in a Walmart bag. He lines them up on her desk.

"Zoloft," Sue says, picking up the first one. "Are you taking this every day? One a day? You feel like that's working for you okay?"

She picks up the second. "Klonopin. Do you take this twice a day every day? Does it help you with your anxiety?"

The third. "Abilify. What do you take this for? Do you feel like it helps you?"

Tausolo laughs. "I don't know. I'm on so many pills," he says.

"Trazodone," she says, moving on. "Do you know what this one is for?"

"Sleep?"

"Yeah," she says. "Now I notice you also have Lunesta. Do you take them both for sleep?"

He nods.

"I guess my question is do you need them both?"

He nods again.

"And then your ibuprofen," she says, picking up the next.

"Yeah. That's for my knee thing."

"And here's another bottle of Lunesta," she says. "And here's another Trazodone."

She makes notes of all this and checks them against a list she'd been given before his arrival.

"Now what about Concerta?" she says, mentioning the drug he had told Tim Jung he takes for attention deficit and memory. "Are you taking that?"

"Yes," he says sheepishly. "I forgot to bring it."

She reaches into a supply cabinet and fishes out two plastic pill boxes, one green, one purple, one for morning, one for evening, each of which can hold seven days' worth of medication. "Would that make it easier?" she asks. She takes out a pen.

Twenty-two signatures.

Later, walking down a hallway with his Walmart bag reloaded, he runs into the sergeant who the day before had asked him what was going on with him, to which he had nervously answered, "Good." That was uncomfortable enough, but now the sergeant, whose name is Michael Lewis, is poking around the Walmart bag and motioning Tausolo over to his desk.

"You got a lot of pills, man," he says as Tausolo once again finds himself seated across from someone he knows nothing about. Jung, at least, seemed friendly. But there's something about this guy that makes Tausolo hesitant to say anything at all, and it's not like he's much of a talker to begin with.

"Wow," Lewis says, taking out a container and looking at the label.

He takes out another.

"You got it bad, man," he says.

He takes out the next one, aware of Tausolo watching and knowing what he is thinking of him. Too bad. This is the way he is now. He's been in this place for three years, and at first he tried to get close to everybody, even the one who threw beer bottles at anyone who came in his room, which he not only tolerated, but understood. He'd lost three guys in the war. But then, back here, came his fourth loss, a high-risk tracker named Jessie Robinson, who on a Friday night called in, right on time, saying he needed to go to his house and cut his grass. Saturday morning, he again called to say he was at the house and about to start mowing. Saturday night, he called to say he was at his house and had just finished. Sunday morning: nothing. Lewis waited until fifteen minutes after deadline and then called another sergeant, who hadn't heard from him, either. They drove to his house, where the grass was freshly cut, the car was in the driveway, the car windows were down, and the keys were in the ignition. They knocked on the front door. No answer. They circled the house, trying to see inside. Everything looked shut and locked. They tried the front door and were surprised to find it open. "Jessie?" the other sergeant called as they went inside. "Jessie?" The house was dark. Lewis started climbing the stairs up to the main level. "Jessie?" A cat came flying out of nowhere and disappeared down the stairs. "Jessie?" Now, at the top of the stairs, he heard a moan and saw a slice of light at the end of the hallway. It was coming from the bathroom, and when Lewis looked in, there was Robinson, on the floor near two empty pill bottles, his head resting in a puddle of blood. "And the blood was black," Lewis would recall. "Jessie, Jessie, it's Lew," he said, lifting him. Robinson vomited. He went limp. Lewis held on to him until, as he would put it, "there was no noise anymore." And that's who Tausolo is looking at, someone who describes himself as "more leery now. More cautious." Because "you have to be. You never know." Because "it kind of messed me up."

None of which he says to Tausolo, just as Tausolo says nothing to him. Instead, he sweeps the pills back into Tausolo's Walmart bag, flips open his briefcase, shows Tausolo the pill containers he carries around, says quietly, "I got my demons, too," and tells Tausolo to take the rest of the day off.

And maybe what happens next doesn't happen if Tausolo, hearing this, gets up right away. But he hesitates for a minute, and when he stands up he nearly collides with Tim Jung, who happens to be rushing by. "Quite a grocery bag," Jung says, and instead of going home, Tausolo is once again lining up his pill bottles on a desk.

"Klonopin?" Jung asks, remembering that Tausolo didn't mention Klonopin.

"Where's the Concerta?" he asks, remembering that Tausolo did mention that.

He reaches for the phone to call Sue the pharmacist. It will take him several tries to get through to her, and when he does this is what will happen:

He will remind her that Tausolo is on the high-risk tracker and say, "Well he's got a small buffet of Trazodone here . . . Well he certainly doesn't need sixty Klonopins while he's in high-risk . . . same for the Trazodone . . . same for the Abilify . . ."

This in turn will lead to Tausolo going to see someone who will painstakingly sort through all of his pills, take out a week's worth of each one, put the rest in a pile for disposal, and ask which of the two pill containers he was given he would like to use for the pills he takes in the evening. "It doesn't matter," he will say, but she will say it does matter, it really does, and will wait patiently until he chooses the green one, and then she inexplicably will write on it with a pen "A.M."

She will then call someone to dispose of the leftover pills, who will turn out to be Sergeant Lewis. "I told him to leave early. He walked right into this," he will say under his breath when he sees Tausolo, and after they've disposed of the pills—some two hours after he told Tausolo to go home—he will shake his head and say, "Next time I tell you to leave early, put some jet engines on your legs."

"Damn," Tausolo will whisper to himself. "How'd I get myself into this mess?"

All because he didn't get up fast enough. Or because he is why the banner still waves, the founding principles still shine, and the United States of America still stands as a force for good all over the world. Or because he once got in a Humvee because someone told him he needed to go from here to there, and because of that he is high risk.

Whatever the cause, all of this will happen as surely as Harrelson will return to his dreams, but first, as Tim Jung dials, once again seeing the look that has returned to Tausolo's face, he pauses. He knows the look. It's the look of the river-bound. He had it himself once, and he didn't leave the river that day so someone would die on his watch, not his soldiers, not himself, and not Aieti, Tausolo, who by contract acknowledges he is in a difficult state.

"You didn't do anything wrong," he says to Tausolo.

"I know," Tausolo wishes he could say back, but he knows he has.

Why else would he be here?

10

Jessie Robinson's trip to the Gardner Room in the Pentagon begins as soon as he is taken from Michael Lewis's arms, rushed to the hospital, and declared dead from an overdose of acetaminophen.

Right away, his unit starts work on completing a Commander's Suspected Suicide Event Report, also known as a 37-Liner, even though it contains only thirty-one lines of questions. The report will be the basis for what Peter Chiarelli eventually sees, and it asks about such things as Jessie Robinson's marital status, financial status, alcohol use, drug use, suicide prevention training, behavioral health history, and "Details of suspected suicide event, including suspected method of death (e.g. hanging, drowning, overdose)."

At the same time, a different army unit, the Army Medical Command, works on its own report, which among other things will say that at the time of his death, Robinson was separated from his wife, Kristy, had been diagnosed with "Major depression, recurrent" and "Atypical psychosis," and was taking twelve prescription medications. It will also say that Robinson "had two spouse abuse cases . . . that were substantiated with him as the offender," and that "there were also accusations of infidelity, conspiracy theories, communication problems, depression (for both), anxiety, obsessive compulsive tendencies, and trust issues. SGT Robinson continually attended therapy sessions, but it cannot be determined if they were successful due to his unwillingness to cooperate, stay on task, and talk about the presenting issues. Towards the end of his life, the Robinsons were pending divorce, and Mrs. Robinson had moved out of their house."

Summer and Kristy Robinson

That report will be sent to Chiarelli as well, along with results of a separate Fatality Review Board being conducted by Fort Riley, which shouldn't be confused with the Initial Death Notification report that is supposed to be sent to Chiarelli within two days of any suicide.

Meanwhile, army public affairs is working on a press release to go to the media and members of Congress about all of the army suicides that happened in the month Robinson died, which will need to contain a quote from Chiarelli or someone else from the army's highest ranks.

This should be easy enough, but sometimes it isn't. After one especially bad month, the proposed quote sent to Chiarelli's staff for approval was:

> The brave individuals who wear the cloth of this great Nation in combat deserve our deepest gratitude. It is remarkable all they have accomplished. I am incredibly proud of them and of their families. That said, they are tired. The persistent high operational tempo of this war, the terrible things some have seen or experienced in combat, have undoubtedly taken a toll on them. Many are struggling with the "invisible wounds" of this war, including traumatic brain injury, post-traumatic stress, depression and anxiety.

A good quote. Seemingly sincere. Even moving. Except:

"The quotes from GEN Chiarelli are accurate, but I'm not sure they fit if we are indeed addressing the highest active duty suicide month on record," someone responded.

"I have a feeling the VCSA will want to be personally involved in the shaping of this message," someone else responded.

"I am not a fan of more meetings, but on this . . ." someone else responded.

There were more e-mails, followed by a meeting, followed by another flurry of e-mails, and finally a new quote was crafted and sent directly to Chiarelli for his approval. "Sir," the e-mail to him said:

> We would propose the following, with the goal of alleviating an "alarmist" reaction to the spike in July, while keeping to our message that suicide, albeit terrible, represents the most extreme end of the spectrum

of at-risk/high-risk behavior. Bottom line: we want the Members and media to read the release and conclude that while the high number of suicides is discouraging (goes to your reputation as being frank/honest), we remain confident we're doing the right things and having the intended positive impact.

"Proposed quote for your approval:" it continued:

As I've said many times, every suicide represents a tragic loss to our Army and the Nation. While the high number of potential suicides in July is discouraging, we are confident our efforts aimed at increasing individuals' resiliency, while reducing incidence of at-risk and high-risk behavior across the Force, are having a positive impact. We absolutely recognize there is much work to be done and remain committed to ensuring our people are cared for and have ready access to the best possible programs and services.

"That is fine," he replied.

"Success! :)" one of his staffers responded.

Meanwhile, Robinson's unit finishes the 37-Liner and starts getting ready for the actual briefing, a process that one battalion commander who went through it refers to as "ass-pain" because of all the attention that's required when "the dreaded 'suicide' word is used." Describing what he went through when one of his soldiers killed someone and then committed suicide, he says, "The unit starts to panic because everyone has been through suicide awareness training, and if this kid hasn't we're screwed. The first event is to circle the wagons and ensure his name is on the roster that he attended the mandatory training, because if he didn't that will be the reason he killed himself. Doesn't matter if he's a murderer—if his name's not on that roster, that's why he did it. The good news in our case is he was on the roster. Lucky for us. Then comes the brief. About six months after the event, much of the original chain of command has moved on, the story has gone stale, but the Vice is going to take a brief, we are told. Really? The Vice? Disbelief at first but others who have been through it come online and confirm the Vice does sit in, so the brigade commander gets spun up. 'This can't be dropped! Double-check the font on the slides! Make sure the info is correct!' The brigade commander rehearses the brief to staff—'Check that damn font!'—briefs the chain of command—'That last line's font is off! Fix it!'—we check again with the Vice's staff. 'Does this type of suicide get briefed?' 'Yes! You better get on board' . . . It took a few weeks of work, not constant but enough time to be distracting."

Versions of this ass-pain are happening at posts around the world as the day of the briefing closes in. On the day itself, at the appointed time, no matter if at that time it might be midnight in Iraq, 1:30 a.m. in Afghanistan, and 4:00 a.m. in Korea, various generals and their staffs gather in video-conference facilities and beam themselves into the Gardner Room, where name cards have been arranged and the SECRET sign has been lit.

"Ladies and gentlemen, the Vice."

Eight months after he killed himself, Jessie Robinson's briefing is under way. As usual, there are too many cases to get through in two hours, and to get through as many as possible, Chiarelli wants the focus to be less on what happened and more on lessons learned.

The lessons learned, then, in Robinson's case:

"Additional training is required to inform soldiers of the dangers of self-medicating along with the associated risk of overdosing" is the first. "Encourage the use of a battle buddy among warriors" is the second. "Increase suicide prevention classes" is the third. "Increase communication to twice a day with high-risk soldiers" is the fourth. "Continue improvements in leader communication" is the fifth.

And that's that. Eight months. Five minutes. The army moves on to the next suicide. Case forever closed.

In Kansas, meanwhile, Kristy Robinson has begun repainting the walls in the house where she stayed with her husband as long as she could, until finally, too frightened to remain, she took their baby and fled. She is thirty years old now, and if her husband's trip was eventually to the Gardner Room, hers is to a place she has yet to arrive at and understand. She's not even sure where her trip began. Was it before the war, when she was at a church dinner, bored to tears by the men talking to her, and Jessie came over, introduced himself, and swept her off of her feet? Was it four years later when Jessie—still the "polite, organized, hard-working, gentle, loving man that remembered everything," as his obituary would say—went to Iraq? Was it a year after that when he came home wanting the towels folded a certain way and calling her a slut, bitch, whore, cunt, and pissed-on fire hydrant?

Her lesson learned: it's different from the army's. To her, what happened *is* the lesson.

"He laid out a blanket on the bed," she says. "It was a quilt his grandmother made for him. He slept on top of the covers, on top of it."

He cut the grass. Cleaned out the drawers in the bathroom. Took out the trash.

"He also turned off the AC."

That's what he did, and now she gets to figure out why.

"I guess to save on the electricity bill," she says of why he turned off the AC, but is that something that someone in the act of committing suicide would think about? The electricity bill?

"I think he was trying to get rid of anything embarrassing because he knew there would be an investigation," she says. Is that why he cleaned out the drawers?

"I think he was trying to make it look like an accident because I don't think he thought insurance would pay out for a suicide." Is that why he left no note?

"To not make a mess"—is that why he slept on top of the quilt?

"I still loved him very much." Did he know that?

"Did he still love me?"

"Did he hate me?"

She is back living in the house now with their daughter, Summer, who was ten months old when it happened. The kitchen floor still has nicks in it from the day he toppled the china cabinet. The door at the end of the hallway is still gouged from the framed family pictures that he picked up and flung. The walls are dented and scuffed from the furniture he overturned.

Those are the walls she has begun painting. Light green for the living room. Dark green for the bedroom. Brown for the downstairs.

"Jessie hated colors," she says. "Walls should be white with nothing on them but mirrors and clocks."

Wherever she's going on this trip, every brushstroke feels like a step. She just doesn't know toward what.

The army has its reports, she has hers.

"Two days ago Jessie shoved me and kicked a laundry basket. Summer was on the floor next to the laundry basket" is how hers begins. The army has a 37-Liner. Hers consists of texts that she typed into her cell phone when Jessie wasn't around, which she hid in a folder called "Tasks" and a subfolder called "Don't Forget to Register." He had been home for four years, and things had gotten bad enough that she wanted a record of what was happening. Hastily written, sometimes with misspellings and always with the feeling that Jessie was about to reappear, it ended up being a record of his disintegration.

November 1: "Jessie overturned the coffee table. He took my cell phone away from me. When I tried to leave the house he held me and pushed me back inside the house. I was holding Summer in my arms durring all of this. He said that if I called the police they would take Summer away from both of us. He wouln't let me near the front door or the back patio door."

November 12: "Jessie said that the only reason he sleeps in our bed is because it is the most comfortable place to sleep."

December 12: "Jessie woke up telling me that he was 'this close to beating the living shit out of me' and tha I was lucky I just hadn't made him mad enough. He spat at me."

December 24: "Jessie got up, yelling at me that I forgot to set his alarm clock. He threw a bugger bulb at me. He said that the only reason he puts up with a monster like me is because of Summer, and that she would be worth giving up to get away from me."

December 25: "This morning Jessie left at 9:00am. When I got out of bed I found the Christmas tree tossed off the deck into the back yard. He came home just after 2pm, took a shower and wend to bed."

January 11: "Jessie yelled loudly in my face, I was holding Summer—she began crying because of how loud he yelled. He said he should smack me so I would know how a battered woman really felt. He threw the bed post across the room. He said he 'could just bash (my) fucking head in.' "

January 16: "Jessie demanded that I leave work early and get home immediately. He said he had been posing as me on Instant Messanger and contacting people I have no desire to be in touch with. When I got home, he left. He came back later with a liter of vodka & orange juice."

January 19: "Jessie yelled, called me a feminist bitch, a live in prostitute. He emptied a vase, thrw it away and then urinated on it from the top balcony of the deck. He said since he's already labeled a perpetrator of abuse, it really wouldn't be a suprise, he should live up to the label. He said he hoped to get arrested—he was aiming to get arrested."

January 20: "Jessie woke me up at 5:00 and began yelling again. He said that tomarrow he is going to raise a stink. He grabbed my hair and ear and shoved my face to the bed while I was feeding Summer."

February 27: "This morning we woke up and played with Summer. When she calmed down I started breast feeding. Jessie started yelling at me 'I'm fucking talking to you!' i'm going to break every knuckle of your conciousness. When I get done with you you'll wish you had only been chocked. He says i'm a yo-yo that he's kept on his finger for the past year and a half, and that i'm falling perfectly into his trap. He said I'd better hope my car doesn't brake down. I'd better be careful because in twenty years or so I might have an 'accident.' . . . he said I should watch out because 'you never know when you're being recorded.' "

February 28: "Jessie said he has the scanner listening to and recording the house and my cell phone conversations. When I took Summer into the bedroom to lay her down asleep, Jessie yelled at me and shoved one dresser into the other. The noise startled and woke Summer crying. In the kitchen I was holding and trying to calm Summer, Jessie yelled loudly in my face and stomped his feet, Summer started crying."

March 4: "6:30am Jessie woke up calling me a fucking bitch. He said he used to think about getting me flowers, now he thinks about punching my fucking nose and watching it bleed."

March 11: "Jessie didn't sleep at all last night. He has barely slept at all since Saturday. He's been telling me that he's been being watched and has been for a long time. On Saturday he said the substitute mail carrier was in on it. Sunday night he went to the store for smokes—said he had a really bad headache, and didn't come home till Monday afternoon . . . He spent Monday night working in the garage. He screwed the windows shut and blocked them with pegboard. He turns on all the outside lights and leaves them on all night. We went to a sevice at Faith Tabernacle Church yesterday. It was very loud. The people were nice, but I didn't get anything out of the service. Afterwords, Jessie didn't come home right away and he didn't come to bed at all last night. This morning he told me our house is wire tapped. He said he could tell because of the telephone jacks and tlephone wire attatched to the house. He said our neighbors are croocked and the house down the street that is for sale is empty so they can spy on us. He has stopped putting the trash out ad started sorting recyclables because he says they look through our trash to get information on us. The treash bill is paid through April, but he wants to cancel service. He wants to use mainly cash because he says they look at our bank transactions and credit reports. He says the daylight savings time adjustment is part of the cover up. Claims US has technology to affect climate/weather. Says there was an anomoly-mistake that resulted in tsunami, was US's fault, that's why US sent so much aid/relief. Says Junction City/Fort Riley are running lots of cables for new doplar radar. He says the doplar radar is a cover—hiding the 'battery' created using the water of Milford lake. He talks quite a lot about preparing for when everything goes sour and what we'll need to live without electricity. He has began saying that things done in the past were done on purpose, and all part of his plan. He said its good for people to think we're not getting along."

March 12: "Jessie says there was a ynegative atomic blast last night—he felt it. Said everything is going to go sour really soon. Said he cut the hard lines of the wire taps."

March 18: "It's 3:40am. Jessie hasn't gone to bed at all yet. I woke up hearing him searching through my dressor drawer and jewelry box. When he saw me awake, he asked for my keys. He took the Jeep key and key fob. He rearranged my keys. I had one on a single ring—he asked what it went to. I answered 'the front door.' 'the front door to what?' 'our house.' He asked if I had, or had seen the key to his locker. He went downstairs and started a vehicle. The garage door went up/down 3 times, after about 5 minutes he drove off. It is now 3:49am."

March 22: "For the past two months, Jessie has insisted that I have a bag packed for me and Summer incase we need to blitz. tonight Jessie decided we needed to blitz. He packed the car with my bag, and blankets, baby toys, two coolers, my medications in a false book of War & Peace, a stroller, frozen dinners and sandwiches. His Jeep was packed—crammed full of duffle bags, suitcases, boxes, totes as well as his rollerblades, our home computer, a reciprocating saw. He also took the dog. Jessie insisted that I trust him and just get in the car and follow him. He gave me a walkie-talkie and had us use that for communication. He insisted that the radio/cd player be completely turned off, and cellphones turned off also. He had us stop several times to change the Walkietalkie station that we were talking on. In Topeka, he had us drive around, in circles, random paths, through parking lots to make sure no one was following us. We drove to my parents house and got there late, i think around midnight. They were already asleep, so we came in and I got myself and Summer ready for bed. Jessie said he was going out for smokes to the corner gas station. Around 2:30am there was a knock at the door—the Raytown police asked to talk with me. They said Jessie called them, and they were stopping by to see if I was okay and what was going on. The police asked me if he had a history of mental illness, I replied 'only suspected.' They asked why I was in Kansas city, I told them because my husband insisted that we pack up and go. After there questions, the police left and went back to talk with Jessie. (another officer was still with him.) They brought him back to my parents house for the evening."

March 24: "I found out that Jessie had been voluntariely committed at the VA hospital in Topeka. My brother Randy went with me and Summer to see Jessie. He told me that everything was okay . . . he was at the hospital for witness protection/safekeeping."

April 6: "Jessie checked out of the VA and came home. Jessie didn't sleep."

April 9: "Jessie took the car to work. Uneventful until evening."

April 10: "Jessie aressted for domestic battery."

That was her last entry. She left with Summer soon after. His suicide at that point was three months and nine days away.

More questions that she asks herself: Why did she stay so long and believe he would get better? Why couldn't he get better? What happened over there?

He told her a few stories when he got home. Volunteering for first truck in convoys. The roadside bomb that hit the truck behind him and the injured sergeant whose skull he held together. The decision that had to be made about who would disarm a bomb—the guy who was leaving for good the next day or his replacement who had just arrived. It was his choice, he told her, but before he could make it, one of the guys volunteered, and when the guy got blown to bits, it was like seeing "a pink mist." Did that really happen? Did any of it happen? It must have, because how else to explain why her funny, charming husband would come home demanding that the towels be folded a certain way and angrily pack to leave when they weren't? "I begged him like crazy," she remembers. "I would do whatever I could to fix it."

She had been told this happens sometimes. Be understanding, the wives were advised before their husbands came home. Give it time. So she gave it time, even as his anger sharpened and he told her she would have to change if their marriage was to survive. "How?" she asked him. "You have to figure it out on your own," he said, and then asked her in a mocking tone if she was smart enough to do that.

He had been back for two years at that point, still a corporal (his promotion to sergeant would come posthumously) whose job at division headquarters included summarizing casualty reports. Did that affect him? How could it not, she decided. The next year, his third year back, was when he started throwing things and describing how he was going to kill himself. He was going to hang himself from the deck. He was going to drive off the Milford Lake dam. He was going to light himself on fire in the shed. He was going to cut his brake lines and go for a drive down a hill. He was going to take off and disappear and she'd never know whether he was alive, dead, far away, just around the corner . . .

Well, okay, she began thinking.

She wasn't without fault in all that came next; she understands that. He accused her of having an affair. She hadn't. He accused her again. This time she had. She stopped it and again found herself begging him like crazy for forgiveness, but this time she had provided him a reason for his rage. They separated. She moved out. Visited. Spent the night with him. Got pregnant. Promised to "stay together and work things through no matter what." Moved back. Stayed.

Through all of this, she sought no help and confided in no one. As for Jessie, he did get help from time to time, but little of it seemed to make a difference. At one point, he spent three weeks in the Kansas City VA hospital, and Kristy remembers visiting him. "His posture was slumped. It seemed like everything just drooped. His eyes drooped. His cheeks drooped," she says. "All they did was drug him."

After that, he was admitted to Fort Riley's WTB, where just like Adam Schumann and Tausolo Aieti and Nic DeNinno, he met with a case manager, the chaplain, the pharmacist. He got to know Kevin Walker, who was his platoon sergeant when he started, and, later, Michael Lewis and the other sergeant who would find him dying in the bathroom, both of whom Kristy would call from time to time for support as he worsened. He got occasional counseling and was prescribed the twelve medications that would be mentioned in the post-suicide medical report. He also attended suicide awareness training and was given a laminated card on how to recognize the signs of suicidal behavior, which was found tucked into his wallet after he was pronounced dead.

The months went by. He spent days at the WTB and nights at home. He kicked the laundry basket. He overturned the coffee table. Kristy began taking notes.

Now it was April. He was arrested and jailed for domestic battery, and Kristy, fearful for Summer's safety, took off with Summer to her parents' house.

May now. He was in the psychiatric wing of the Topeka VA, medi-cated, calmer, and to Kristy's eyes almost worn down. "I think he was starting to find his solution."

June 12 now, and he was barraging her with texts. 7:45 a.m. "Are you awake yet?" 8:08 a.m. "Please know I love you very much." 8:09 a.m. "Thanks for taking such great care of Summer." 9:14 a.m. "I love you more and more with each passing day." 9:41 a.m. "Would you please call me?" 10:04 a.m. "Please find some time to talk with me." 10:11 a.m. "Please don't just turn your back on me. I need your support. I can't do this by myself." 10:23 a.m. "Please work with me." 10:27 a.m. "I need you to stick by me." 10:38 a.m. "Please find a way to enjoy my company." 10:49 a.m. "Would you please call me?" 10:55 a.m. "Please find some time for me?"

July 8 now. He would be getting out of the hospital the next day, and Kristy stopped by the house with a gallon of milk, a dozen eggs, a loaf of bread, and a box of Lucky Charms so there would be food waiting for him when he came home.

July 15. "Are you doing ok" Kristy texted him.

"No."

"What's going on? Did you eat dinner"

She waited for him to answer.

"Summer says 'hi' (actually just dadada)" she texted.

No answer.

"Mom & I are going to Sears to look at washing machines"

No answer.

She texted him a phone number of a crisis hotline someone had once given her. "If you are not going to reply to me, please call"

"I called that number and its not in service" he wrote back a few minutes later.

"I'm sorry—I will get you a good number"

"Ok"

"This is a good number to call," she texted, passing along a different one. "I just called to check and make sure. They are there 24/7 if you are struggling"

"Ok"

July 17. "Did you call that number I gave you?" she texted.

"Not yet," he wrote back.

A little later, she telephoned him.

"Did you call?"

"Yes."

"Did it help?"

"Not really."

July 19. Now someone was telephoning her. "Corporal Robinson didn't check in," one of the WTB sergeants said. "Do we have your permission to go to the house?"

Lately, she has been taking all of Jessie's e-mails and text messages and assembling them as a chronology. She worries that her memory is distorting things. If she can think about what happened as an unfolding timeline, and be taken again and again to her moments of trauma as they were unfolding, maybe it will help her make sense of it all. It's an idea, anyway, and she's willing to try it. "Little by little" is what those messages have told her so far about how Jessie died. It is the same phrase she uses in describing her coming back to life.

She has gotten rid of the bedroom furniture, including the bedpost she came to fear. That felt good.

She has sorted through his clothing and sent all but one of his uniforms to his beloved family in Sacramento, California, where he was born and where he was buried.

She has begun seeing someone new, a man named Kent Russell, who was her math instructor at the community college she enrolled in a year after Jessie died. "I kept talking to her and thinking, 'Wow,'" Kent remembers of their first conversation. He liked biking. She liked biking. He liked plays. She liked plays. He had been married once. She had been married once. He had a son. She had a daughter. "I'm divorced," he said. "My husband died," she said. "I'm so sorry. Was it in the war?" he said. "No. He committed suicide," she said. *Okay. That's a lot of candor*, he thought, not in a bad way. A few weeks later, he was at her house, having barbecue on the deck from which Jessie had once tossed a Christmas tree and threatened to hang himself. A few months after that, she was showing him all of the messages hidden in her cell phone. Eventually he bought her a ring and proposed, and Kristy began planning their wedding. With Jessie, she had eloped. This time would be different. She would wear an actual wedding dress. Kent would wear a tuxedo. There would be a buffet dinner and a buttermilk cake. And then she called off the engagement because she decided one day to get her hair cut, then decided she shouldn't because Kent wouldn't like it short, then realized it was Jessie who didn't like it short, and then realized she was nowhere near ready to get married if she was still making decisions based on her fears of Jessie's reactions. So she returned the ring, and when Kent said he would marry her whenever she was ready she believed him, and when she got her hair cut and he told her how much he liked it, she believed that, too.

Is that progress? She thinks it is, as are her decisions to repaint the walls and start seeing a counselor, who often reacts to what Kristy tells her by saying, "Oh my gosh." Hers is that kind of story, apparently. At the end of the first visit, the counselor said Kristy was suffering from depression. After a few more visits, she changed it from depression to PTSD and gave Kristy something called a "Feeling Word List" with instructions on how to use it. Pick a word, she said, write it down with the words "I feel" or "I felt" preceding it, finish the sentence with whatever comes to mind, and soon enough you'll own the emotion that at the moment is owning you.

Kristy looked over the 347 choices on the sheet of paper and chose the word "angry." "I feel angry that Jessie is still impacting and controlling my life," she wrote.

She chose "demeaned." "I felt very demeaned when he would drag me around to all the offices on Fort Riley and make me smile and show what a happy family and perfect couple we were."

She chose "petrified." "I felt petrified when Jessie overturned the china cabinet."

She chose "degraded" and "demoralized." "I felt very degraded and demoralized when Jessie would yell at me and tell me how much of a whore and a slut I was."

She chose "enraged." "I felt enraged when I got to the point where I beat Jessie with a baby blanket."

Then, trying to think of something that sounded more positive, she chose "relieved" and "unburdened."

"When Jessie died, I felt relieved and unburdened," she wrote, and it's true, she says, she did, but of course the more time that has gone on, the less that's been the case. Sometimes she envies the army, with those five lessons learned about her husband's suicide. How did they come up with so many? Because when she goes over the circumstances of all that happened, culminating in the phone call when she learned that Jessie hadn't checked in with the WTB, she can come up with only one.

She was in church in Kansas City when that call came, and at first she wasn't terribly worried. He was probably asleep, she told the sergeant who was calling. Or perhaps he had turned his phone off and forgotten. She hung up and went back into the sanctuary. Then came a second call an hour later, asking for her permission to go to the house. Now she was worried. She hung up and began pacing outside of the sanctuary as Michael Lewis and the other sergeant drove to her house, noted the car in the driveway, noted the keys in the ignition, noted the mowed lawn, opened the door, climbed the stairs, and headed toward a light at the end of the hallway. Here came the cat. Here came the moan. "Jessie?" they called out. "Jessie?" Now came the third call to Kristy, and soon she was on her way to the hospital in Junction City where Jessie had been taken. Her father drove, and she sat in the back with Summer, thinking, "This is not how it's supposed to be," and then correcting herself: "I'm not the one who says how it's supposed to be." It was a long ride in a quiet car. Mostly she tried not to think at all. At some point, someone called to say the doctors had managed to coax a few breaths out of Jessie, so there was some hope, but the hospital was still an hour away, and by the time she got there he was dead and his trip to the Gardner Room was under way.

Her lesson learned, then: it came to her six days later.

She was in Sacramento, at the funeral home, just her and Summer and Jessie, who was in a propped-open casket at the front of the room. Visitors would be along in a while, but for now, on this day, the day before his funeral when he would go in the ground and she would have nothing to figure things out by except for her bruised house and her hidden texts, she had two hours on her own to consider him as he lay in front of her. It was the same amount of time as a meeting in the Gardner Room, but here there was only one case to consider and one person to do it.

She went up to the casket and held his hand for a while. She used her fingers to brush his hair. She took a seat in the first pew, all the way to the right, and while Summer crawled around her legs, she thought about who Jessie had been before he died, before he kneeled in his own blood, before he sent her so many texts that began with the word "please," before he thought about punching her fucking nose and watching it bleed, before he needed those towels folded, before he saw a pink mist, before he held a skull together, before he went to war. She thought all the way back to the beginning when she was at that church dinner, so bored, and he took the seat across from her.

"What do you do?" she asked.

"Paperwork," he said.

That's all it took. One routine question, one silly answer, and right then she felt herself tipping over the edge and falling in love. Just like that. No way to explain it. It just happened. And that was her lesson learned, that she had married a wonderful man.

11

N ow it is Adam Schumann who is in Sacramento, standing alone at the airport curb. It's warm out compared with what Kansas had been, and yet something about the air makes him want to shiver. Even in Iraq, at least on the good days, he didn't feel this unnerved.

The flight from Kansas City to Salt Lake City might be part of the reason—he wanted to sleep but ended up next to a snorer who kept sprawling onto his shoulder. The flight to Sacramento was worse—this time he was next to a man who reeked of liquor and could barely buckle in, even with a seat belt extender. But the bigger reason, and probably the real reason, was the older man now approaching him, who is decked out in an earring and one of those California tans.

"Fred," the man says, extending his hand.

"Adam," Adam says warily, and then, wondering what he is getting himself into, climbs into Fred Gusman's car.

Patti Walker is responsible for this. Since Adam had stopped by her office that day, she had been looking for a program for him, and when neither Topeka nor Pueblo had room, she found one in California called the Pathway Home. Fred Gusman was its director. The program was fairly new, not well known, and much more unconventional than the others. Topeka, for instance, was part of the VA system, and Pueblo relied on insurance payments; this one was opened with a five-million-dollar grant from private benefactors that covered the first three years, and was now scraping by on fund-raising and donations. Pueblo was four weeks and Topeka was seven weeks; this one was four months minimum and often longer. Still, when Patti called Adam to tell him

Saskia Schumann

about it, he said yes on the spot. He had lost fifteen pounds over the past few weeks and was up to two packs of cigarettes a day. Patti was thrilled.

Saskia was not. The idea that Adam would be gone for so long, and that he had decided to go without even discussing it with her, had left her fuming. She wanted him to get help. She had been the one begging in the furnace room. But four *months*? And not sixty miles away in Topeka, where she and the kids could drive over and visit him, but seventeen hundred miles away in California? "Well, Patti wants him to go to the California one, so I guess he's going to the California one," she said angrily. "Guess Patti was able to decide my life for me." Later, after talking to Patti, angrier still, she said, "Of course, Patti used my favorite quote: 'Stay strong. You're a soldier's wife.' Makes me want to puke." But an opening was an opening, and in the same way that Tausolo Aieti had ended up in Topeka and Nic DeNinno had ended up in Pueblo, Adam was off to California, leaving behind for Saskia a flower on the nightstand and a note that said "I promise to be a better man when I return."

In the car now, Adam looks out the window as Fred steers away from the airport and asks how his flights were. They had talked once by phone, but that was it. They know nothing about each other.

"Miserable," Adam says.

"So how's your wife?" Fred tries.

"She's okay," Adam says. "Just nervous. Like I am."

"Well, when you see the place, you'll probably think this is beautiful," Fred says. "A lot of trees. A lot of grass. Green."

Adam is far from the first person to sit across from Fred Gusman in these circumstances. In the three years since he left a high-level job at the VA to open Pathway, a few hundred combat vets have been through the program, and every one of them had been as nervous as Adam. Fred keeps a running tally of who has come his way. Sixty percent had tried to kill themselves. Seventy-three percent had quit or been fired from a job. Eighty percent had tried school, of which eighty-three percent dropped out. Most pertinent to this moment, every one of them felt disgusted with himself for needing to come here, and Fred knows to keep these drives low-key.

"What'd your case manager tell you about the place?" he asks.

"Not much. I'm in the dark," Adam says.

Fred points to some distant buildings on the horizon. "That's Sacramento, our capital city. Not the biggest city in the world," he says.

"A lot bigger than what I'm used to," Adam says.

Now Fred angles southwest, away from the city, and soon they are cutting through farmland that is at least a little reminiscent of Kansas. "So what's the population where you live?"

"Junction City?" Adam says. "I think about thirty thousand." He has an empty soda bottle in his hands, and he begins crushing it over and over.

"So how many deployments have you had?"

"Three," Adam answers, and then, after a pause, says, "It's the last one that did it."

"Well, what you're going to have the opportunity to do is push through some of these things," Fred says. "A better quality of life. That's the main thing." He mentions that the program has three psychologists and three family therapists, that there's a massage therapist who drops by sometimes and a yoga instructor, too, that the guys go fly fishing and at the moment are out bowling. There are no locked doors, he says. No demerits. No privileges to be earned or lost. Nothing like that. "Over time, you'll figure it out," he says. "We tell everybody to keep an open mind. Especially the first week or so. It can feel a little awkward."

"How long you been doing this?" Adam asks.

Fred laughs a little. "For forever," he says.

"Yeah?" Adam says.

"Since four years after the Vietnam War."

"Oh. That *is* forever," Adam says.

They keep going and are now flanked on both sides by high hills, and Adam is staring out at them in silence, thinking how odd they look, how smooth, like they're coated in velvet or something, when a sudden noise startles him. It's an approaching motorcycle zooming between cars at full throttle. It pulls even for a moment and then flies past, and if this were ten years ago, the young guy straddling it with his shirt tail flapping behind him could have been Adam himself, on his way home to sit in the sun and meet the new girl in the basement apartment.

"Jesus!" he says as the motorcycle disappears somewhere ahead and the noise fades.

He takes a deep breath.

"Everybody has ups and downs," Fred says.

"Story of my life," Adam says.

"Well," Fred says, telling him one more thing about the program, "you'll be with a lot of ups and downs."

They've been driving for more than an hour now, and as they emerge from the high hills and head north past the town of Napa into a landscape of vineyards, Adam says to Fred, "It just feels like I'm in another country."

"I've never seen a tree like these," he says a few minutes later.

"I'm so damn nervous."

Now Fred is pointing again. This time it's at a hill, on the slope of which is a collection of white buildings. Inside one of them is Adam's room. It has a mattress, a closet, a sink, and a window, and outside the window is a hundred-foot-high palm tree that Adam will soon be obsessed with climbing to the very top.

Maybe he'll just jump.

Maybe a swan dive.

"There's the Pathway Home," Fred says, turning toward the entrance, and a few minutes later, Adam is inside.

A week later, the flower on the nightstand dying, Saskia sends her vanished husband a text message, sends him another, sends another saying "Call me," sends another, calls him and leaves a message on his voice mail, wonders if he's not answering because he's in therapy, wonders if he's out fishing, wonders if he's out bowling, wonders if he's at a restaurant, wonders if he's picking up a knife pretending to cut into a steak, wonders if he's aiming it at his chest instead, wonders if he's stabbing himself, wonders how she'll tell the kids, wonders what she'll do now that he's dead, and after sending twenty texts without getting an answer, her stomach hurting, her nerves shot, she says: "It's not going well. I'm a mess. A hot mess. Right now, I've probably lost five or six pounds since he left. I have yet to eat a meal. We constantly fight. If I see Patti Walker, I might punch her in the face. We've been fighting all week. Yesterday afternoon we kind of patched things up. At five-thirty, I called him and said, 'You need to talk to Zoe. She's not listening to me.' He talked to her, and then I got back on the phone and he started yelling at me. Screaming. You could hear him smashing things. You could hear things breaking."

She says: "I can't do this anymore. I'm an absolute mess. He never should have gone out there in the first place, and it irritates the hell out of me that Patti Walker is his little pawn. She called the other day and asked if I needed yard work to be done. Well, I can do the fucking yard work. I told her how bad he was doing, and she said, 'Well, you have to be patient.' I'll tell you what. If one more person tells me to be patient, I'm going to need a fucking institution. I mean I know she's trying to help, but she's influencing him. The 'stay strong, you're a soldier's wife'? I could have taken a gun and killed her that day. He's not a soldier any-more. He's fucking screwed up."

She says: "I knew this thing was a bad idea from the start. When I have a bad feeling about something, I'm usually right."

She says: "I'm pissed. I'm pissed. I really am fucking pissed. I won't get over it. He gets to go fishing. He gets to go out on weekends. I can't do any of that. I'm always getting the short end of the stick. I am here, taking care of everything. This is not why I got married and had kids, to do this on my own. If I could take it all back, I would. I wish I had never met the man."

She says: "*I'd* like to stay in a hospital for a couple of weeks. And sleep. That would be great. Medicate *me*."

She says: "Fuck. I didn't even have any help after I had a baby. And then he *dropped* him."

She says: "I feel like my heart is ready to explode."

She says: "I hate that man so much right now."

She says: "All I can think about is how much I hate him but how much I want him home."

―――――――

When did she become this way? That's something else she keeps wondering, because ten years ago, when she was the girl about to meet Adam, she had a vision of how her life was going to go and it didn't include such rage. The basement where she was living was supposed to be a first stop, not a continuing theme. She had moved there straight out of high school because she was tired of having a curfew and it was what she could afford. "I had fun. Partied. Drank. Hung out with completely older people. I wasn't bad, though. I didn't do stupid stuff. I didn't drink and drive. I didn't sleep around," she says of the girl she once was. She understood that some people paid attention to her because of her looks, and she didn't mind that, but she had her own way of seeing herself. She was going to have a career of some sort, in some kind of office, and a closet full of business clothes. Single, strong, dependent on no one—that kind of life. She'd start in a basement, save money, go to school, and end up wherever. She was open to anything. She glowed in those days. She had so much confidence, and compassion, too, and now the most compassion she can muster is when she is running errands around town and sees young wives with their soldier husbands. *You poor fuck*, she thinks. *You have no idea what it will be like in five years.*

With Adam gone now, she is back to doing it all, just like in a deployment. The difference is that in a deployment, doing everything felt like a contribution, even a source of pride. Why, this time, is she telling no one about where Adam has gone? Her family knows a little, but, weirdly, the person so far she has been the most honest with was a stranger at Walmart who was sitting at a fold-out table, collecting donations to help hospitalized soldiers with their bills. "My husband's hospitalized right now," she surprised herself by telling him, and then she handed over fifteen dollars, even though the wiser thing would have been to ask him if he had any money for her.

The truth is that they have no money at all, and she is worried about losing the house and cars in these four months while Adam is fishing and bowling and doing God knows what else out there. Just as Adam will be obsessing about the tree outside of his window, she will soon begin obsessing about the growing pile of past-due notices on the dining room table. There will be no paychecks while Adam is away. Hoping to bridge that, Patti Walker arranged for an e-mail to be sent out army-wide asking for people to donate leave time to "Mr. Adam Schumann," a wounded ex-soldier "approved as a voluntary leave transfer program recipient under 5 CFR 630.904," but Saskia knows that similar requests go out all the time, and she's not holding her breath that anyone will read such a message, much less respond.

Her solution, since she is the one who will have to solve it: to work, and to bring in enough money to cover day care costs and keep an inch in front of the collection agencies. Even before Adam left for California, she had been thinking about this. With his help writing some of her papers, she had gotten a bachelor's degree in criminal justice from a school based in Iowa that offered distance learning. Then she began applying for whatever jobs were out there in Junction City, including a data processing job with a local mental health agency. To her surprise, they called her in for an interview, and to her greater surprise, they offered her a job—not as a data processor but as a case manager.

A case manager? she thought. *Like Adam has? Me?*

The pay was lousy, but there was a part of her that was flattered to be wanted, and so she went in one day to find out about whose cases she would be managing. These are some of the poorest, saddest, and neediest people in Junction City, she was told, and then came an example: a woman who had been raped and abused, and as if that weren't enough her cat had been burned to death in front of her. That kind of thing. Saskia sat there, trying to imagine what she could do for such a woman. "She's deathly afraid of men," the person telling this to Saskia said, and added, "Maybe you're the one she needs."

Well, maybe so, Saskia decided. Maybe this was the way her compassion could return, and her life could become what she had intended it to be.

She said yes to the job. She bought a few clothes to look professional, arranged day care for Jaxson and after-school care for Zoe, trained for a week, and got her first client. It was the woman. They met at the mental health agency so the woman could decide if she wanted Saskia as her case manager.

"Are you going to tell your boss everything I say?" she asked.

"It depends what you say," Saskia answered.

"If I say I'm going to kill myself?"

"If you—"

"I'm joking," the woman said. "If I say I'm going to kill myself, I'm joking. It's when I'm quiet, you need to worry."

What have I gotten myself into, Saskia thought.

"I think I'll take her," the woman said to Saskia's boss when he came into the room.

She got a second client and a third, and by the time Adam was on his way to California, she was up to a dozen. Her job wasn't to counsel them—psychologists were supposed to do that—but to sit with them in their lonesome homes, run them to the grocery store or the pharmacy, do whatever they needed to help them get through their days. Several had been sexually assaulted. Several had multiple personalities. All had been traumatized in one way or another and diagnosed with severe and persistent mental illness.

These were becoming the people filling her days now that Adam was away.

She wakes up before sunrise now and is slowly getting used to it. She likes to be at the office before anyone else, do her paperwork, grab the keys to the van they want her to use, and haul out of there before any of the others arrive and can trap her in a conversation. "How Am I Driving?" reads the bumper sticker on the van, and the answer is the same as ever, except now, instead of tailgating her way along the interstate to another appointment for Adam at the Topeka VA, she is turning into a trailer park, this one on the outskirts of town near the strip clubs. All these years in Junction City and she never realized until she got this job how many trailer parks a little town could have.

This one, one of the oldest, surely is one of the worst. Everything is cockeyed, knocked around, and dented. Weeds and puddles have the run of the place, and some of the trailers have been abandoned. One yard is decorated with the flipped-over cab of a pickup truck, rusting and filled with sofa cushions. Saskia drives past a woman leaning on a cane and giving her the evil eye. She turns left on a sort-of street, where the road sign is obscured by a torn shirt someone has wrapped around it. She approaches a particularly shabby trailer with an American flag and a Tweety Bird in the window. An older woman without teeth is sitting on the steps leading to the front door, reading a Louis L'Amour paperback, and when she looks up and waves to Saskia, Saskia waves back.

The woman is her first client of the day, and Saskia is glad to see that she's already outside, because inside there's nowhere to sit. Junk and paper stacks are everywhere. So are roaches. The floors have rotted through in parts, and the smell suggests that something else is rotting, too. The first time Saskia came inside and saw all of this, she asked the woman why she didn't do dishes more than once a week, and the woman said that she knew she ought to but it's easier to keep watching TV. Her depression runs deep, she explained, to the point of not wanting to bother with very much at all. Nonetheless, she has fixed herself up today for the only visitor she gets, brushing her graying hair and tucking a purple shirt into her blue jeans.

"You look nice," Saskia tells her. She is scheduled to be with the woman for an hour, to do anything the woman needs other than wash her dishes and kill her roaches, and when the woman says she has twenty-five dollars and wants to go to the grocery store, Saskia takes her to the grocery store. The woman leads the way on a walker, and Saskia follows with a cart. With limitless patience, she watches the woman pay. She loads the bags into the van. She helps the woman into the passenger seat. Back at the trailer, she takes the groceries and the walker inside. The hour is up. The woman settles back onto the steps with her book. Saskia gets in the van, ready to go, and then, thinking for a moment, steps back out and walks over to the woman. "I'll see you Friday," she says.

From there, she goes to see another client, this one a forty-year-old woman who lives in a small wooden house so crowded with relatives that she sleeps on the living room couch. Her house stinks, too, of cigarette smoke, and when she asks Saskia to take her somewhere so she can get away from all of the people living with her, Saskia is happy to oblige. They go to a park with a few scattered picnic tables. The woman is obese and sickly and can walk only a few steps before pausing to catch her breath, but, again, Saskia shows none of the impatience she shows with Adam and the kids and drivers on the interstate and everyone else in her life. She takes the woman's arm and helps her along, and when they are at last sitting and the woman is saying how depressed she is, how she was abused as a child, how she cuts herself sometimes and wishes she were dead, Saskia listens to every word.

Her next appointment takes her to an old apartment complex not far from where she and Adam live. The client waiting for her is her most difficult, who fifteen minutes into their very first meeting lifted her skirt, pulled down her underpants, and said, "You want to see my scar?" At least it was a real scar, from a hernia operation, but still. And it got worse from there. Saskia took her to a doctor's appointment that day, and when the woman asked her to come into the bathroom to see if there was blood in her urine, Saskia sent Adam a text message.

"This lady I'm with is nuts."

"Well I'm stuck in a building with 35 nuts," he wrote back.

"I think this 1 might have you topped."

"Really?"

"She made me look at her piss, her vag at the doctor's, and then told me about all of her traumatic events. Fucking cuckoo."

"Wow."

Now that Saskia was getting to know the woman, though, and the woman was trusting her, she regretted how coarse her reaction had been. She was feeling a little tenderly about all of them, actually. In their own oddball ways, there was something honorable about them, Saskia was realizing, which she had first noticed on a day when they were all at the mental health facility, gathered at tables and working on a craft project. One of the women who was using some beads to make a rosary for herself tried to say something and began stuttering, and Saskia fully expected the others to make fun of her. That's what people did to stutterers, at least the people Saskia had grown up with. Instead, these people listened in silence as the woman stammered on, continuing with their business as if she weren't taking forever to get to the end of a sentence, and when she finally finished her thought and sighed, one of them said, "Good job," and several others clapped for her. "You're doing awesome," another said, and as the woman beamed, Saskia found herself unexpectedly moved.

Fucking cuckoo or not, they were decent people, she thought that day, and in some ways it made her more irritated with Adam than ever.

Now, this day, she spends an hour with the pee woman, as Saskia refers to her, who talks about how much she hates herself, and then she heads to an appointment with a new client she will be meeting for the first time. From what she knows, it is a twenty-eight-year-old woman with three kids who has just been released from a lockdown psychiatric facility. She had been hallucinating, apparently. Something about her husband being abusive, or maybe her ex-husband. For some reason, she hadn't slept for weeks and had finally melted down.

In Saskia goes to meet her, and an hour later she emerges knowing a little more.

The woman's husband turns out to be a soldier who had returned from a deployment and steadily grew more abusive until she finally got him out of the house with the help of a restraining order. That hadn't stopped him, however. While she was in the shower one night, she heard the sound of a window being smashed, and there he was, in the house, in the bathroom, screaming that he wanted his children.

She was terrified, she told Saskia. She had never had a problem in her life, rarely had a bad dream, never seen a therapist, nothing like that, and suddenly she was breaking down so thoroughly that she had to be placed in a psychiatric facility. She spent two weeks there, and now she was home, unable to sleep.

She kept talking as Saskia took in the surroundings.

An immaculate apartment. Not much furniture. An old TV. A painted kitchen table. A couch with a slight tear in it. Three well-dressed children, listening politely as their mother said she hears him knocking at the door all night long.

She hears his footsteps.

She hears his voice.

Now, afterward, Saskia seems a little shaken.

"I mean, I'm the same way at night," she says.

She goes back to the office and does some paperwork. She picks up the kids and throws some fast food on the table for dinner. She feeds the dogs and changes Jax's diaper and tells Zoe for the third time to do her homework. She does the dishes and takes out the trash and gets the kids to sleep and texts Adam and texts him again and texts him again and feels her panic rising while waiting for his reply until she is clutching her stomach. It has been twenty-four hours since she last heard from him.

"Group was okay," he had written from the land of the velvet hills. "Just finished some meditation and relaxation. Ready for another nap before bowling tonight. lol."

What is he *doing?* she wonders. *What kind of program is this?*

It's been two weeks, and the only person she's heard from, other than Adam, was a family therapist who called after they'd had a fight to say that the cause of his erratic behavior was PTSD. "Well, no shit," Saskia said after hanging up. "I'm not an idiot."

She has looked at Pathway's website and its descriptions of goals and treatment protocols, but it was the part labeled "Our Environment" that caught her attention. "We offer a beautiful, tranquil residential environment in the Napa Valley, CA 'Wine Country.' Because we are located on the grounds of The Veterans Home of California—Yountville, we can also offer a variety of 'free time' and recreational activities (e.g. swimming pool, bowling lanes, golf course, fitness center, base exchange store, chapel, and coffee shop)," it said.

"Well, this is bullshit" was her reaction to that.

She has tried asking Adam what he does all day, but he hasn't wanted to talk about it, even though, on the ride from the airport, Fred Gusman had told him how important it was for a wife to hear about her husband's progress. He gave an example. "I'm learning how to deal with my anger." "Okay," Adam had said. "You better not tell your wife there's a golf course here," Fred had added for emphasis, knowing how some wives have reacted to that fact. "That's all she needs to hear."

So of course Adam has mentioned the golf course, the bowling, the fishing, and has neglected to mention all of the hours he has spent in group therapy and his suspicion that it might be helping a little. Neither does he mention how the four months are supposed to go, that Fred has said he would start at the very beginning of Adam's life and work forward from there, looking for patterns that were already in place by the time he went to war and reacted the way he did. Instead, he texts about a "cool ass tackle shop" he went to and a fishing rod he saw that he'd like to have. "What are the odds of you letting me get one?" Or he telephones when it's clear she doesn't have his attention. "Are you *peeing*?" she asks him, and there goes her patience. "Mute it or something," she snaps.

Worse, the calls and texts are sporadic, leaving her waiting at night to hear from him. If it were a deployment, she'd be more understanding. But this is California, not a war zone, and here she is, once again spending another night at home, waiting for any word at all from a man always in possession of his cell phone. She pulls Jaxson onto her lap. It's been sixteen months since Adam dropped him, and she's always checking him out. Why isn't he talking yet? she wonders. Physically, he's a little acrobat—just last night he climbed onto the couch, balanced on the back edge, and beat the wooden blinds until he broke a couple of slats—but developmentally she worries that he's behind. She wraps him in a blanket and kisses him again and again on his cheek until he's asleep, and then she holds him for a while more, just looking at him. He looks so much like Adam in this moment, down to the way he is sleeping with his mouth open. "Must be a boy thing," she marvels. She taps his forehead. "Like nothing's working up here. Mouth wide open. Flies buzzing. Mouth-breathers."

She needs to get out of the house, she realizes.

Even one night would help, and so she arranges to leave the kids with Dave and his wife, Donna, across the street and go out somewhere with her friend Christina, who happens to need a night out, too, because her husband has gotten into photography lately and she has been driving him all over Kansas so he can take pictures of cornfields.

A Friday night now. Donna comes over for the kids. It's race night at Whiskey Lake, and that's where the kids will be going. Saskia gathers up extra bottles and diapers, and as she does, Donna tells her about a dream she had. She was on her front porch smoking, and when she looked across the street, Adam, Zoe, and Jaxson were standing in an empty lot. Their house was gone, and Saskia wasn't there, either. "It was so weird," she says, and wonders if it was some kind of premonition.

Saskia shrugs. She's not a premonitions type of person, although when she goes out on the front porch and sees that a bird has built a nest in her hanging plant overnight, she mutters, "That can't be good." She turns to Zoe. "You better behave yourself."

"She will," Donna says.

She goes inside to change. She has an outfit in mind. Something kind of fun. Other than for her job interview, she hasn't dressed up, really, since she and Adam went on a date to the Cozy Inn. When she emerges a few minutes later, though, she's wearing jeans and a T-shirt. "I got no one to impress, huh, Eddie?" she says, petting the dog, whose leg seems to have fully healed. She hugs Zoe, who asks, "Where are you going?"

"To the mall."

"All night?"

The mall is a half hour away. She and Christina start off with a jumbo margarita at Carlos O'Kelly's Mexican Cafe. They go into Victoria's Secret. They go to Maurices and the Children's Place and get French manicures at Cali Nails and are in Dillard's, looking at purses, when Saskia's cell phone rings.

A California number.

"Hello?"

It's Fred Gusman, calling to introduce himself and to let Saskia know that Adam has been having a bad day.

"Really?" Saskia says, thinking of him fishing. "It sounds like he's having a pretty good day."

Someone went in his room and flipped things around, Fred explained. Weekends are hard out here, especially at first. He was missing Saskia and the kids. Maybe she should come out, Fred suggested. They'd pay for it if she would come.

"Maybe," she says. They talk for a few minutes more. Fred promises to call again and tells her to call anytime she has questions. She says she will and hangs up. How could she go out there? How could she take time off from work? Who would watch the kids?

Eight o'clock now. The margaritas have worn off, and they've exhausted the mall. Christina goes home, leaving Saskia standing outside in the last gray of the day. She calls her sister. "What the fuck do I do now?" she asks. She calls her mother, who suggests going to the Cozy Inn, sitting at the bar, and striking up a conversation.

She goes to Walmart and buys toothbrushes and a set of shelves for Jaxson's bedroom.

Home now. It's just her.

She looks around for a hammer to assemble the shelves. Maybe it's in the furnace room, but there's no way she's going down there, not when there's no one else in the house. She sits in the living room. She's tired, but she dreads going to sleep nearly as much as she dreads the basement. She always lies awake thinking over and over about money, the bills, the kids, and Adam, and now the women who are her clients and who all seem so utterly alone. Her version of footsteps and voices.

The phone rings.

Adam.

She grabs for it.

"Hello? . . . Hey . . . What'd that guy do to your room? . . . Well, who did it? . . . Why? . . . Mm-hmm . . . Mm-hmm . . . What do you mean? . . . What do you have planned for the rest of the night? . . . Tacos? . . . Really? . . . Okay, I guess . . . Well, no shit . . . Do you know where the hammer's at? . . . Okay, I'll just go buy one . . . Because I can't find anything in the garage, and I'm not going through the basement . . ."

She starts chewing on her nails. There goes her manicure.

"Must be nice . . . Okay . . . All right . . . Love you, too . . . Yeah . . . Love you, too . . . You, too . . . Okay . . ."

All the next day, a Saturday, she feels better, and, as a result, the house feels almost normal. Zoe reads a book. Jax finds a plastic bucket, puts it on his head, and staggers around. One of the dogs curls up next to her on the couch. "You stink," she says, pushing the dog away, which reminds her that she needs to clean up the piles of dog shit in the backyard. Jax removes the bucket and starts throwing toys across the room while hollering at the top of his lungs. "Here," she says, picking up the bucket and dropping it back over his head.

She checks her phone. Nothing from Adam, but instead of texting him, she texts Dave and Donna's young son, a middle-schooler who thinks the world of Adam. Adam would take him fishing. They'd play video games together. When Adam was leaving, the boy hugged him so hard that Saskia got a little teary. "Want to pick up dog poop?" she writes.

"How much?" he texts back.

"Little punk," she says.

"Ten dollars," she writes back.

He comes right over. Saskia hands him a trash bag and a scooper and follows him into the yard, where he heads for the biggest pile.

"Damn," he says as he gets closer. "Dead bird."

He moves to another pile.

"You wanna work for me this summer?" Saskia asks.

"What, picking up dog shit?"

"No. Watching Zoe. Fifty bucks a week. That's two hundred dollars a month. And all you have to do is make sure she doesn't kill herself."

He approaches another pile. Another dead bird. He says he'll think about it. Saskia leaves him to it, goes inside, roots around her kitchen cabinets and finds a mix for a lava cake that she bought six months ago with big plans to make it right away. Today's the day, she decides. It's the right day for a cake.

A good day, this day.

But then it is the next day—Mother's Day, as it happens—and she becomes so mad at Adam that she hangs up on him and slams the phone onto the table. She had awakened to Zoe bringing her breakfast in bed, and even though it was a bowl of cereal so sugary that she threw it out as soon as Zoe left the room, it was at least a good try. All morning long she waited for Adam to call, and when he finally did, at two in the afternoon, after he had been on Facebook, which was all the proof she needed that he was awake and could have called well before two o'clock, she hung up, slammed down the phone, and says now to Jax, who is staring at her, "He can kiss my ass."

"I'm not going to play this game with you," Adam texts a few minutes later. "I don't know what I did. I called to wish you a happy mother's day. I got u rings and something else, which I'm assuming hasn't got there yet."

"How am I playin games??" she writes back. "Imagine how u would feel when everyone around u is made to feel special all day and I don't even get a card and rings that I told you to order and then you get on facebook before u can even call me."

"I woke up at 11 sent u a message on FB ate lunch then called u," he writes. "The days not even over with and ur already assuming thats all I was going to do."

"Put yourself in my shoes for 5 min and see how u would feel," she writes. "I feel like shit and im alone."

"This is getting out of hand," he writes.

"U cant answer your phone?" she writes after she tries to call him and he doesn't answer.

"No. Im not going to fight with u," he writes. "Im sorry."

"This is so fuckin ridiculous. Im so tired of fighting with you," she writes, and waits for his answer.

A few minutes later, after trying another call to him, she writes again.

"Can u pick up the phone please."

Five minutes later:

"Im not doing this. U dont wanna b mature and pick your phone up then im done."

Eight minutes later:

"Way to show me your true colors, u cant even talk to me."

Five minutes later:

"Damnit adam, I cant fucking go through this again, pick up your phone."

Six minutes later:

"if you give a fuck about me then call, i cant do this anymore. I dont understand, all this is doing is tearing us apart and u dont even try."

Five minutes later:

"Point fucking taken, i guess. Im done, im leaving. Good luck taking care of everything."

Twenty-four minutes later:

"Can you please call me, i need to know what u want me to do with everything."

Another twenty-four minutes later:

"Can u please talk to me, i dont know what to do im a fucking mess, do u just not give a fuck anymore? Im trying to say sorry and all your doin is making things worse."

An hour and nineteen minutes later:

"why r u doing this."

So he's not going to call. So she is going to leave him. She will go back to where she grew up and get a goddamned basement apartment if she has to and he can come home from his fishing to a foreclosed house and a furnace room where he can pull the trigger at last. No, she can't do that. He went to war. He needs help. He's in a good place. She will call back Fred Gusman. She will get herself under control. That's always been the goal: control. And hope, too. Hope and control. She calms down. She cleans up. She sits on the couch and instead of checking her phone for messages decides to look at her calendar to see what she has tomorrow.

First appointment: the pee woman.

"God*dammit*," she says.

A few days later, she goes into the office after hours, when no one is there, and drops her keys and ID tag on her boss's desk. Too much sadness. She can't do it. She doesn't leave a note but figures she doesn't have to. He'll know what it means.

The one who needs help is her.

12

"Dispatch. Sharon."

"Sharon, it's Elaine over at Fort Riley."

"Uh-huh."

"I have a domestic physical in process for you."

"Okay. Hold on."

"Tell me when you're ready."

"Okay. What's the address?"

"One one one nine Cannon View, apartment number 8, in Grand-view Plaza. Your victim is Theresa—"

"Mm-hmm."

"—last name Aieti. I'll spell. Alpha India Echo Tango India."

"Okay let me make sure on the last name. A-i-e-t-i?"

"Correct."

"Okay."

"Husband's first name is, uh, Tausaloa. It's t like Tom, a, u, s like Sam, a, l, o, a. Same last name. He's in the house with her wearing T-shirt and jeans. He does not have weapons. Abuse was fisticuffs only."

"It's what?"

"Fisticuffs. Hitting her."

"Oh okay. Physical domestic."

"Yes. And she is locked in the back bedroom with her baby, and he is in the front of the house. And she said that, yes, you could call her . . ."

———

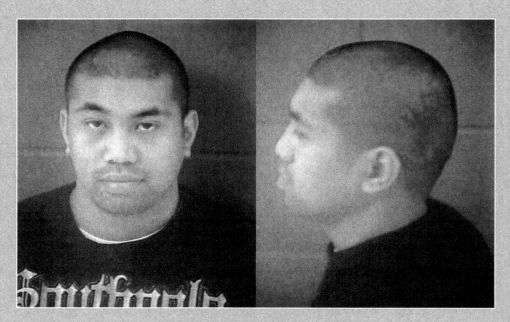

Tausolo Aieti, after his arrest

"Hello?"

"Hi, ma'am? Theresa?"

"Yes."

"This is Sharon in dispatch with the Geary County Sheriff's Department. I had a call from Fort Riley. Are you okay?"

"Yeah, I'm, I'm, okay."

"Are you still in the back bedroom?"

"Yeah, I'm in the bedroom."

"Okay, and where's he at?"

"He's in the front living room."

"He's in the front living room still? Has he calmed down?"

"I don't know."

"Okay, what did he do?"

"He hit me. So many times. With his hands."

"Do you need an ambulance?"

"No."

"Okay. Is your child okay?"

"Yeah. My, my, my baby's okay. I was holding him when he, um, beat me."

"Okay. Does he know the police are coming?"

"I don't know. I'm making the phone call in the room."

"Okay. I understand. Do you think he'll open the door when they come?"

"I'll open it."

"Okay. Can we stay on the phone with you until they get there?"

"What was that?"

"Do you want me to stay on the phone with you until the police get there?"

"No, it's fine."

"Fine?"

"Yes."

"Okay, I'll go ahead and disconnect. If he starts trying to make it through the door, just give a call back, but they should be there in the next few minutes."

"All right, thank you.

So his dream about Harrelson continues, as do its consequences, and now there's nothing to do but wait for the police to knock on the door.

Tausolo sits on a couch in the living room, where the old gouges in the walls have been covered with photographs of the new baby.

Theresa remains in the bedroom, where a blank piece of notebook paper has been carefully taped over the old fist-sized hole in the door.

Meanwhile, Brad Clark, who is the chief of police in Grandview Plaza, turns on the siren and speeds toward Geary Estates. He is no longer surprised by domestic-disturbance calls that turn out to involve a soldier. When he first took the job in 2004, when the wars were in their early years, the police force consisted of him and one other officer. Since then, as the population of Grandview Plaza more than doubled, mostly with military families moving into Geary Estates, the force has grown to six full-time and three part-time officers, and the equipment they carry now includes semiautomatic rifles, a door ram, and a ballistic riot shield. There have been fights to break up, marriages in violent free fall, and a notable increase in drug-related arrests. There was the case of a crazy high soldier who climbed to the top of a dirt mound and began waving around what seemed to be an assault rifle, and thank heavens the officers took enough time to realize it was a paintball gun. There was the case of a woman so unhinged after her husband deployed that she covered the walls of her apartment with feces and her children were taken into protective custody. There was the case of a woman from Korea who had no idea what to do when her American soldier husband died in a training exercise. "Where do I pay the electric bill?" she asked. "Where is Walmart?" The worst cases, though, were the two suicides. As police chief, Clark responded to both, saw the rooms, saw the bodies, and each time found himself thinking all over again of his first suicide, years before, when he was just starting out as a cop, which involved a garage and a nicely dressed woman hanging in the most absolute stillness. There she was again, directly in front of him, and it made him wonder: If that kind of triggering could happen to him, what must it be like for these soldiers?

"Dig a little deeper," he has told his officers when they get a call involving a soldier. "See what the problem is." It's something he has in mind when he and two other officers knock on Tausolo and Theresa's door. But when he goes into the bedroom and sees what appear to be marks on Theresa's cheeks and neck, he has no choice. He arrests Tausolo for assaulting Theresa, and when Tausolo protests, saying nothing happened, he says, "Don't stand there and bullshit me."

That's the way Clark will remember it. Tausolo will remember it differently, that Clark snaps at him, "Look at me when I'm talking to you," and he decides right then and there that there's no point in trying to persuade Clark that he hadn't hit Theresa, that he'd cussed her out because he discovered some cigarettes and didn't want her breast-feeding the baby with nicotine in her, that she'd said she was going to take the baby and go home to Samoa if he kept yelling, that she was terrified he was about to become violent because of how violent he had been before. Instead of saying any of that, though, he holds still while he is handcuffed. This is the way things go. He knows it, as surely as anything. Life involves following orders. If he is told to collect thirty-nine signatures, he will collect thirty-nine signatures. If someone says, "Do you want a quilt?" he will want a quilt. If someone says, "Put some jet engines on your legs," he will put some jet engines on his legs. If someone says to get in the Humvee, he will get in the Humvee. If someone says, "Look at me when I'm talking to you," he will look at him, and then he will get in the police car and say nothing more.

So he is surprised when Brad Clark—who will later remember thinking, "I wanted to give the guy one more opportunity. This guy's not a jerk. This guy, it appears to me there's a problem. The guy needed frickin' help"—breaks the silence with a question.

"Hey, man, you've got some issues here, don't you?" he asks.

Silence again, until Tausolo mumbles something about PTSD and multiple deployments.

Well, be sure to tell the judge, Clark suggests, so it can be taken into account.

They are at the jail now. Tausolo is processed in, given a yellow jumpsuit to change into, and put in a cell with four other inmates. The only place for him is a middle bunk. His heart is racing from nerves. He doesn't have his Zoloft and Lunesta and Trazodone and Abilify and Concerta and Klonopin. For three nights, he dreams of Harrelson. On his meds, it happens once a week. Here, it happens every time he shuts his eyes.

Finally, after the weekend, he is released. He goes to court, pleads guilty to a charge of disorderly behavior, pays a fine of a few hundred dollars, and promises to get marriage counseling.

Back at home, he apologizes to Theresa, and Theresa apologizes to him.

And then he is back to where he was before all of this happened, at the WTB, where he reluctantly seeks out his case manager to tell her what happened.

The reluctance is because she is new—his third case manager in as many months. Such is the nature of personnel churn at the WTB. Sergeants who are squad leaders and platoon leaders come and go, often with destabilizing effects as the new ones adjust to the peculiarities of the place. It's the same at the command level—just when things are going fairly smoothly, it's time for a new battalion commander, who, on his first official day, assembles the soldiers at the parade field for a change-of-command ceremony. It's a gray, drizzly day, and the soldiers stand in the wet grass with their hands clasped behind their backs, and only when a few of them drop to the ground quaking does he realize that the customary cannon blast wasn't such a good idea.

Of all the personnel changes, though, the change of a case manager can be the most destabilizing of all. This is the person who is supposed to coordinate a WTB soldier's day-to-day care, and when Aieti met this new one for the first time—it was just before he was arrested—he didn't know what to make of her.

"Well, welcome, sir!" she had said when he walked into her office. "I'm going to be your new case manager."

She motioned him to a seat. He sat. *What happened to the old case manager?* he thought.

"Okay. My role. What is my purpose in your life?" she continued. "This is my purpose in your life. I am like your mom."

She smiled at him and winked.

A winker, he thought.

"We're gonna do a risk assessment right now," she said. She brought up a form on her computer. "Okay, on a scale of zero to three, three being, 'This is horribly heavy on my heart,' zero is, 'I'm all cool, everything is copacetic,' where are you on that scale?"

"Uh, two," he said, wondering why he was doing another risk assessment after having done so many.

"Two," she said. She noted his answer and turned her attention to his treatment at Topeka. "Did it help? Did it help at all? Was it a first step to helping? I'm talking about the PTSD program. How'd you feel afterward?"

"Good," he said.

"Okay. Good means, 'I'm on my road, on the way to recovery,'" she said. "Good means, 'Okay, now I understand the scope of what PTSD means, but I still have a lot of issues with my symptoms.'"

"Mmm."

"Okay," she said, translating his *mmm* to an answer. "Any history of domestic violence or neglect?"

"No."

"Okay. History of suicidal-homicidal thoughts."

"None."

"None," she said. "When was the last?"

"I never had any," he said.

"You never had any?"

"No."

"Okay. PTSD symptoms. Zero is, 'I have no idea what you're talking about,' six is, 'My anxiety level is out of the roof, I'm gonna beat somebody up if they even talk to me, look at me wrong, I can't sleep, I'm having nightmares, the whole realm.' Where are you in that? Six is horrible, zero is none."

"Two," he said.

"Two? Okay," she said.

He waited for her to wink again.

"Okay. I think we're good," she said after a few more minutes of this. "If you need anything and you have a question about something, if I don't know the question, if it's not in my lane, I can find out. So. Anything I can do for you, that's my yob. Okay?"

Did she say "yob"? he thought.

"I'm mom away from Samoa," she said. "So I'm the Samoan mama."

She is the Samoan mama, and now, as he goes to see her for the second time to explain that he has been arrested and jailed, he is wishing he still had his previous case manager. Or the case manager before that.

This time, though, instead of talking and winking so much, she listens, and when he is done, she reaches into her purse, finds fifteen dollars, gives it to him, and tells him to go buy some roses for Theresa.

So many people are rooting for Tausolo, it seems. Case managers. Police chiefs.

"Thank you," he says.

He leaves her office. He has never bought roses before. Where does a person buy roses? He goes home.

"Where can I buy roses?" he asks Theresa.

"Why?" she answers.

This is getting too complicated for him.

He hands her the fifteen dollars.

Before he got blown up, he could have figured it out. How hard is it to buy roses? There's a flower shop on Fort Riley. They sell them at Walmart. But such are the effects of being in a Humvee that rolls over three buried 130-millimeter artillery shells, which explode at the perfect moment. Up he went, and down he came, and once his brain was done rattling around from a blast wave that passed through him faster than the speed of sound, here came the rest of it. Memory, fucked. The ability to pay attention, fucked. Balance. Hearing. Impulse control. Perception. Dreams. All of it, fucked. "The signature wound of the war" is what the military calls traumatic brain injury, and that's one way to see it, but another is in a conversation that Tausolo has one day with a woman named Meg Vernon, who is a clinician at Fort Riley's TBI clinic.

"Like one time, I came in the gate, I forgot to register my car and I got pulled over, and the guy said I could keep going—and then when I get going I don't know where I'm going," he tells her with some embarrassment at how forgetful he has become.

He has come to see her so she can help him with his memory, or at least give him some tricks for remembering things. One more person rooting for Tausolo—that's Meg Vernon, who begins a session with him by holding up a photograph of a young woman.

"Her name is Catherine Taylor," she tells Tausolo. "Say it back to me so I know you heard it right."

"Catherine Taylor," Tausolo says.

"And what are you going to do to remember her name?" Meg asks. "Walk me through what you're going to do. Because we're probably not going to remember it unless we really take some effort to commit it to our memory. So what are you gonna do?"

"I don't know," Tausolo says. " 'Cause I can't associate it with—"

"Because it doesn't look like anyone?" Meg asks.

"Yeah."

"Do you know a Catherine? Or a Taylor?" she prompts.

"No."

"Okay. We can use multiple strategies. You might say it over and over. Or you might think of CT. I think of, like, a CT scan when I see CT. But whatever comes to you that you might be able to use."

Tausolo keeps staring at the photograph.

"Think you've got that tucked away?" Meg says after a while. "You want to look at it a little longer?"

Tausolo shrugs.

She puts the photograph down and picks up another, this of a man.

"His name is Henry Fisher."

"Henry Fisher," Tausolo repeats.

"Henry Fisher," Meg says. "So walk me through how you're going to remember his name."

"Fisher . . ." he says, trailing off.

"Do you fish?" she asks. "Are you a fisherman? Or do you know somebody that fishes?"

"Yeah I know somebody that fishes."

"Okay." She lets that idea settle in and turns to the first name. "Henry." She points to some of his facial features. "He's kind of hairy."

"Yeah."

"Henry," she says. "Hairy."

"Hairy Fisher," Tausolo says, nodding.

"Think you got that one committed to your memory?"

"Yeah."

"So what's his name?"

"Henry Fisher."

"What's the first lady's name?"

"Um . . . Catherine. Taylor."

"Catherine Taylor. And Henry Fisher. And the third person," she says, holding up a third photograph, "is Andrew Harris."

"Andrew Harris."

"Do you know an Andrew?"

"Yeah . . ."

"Do you know a Harris? How could you associate Harris with that picture? Hairless? Harris? Something like that?"

"Oh, okay, I get it."

"So what's his name?"

"Andrew Harris."

"Okay, so the first lady?" she says, holding up the first photograph.

"Um, Catherine . . . Taylor?"

"Mm-hmm." She holds up the second photo.

"Uh, Henry . . . Fisher?"

"Mm-hmm." She holds up the third photo.

"Andrew . . . oh, I can only remember hairless."

"And that's supposed to bring you to . . ."

"Harris," he says after a few moments of concentration.

"Harris. Yes," she says.

"Harris."

He smiles, pleased. Three names in a row.

Meg continues with the session. She picks up a clock and sets the alarm. "When the alarm goes off, I want you to ask me two questions," she says. "Okay? The two questions are: 'When do I have to see you again?' and 'When does the session end?'" So when that alarm goes off, whatever we're doing, we'll be in the middle of something, stop and ask me those two questions."

"Um, what are the two questions?" Tausolo asks.

Meg repeats them.

"Wow. That's a lot," Tausolo says.

She moves on with the testing. "I'm going to read you a story, and I want you to recall back as much of the story as you can. Any detail that you can recall. Any highlights. The gist of the story. Just do the best that you can. Ready?"

She reads him the story. "Mr. Brian Kelly, a security express employee, was shot dead on Monday during a bank raid in Brighton. The four raiders all wore masks, and one carried a sawed-off shotgun. Police detectives were sifting through eyewitness accounts last night. A police spokesman said, 'He was a very brave man. He went for the armed raider and put up a hell of a fight.'" She pauses. "Tell me what you can remember from that story."

"I got confused," he says. "I was trying to listen to you, but my mind keeps going back to the different things."

"Do you want me to read it again?"

"Yeah."

She reads it again.

"Okay," Tausolo says. "Somebody got shot, and, um, they, um, and someone said he was a brave man. He went after the four raiders, and . . . that's it."

"Anything else coming to you?" Meg asks.

"No."

The alarm goes off.

"Um, um, what time are we done with the test?" Tausolo says.

"Yes!" Meg says. "Very good!"

"And, um, oh! When am I going to see you again?"

"Excellent! Terrific! You got it!" Meg says. "Now the story I read you earlier—what was it about?"

"Umm, a guy who died, and there was an investigation, and, um, someone said he was brave, he was a brave man for taking on four . . . four . . ."

"Okay," she says. She picks up the very first photograph she had shown at the beginning of the session and shows it to him again.

"Oh shit," Tausolo says. "Catherine . . . Catherine . . . that's all I can remember."

"I want you to think longer," Meg urges. "Think of some of the things we talked about."

"Catherine . . . Catherine . . ."

"Do you remember the initials?"

"No."

"Okay. Her last name starts with a T."

"Trevor?"

"Taylor."

"Taylor," Tausolo repeats as Meg holds up the next photo.

"Um, Henry . . . Fisher," he says.

"Very good! And the last one?"

"Andrew," Tausolo says. He concentrates really hard. "I remember hairless. But . . ."

"It's close to that," Meg says.

"Hairy?"

"Harris," Meg says.

She looks at him, waiting. "You did very well on that overall," she finally says. "There was a *ton* to remember."

He knows better. He looks at her and shakes his head.

They're out of time.

"Somebody up front will get you scheduled for next week," she says.

He gathers his things and goes out to the receptionist, who asks him, "Who's your appointment with?"

He thinks for a moment. "I forgot her name." He keeps thinking. Laughs in embarrassment. "What's her name?"

Now he is back at the WTB, at formation. He goes every morning without fail, even in the rain, even when the temperature is sub-zero.

Formation is usually at 6:30 a.m. and attendance is mandatory. It's still the army, after all, so they all show up, form into lines, and wait for their name to be called—"Aieti!"—so they can indicate that they've made it through another night—"Here!" They're all here, morning after morning, all alive, until one morning when one of them isn't.

He was twenty-one years old, had been sent home from the war early, and killed himself in the middle of the night in his barracks room. According to his obituary, he had been a Boy Scout, a member of his church's Celebrate Life Science Quiz team, and "loved his dog 'Sarah.'" Aieti didn't know him well, but they stood near each other in formation and sometimes went to the gym together. So much for that. Now one more soldier is on his way to the Gardner Room, and a lot of other soldiers are on their way to a memorial service at the chapel, where the electronic sign out front has some flashing messages:

"It is your responsibility to get help for a fellow soldier."

"Never let your buddy fight alone, be willing to lend a hand."

Heads down, they fill seven rows of the chapel and watch a woebegone family file in and take seats in the front row, within touching distance of an easel, upon which is a photograph of a defeated-looking young man. "What next?" his expression might as well be saying, and his family's, too. Next to the easel is a display of his boots, helmet, and rifle, and near that is a podium for one of the eulogists to stand at and declare in the most mystified voice, "What is there to say at this point except thank you for your service?"

Tausolo is not on hand to hear this. He is avoiding all of it: the bugler playing "Taps," the gunshot salute that causes a few of the soldiers to wince, the father of the young man wiping his eyes and coughing, the tears of a woman a few rows back who had come alone, holding a book called *The One Year Book of Hope.* Whoever she is, the last thing Tausolo wants to hear are her memorial tears, or anyone's. He's been to enough of these services. They are Harrelson's service all over again, and Doster's, and the twelve others killed in his battalion. He knows what bad memories these things conjure in him, and that's not what he needs to be remembering. He needs to be remembering Catherine Taylor, Henry Fisher, and Andrew Harris. He can't keep going backward. He can't go back to jail. He can't go back to Topeka. He can't keep going back up into the air and down into another dream. Backward, up, down—those are all the wrong directions. If he's going to get better, he needs to be moving forward, nothing but forward, and so he stays far away from the chapel until the day after the memorial service, when he happens to pass by it as he heads toward the next thing he's supposed to do in his recovery.

He is on his way to his first day of class at one of the colleges offering courses at Fort Riley. "They told me to go to school," he says. "Well I'm going to school." The electronic sign is still flashing—"Have the courage to seek help," it reads as he drives past the chapel—but he ignores it. Back in Samoa, he excelled at math. Does he still have the mind for it? He doesn't know. Probably not is his guess. But he has signed up for an algebra class and is about to find out.

He parks near an old building and climbs a flight of stairs to a classroom on the second floor. Shyly, he slides into an empty seat in the back row and takes out a pen, and is using it to poke himself in the arm as the instructor stands to introduce himself.

"All right. Probably most of you don't know me," he says. "I'm Mr. Russell."

It is Kent Russell, Kristy Robinson's boyfriend. He is Tausolo's next rescuer.

Kent, who knows some things about wounded soldiers and the effects those wounds can have.

Who took the engagement ring back from Kristy and said to her, "I'm going to hang on to it, and if the time is right, if it ever comes, I'll have it." "Thank you," she had said.

Who took the ring home and put it in a drawer, and now, trying to move on, has turned his attention to a new class of students, including one in the back row who is using his pen to poke himself in his arm.

He turns around and writes his name on the board.

"Mr. Russell," Tausolo writes in his notebook, and forty-five minutes later, he walks outside feeling pretty good, as if he's getting somewhere at last. "So I'll see you back tomorrow" was how Mr. Russell ended the class, and Tausolo thought: *Yes you will.* He likes Kent Russell.

As a matter of fact, he likes Meg Vernon, too. And Sergeant Jung and Sergeant Lewis. He even kind of likes the winker.

Some days he wonders why he ever wanted to be in the WTB. But there are also days when he can sense some progress, and on one of those days he heads over to the main building to meet with a new sergeant and get a travel request approved. The sergeant looks it over. "Go see the human resources lady," he says.

So Tausolo goes to see her. "Leave? Emergency? What?" she says. She tells him to go back to the sergeant.

"Ask *her*," the sergeant says.

"He told me to ask you," Tausolo explains to her when she asks him why he's back.

She signs the request and tells him to take it back to the sergeant.

He takes it back, but the sergeant is busy now, having a heated discussion with someone else about which is better, Whataburger or In-N-Out. It seems like it might go on for a while, so Tausolo takes a seat and looks around the sergeant's cubicle. There's not much to see, since the guy just arrived at the WTB, only a blank form tacked to a wall that looks like every other army form in the world.

"Hurt Feelings Report," it is titled.

"Whiner's name," it says under that.

"Which ear were the words of hurtfulness spoken into?" it says under that. "Is there permanent feeling damage?" "Did you require a 'tissue' for tears?" "Has this resulted in a traumatic brain injury?"

"Reason for filing this report," it says under that. "Mark all that apply."

"I am a wimp."

"I am a crybaby."

"I want my mommy."

"I was told that I am not a hero."

"Narrative," it says under that. "Tell us in your own sissy words how your feelings were hurt."

Finally, at the bottom of the form:

We, as the Army, take hurt feelings seriously. If you don't have someone who can give you a hug and make things all better, please let us know and we will promptly dispatch a "hugger" to you ASAP. In the event we are unable to find a "hugger" we will notify the fire department and request that they send fire personnel to your location. If you are in need of supplemental support, upon written request, we will make every reasonable effort to provide you with a "blankey," a "binky" and/ or a bottle if you so desire.

It's a joke, Tausolo supposes. He waits for the sergeant to finish his conversation, suddenly feeling tired. The dream was so vivid last night he couldn't get back to sleep. Up he went. Down he came. "Why didn't you save me?" Harrelson asked.

Some things he can't remember. Some things he can't forget.

13

When Fred Gusman was little, his father came home from World War Two and began beating him with a belt.

Too young to know why, what he did know was that anything could trigger it. One time it was some Spanish rice that his mother had piled onto his dinner plate, the smell of which was making him sick. Eat it, his father said. I don't want to, he said. *Eat it*, his father said again, laying his belt on the table. Fred remembers using a fork to push around the rice until a single grain was stuck to it. He lifted it to his mouth. Stop it, his father said. He ate another grain, thinking he might vomit, and his father picked up the belt and took aim.

Sometimes, anticipating, he ran to a closet and hid. It didn't matter. Eventually the door swung open.

Even now, Fred doesn't know what was wrong with his father. The war, of course, had affected him—"If he didn't have post-traumatic stress, he was *really* weird," Fred says—but what about it? What specifically would fill a man with such fury? The one person who might have had an answer was a neighbor, also a war veteran, who one day asked Fred's father to help him build a boat. They spent hours together in the neighbor's yard, talking now and then as they worked, but any chance that friendship had of loosening something in Fred's father came to an end when he went over one day and found the man hanging dead in his garage. He cut the man down and continued his beatings, and at last Fred's mother fled with Fred to live with her mother, a church-going woman who believed in redemption. There's goodness in everyone, she told her grandson over and over, which was news to an eight-year-old

The Pathway Home

struggling against bad dreams and wetting the bed. Even the worst people have some good in them, she said, and made him a promise. If he looked for it in anyone, he would eventually be able to find it.

Sixty years later:

He had gotten through the rest of his childhood in California's Central Valley by working in middle school as a janitor's assistant and in high school as a picker in the vegetable fields. He had spent a few years in the military and come out with money for college. He had received an undergraduate degree in child development and a graduate degree in social work, and gotten a job at a VA hospital. He had tracked down Vietnam vets who had come home to scrapheap lives and coaxed them into therapy. He had started the country's first residential treatment program devoted to those vets and, after treating thousands of them, had come to believe that their best hope depended on their having enough time to understand their illness in the context of an entire life, that what mattered wasn't just who they became after a traumatic event, but also who they had been the moment before. Deep digging, without time limits, back to the beginning and down to the soul—this was Fred's approach, and after decades of success with it, he had become concerned when the VA and other providers switched to treatment models with maximum stays. Seven weeks. Four weeks. One week with optional renewals. Eventually, he had grown discouraged enough to consider retiring, and that was when the call had come about Pathway. It would be entirely donor-supported, they told him. No insurance companies to answer to. Independent of the VA. He would have his own building on the vast grounds of the California Veterans Home in Yountville, and the program would be his to design and oversee. "One last run" was the way he explained his decision to people who asked why he was doing it, and now, on a Friday afternoon, three days from starting the hard part of treatment with his newest group of war-wounded vets, the part referred to as Trauma Group, he walks over to a visibly distressed Adam Schumann.

"Looking forward to Monday," he says.

The distress is due to a text that just arrived from Saskia.

He was upset even before he looked at it, just by hearing his phone buzz. Why can't she leave him alone? Just let him get better, and one day he'll come home to her healed. Instead, since quitting her job, she has been texting more and more, fifty times a day sometimes, about anything, as if he were still in Junction City. What did he get at McDonald's? That was a text. Jax growled at her when she told him to go to bed. That was a text. What now?

"Any way you can be home by Monday nite? They're doing tubes Tuesday morning. He's got complete hearing loss in his left and mild in right."

It was about Jaxson, who still wasn't talking, in spite of being eighteen months old, and as soon as Adam read it, he was once again thinking of the night he fell asleep and Jaxson rolled off the bed.

"Jesus," he said.

So he will go home. He is needed there. But Monday is when Trauma Group begins. How can he not be here?

He goes outside, where some of the other guys in the program are hanging out on a second-story landing of their building. From a distance, they look no worse off than any other young guys with dangling cigarettes and softening muscles. Only up close does the nervousness in their eyes become noticeable, along with the three bubbly scars on a guy who is now describing the great sex he had once with a girl he met on a psych ward. One scar crosses his left wrist. One crosses his right wrist. One covers the length of his left forearm.

Fred was right in what he had said on the drive from the airport: a lot of ups and downs in this place, and after two months, Adam is feeling at home among them. He doesn't know if he's any better yet, but after a shaky first couple of weeks, the thought of going back to Kansas at this point, even temporarily, makes him feel like he'd be betraying the best chance he might ever get. The counseling sessions, the anger-management classes, the Monday-night bowling with the Rotarians, the meditation lessons—he likes all of it. And he has been looking forward to Trauma Group, even though he has heard it described by someone who went through it as "a kick in the face." Is that progress? He supposes it is.

The conversation switches to things they used to do to kids during the war. One guy mentions putting Tabasco sauce on the M&M's they handed out. Another says they used to throw dollar bills to kids and bet on who would win the inevitable fights. Someone flicks away a cigarette butt, and they all watch it pinwheel to the ground in a satisfying shower of sparks.

Adam finishes his own cigarette and goes inside to check on his roommate, Will, who, after nearly a year in the program, is leaving. Another thing Fred says: it takes a guy a few months to overcome the sense of hopelessness he arrives with, and Will was a case study in that. For a long time, he didn't want to talk to anyone or even come out of his room, and now here he is, swearing he's ready to return to the wicked world that sent him here in the first place.

"You need help packing up, shitbird?" Adam asks him.

Will shakes his head. He's all done. The only thing left is to get rid of his TV, which is too big to take with him. Adam borrows Will's car, runs to an ATM, grabs two hundred dollars, and comes right back. "All right, let's do this," Will says to himself. He turns to Adam and extends his hand. They've been roommates since Adam's very first night here, when an attendant searched Adam's duffel bag for weapons and drugs and discovered a hidden note from Saskia that said "Baby, I love you so much." He's the only one who Adam has told about Emory and Doster. "I'll see you later, Kansas," he says.

"You're not gonna take the trash out?" Adam says to him as he walks out.

The door closes.

"That's a dickhead move," Adam yells.

The door opens. Will is laughing. He grabs the trash.

"See you, man," Adam says, and there goes Will for good, leaving Adam to wonder if it'll take a year for him, too.

A moment later, his phone buzzes with another text. What does she want this time?

"Why'd you take so much money out of the account?"

He sighs. It's been, what, twenty minutes since he went to the ATM? "It fucking feels like I have a fucking satellite watching me," he says, and instead of replying, he turns off the phone and goes back outside.

The others have gone somewhere, so he lights a cigarette, and then another, trying to figure out what to do. From his first day, the place has unnerved and seduced him: hundreds of acres, grape air floating over from the bordering winery, and trees everywhere, of all types, including the tall, skinny palm with the weird leaves outside of his window that, when the wind is blowing, he can't help but hear. It's a different sound than in Kansas, when the wind moves through the cottonwoods and he's hidden up in a tree stand. That has a scratchy sound to it that can make him feel chilly, especially in autumn, when everything is turning brittle. This is more lush, and comes with a chill of a different kind. It would be easy to shimmy up it, he thinks, and the jump, if not soul-cleansing, at least would guarantee relief. That's the chilling part, the way the leaves in this lovely place seem to be calling to him.

He watches now as one of the elderly people who live here year-round comes toward him on a sidewalk. There are said to be eleven hundred of them tucked into the various buildings, most of them old, some of them disabled, most of them men, and all of them with military service at some point in their lives. Judging by the caps they wear, most of them were in Vietnam, but this one, so old and moving so slowly, must be World War Two. He is using a walker. He takes a step and rests, takes another step and rests. He keeps coming, and as he nears Adam, he stops, turns as if he's about to break, and stares at him. Adam stares back. The man takes off his sunglasses and keeps staring. Adam finishes his cigarette. Finally, the man turns away and walks on.

"Goddamn," Adam says, a little creeped out.

More of them are coming now, headed to the dining hall. Some walk on their own. Some use walkers. Most are driving motorized scooters adorned with American flags. Adam keeps watching along with another guy in the program, Rob, who has come out to join him. Now one of those scooters is swerving along the sidewalk instead of going in a straight line like all of the others.

"Wasted," Adam says.

"No, if he was wasted, he'd be going off the sidewalk," Rob says.

They keep watching as the scooter goes off the sidewalk. "Oops," Rob says. But the old man driving it only wants to stop under a magnolia tree for a cigarette, and after finishing it and doubling over in a fit of coughing, he steers onward toward the dining hall.

Another old vet comes along now who probably *is* wasted, one of the hard-core guys who spend every day drinking beer at the picnic tables behind the Pathway building, which has a snack shop on the ground floor. They never say hello, or even wave. They just sit there and drink.

"They're always fucking drunk," Rob says of them.

"They look alone" is what Adam says. "They look broken."

"Six in the morning and they already have a beer pyramid going," Rob says.

"That's me in thirty years," Adam says. "If this doesn't work out, that's me."

Actually, it's ten in the morning when the beer pyramid gets going.

Six in the morning is when Raymond Sherman shows up. He's the first. He often is, the result of a day in the army a long time ago when he was sent on a clean-up detail to Guyana, where nine hundred people at a religious compound had poisoned themselves in a mass suicide. A few years later, he began having dreams about those nine hundred people, and now he sits alone in the morning chill, his hands wrapped around a cup of coffee, waiting for beer sales to begin. At 9:59, he goes into the snack shop. "Three Keystone Lights and three Natural Lights," he tells the cashier, and a minute later, the pyramid is under way.

Paul Alexander—army, World War Two—is the next to arrive. He is wearing a cowboy hat and driving a scooter with two beers in the basket, and after him comes Jim George—Marines, Vietnam—who has neither beers nor legs and is balanced high on his hips on his motorized wheelchair. Soon there are seven of them, all drawn here by the snack shop, which for years was the only functioning part of a vacant two-story building. One day, they were surprised to see painters show up. Next came furniture movers hauling beds and bureaus to the second floor. Then came the first of the haunted soldiers from America's two latest wars, and now a voice is floating down from an open second-floor window:

"Wake up, motherfucker."

It's Rob, trying to wake up Adam, who wants to sleep in on a weekend.

"Wake up, bitch," Rob tries again a few minutes later, laughing, and meanwhile, at the picnic tables, Jim George is telling about the day he was shot three times. "September 21, 1971," he is saying. "I'll always remember that date." He says it happened in Laos, when he was part of a five-man reconnaissance team that was ambushed. The others were killed, and he lay alone for a long time under a bush, blood seeping out of three holes in his stomach and who knows what seeping in. The area was coated in Agent Orange, and after several days under the bush, he was down to hallucinations when rescuers finally arrived. The years passed. His immune system deteriorated. One day, thirty-three years later, he got an ingrown toenail that became infected, and when it wouldn't heal, they amputated half of his right foot. The infection continued to spread, and next they amputated the rest of his foot above the ankle. The next amputation was below the knee. Then above the knee. Then mid-thigh. Then all the way up at the hip. The entire leg was gone. And then, he says, the infection showed up in his left foot. Six more surgeries. Six more amputations. Both legs entirely gone. "I enlisted," he says, thinking back to how this began. "I was mad at the world. I wanted to be a Marine. Big, tough guy. Did me a lot of good. I went in the corps, I was six-foot-two. Thirty-three years later, I'm three-foot-one."

He laughs. No one else does.

"I mean, all wars are the same," he says.

"Only the landscape changes," someone else says.

The beer pyramid grows higher. One person plays solitaire. A few others watch until one of the Pathway guys walks past with a dog he is training to be his service dog, and two more come out and head to the parking lot. The young soldiers don't say good morning. The old soldiers don't say nice-looking dog. No one acknowledges the others at all.

"They won't talk to us." Raymond Sherman shrugs.

"Most of them won't even look at us," Jim George says. "It's like we done something wrong."

"They act like they don't even see us, and yet they'll come to our home—and this *is* our home, for them it's just a stopover—and they'll bring their dogs out to take a shit and not even pick it up," Raymond Sherman says. He is sitting with his knees together, apart, together, rocking back and forth.

He's the most visibly nervous, but they all have their own ways of coping with what they've become. They drink and have the faces to prove it. Some of them scooter up to the cemetery at night and smoke a joint or two among the headstones of five thousand dead soldiers. Jim George says he spent fifteen years high on methamphetamine. Paul Alexander rarely says anything at all. Another of them, Mark Fischer, checks his watch over and over as noon approaches because noon is when a whistle goes off and forty-five years after Vietnam he's still getting used to loud noises.

Now, from the open windows on the second floor, comes the sound of Rob saying to Adam: "I flew to the Green Zone once to see a guy who got shot. There was all this gunfire, and I was thinking, shit, I don't wanna die doing this. I don't even like that guy that much . . ."

Every so often, the old guys wonder what goes on up there. How could they know, though? Most of them came home from their wars to no help at all. There was nothing set up for them, only what they could figure out on their own.

"I would get next to my wife as close as I could, as hard as I could, because I know I was going to dream about it. I was afraid to go to sleep," Raymond Sherman says of what he did after Guyana, which came down to crushing himself against a woman until their marriage came to an end.

"I used to have dreams of rocks coming out of a machine gun," Mark Fischer says of the help he got. "I was in a bar and I told a guy this, and the guy said he learned every night when he was going to bed to lay there, go to your higher power, whatever, and say, 'God, I don't want to dream about Vietnam anymore.' He said, 'Just say that every night for a month, and I guarantee you, you won't have any more dreams.' That was in the mid-1990s, and by God, it worked. I don't have dreams."

The whistle goes off. He's ready for it. He's fine.

The pyramid grows.

Among the seven, the only one who had gotten any kind of professional help was Jim George, who had become suicidal twelve years after he was shot. "My dad caught me with a .45, at the table, about to do it," he says, and because of that he was admitted to a fledgling residential program for Vietnam vets, where he stayed for a year. What he came to understand: "The worst thing about being in it is killing," he says of war. "The worst for me was that I got to like it. I got pretty good at it. I hated myself for a long time for getting that good, liking it that much."

The program, as it turns out, was Fred Gusman's.

"Saved my life," Jim says.

That saved life allowed him to marry and divorce four times and eventually brought him to the Veterans Home, where he lost his legs, got his wheelchair, and was at the picnic tables one day when he saw Fred Gusman going into the vacant building. He tried to talk to him, he says, and was disappointed when Fred didn't seem to remember him.

Maybe it was his appearance. Fred knew him when he was six-foot-two.

Maybe it was something else. "Why would he remember one person when there's probably thousands and thousands that he's seen?"

He changes the subject to life at the Veterans Home and the good things about it. He has his own room at the hospital. He gets twenty-four-hour care from nurses who have learned to keep their distance when he's having a violent dream. He almost never gets visitors, and so he is thankful at Christmas when all of the residents are given a gift, although for the past two years the gift has been a pair of socks.

"What am I supposed to do, put 'em on my dick?" he says.

This time, everyone laughs.

The beer pyramid keeps growing. Saturday goes by.

Now it's Sunday. New pyramid. Same thing.

Now the weekend is over and, at last, two months after Adam got here, Trauma Group is under way. The guys are gathered around a table. Fred is about to say something. Here it comes, the kick in the face. All of a sudden, loud laughter drifts up from the picnic tables.

"Somebody's having fun down there," Fred says.

———

Not that Adam is around to hear it.

His decision was to fly home, spend a few days, and drive back so he would have a car. Five days at the most, he promised Fred.

"Don't forget to come back," Fred said, not at all sure he would.

Adam wasn't sure, either. "It's a fucking black hole, sucking me in," he said of home.

Six days later, he's back. The surgery had been successful. But if Jaxson was suddenly hearing, one of the things he got to hear in its full volume was Adam yelling and throwing his wedding ring at Saskia as she screamed that she couldn't do this alone. They were going broke. He could get help in Kansas. She was going to a therapist because of him. She was on antianxiety medication because of him. He needed to stay home, be a husband, be a father. "Grow some fucking balls and man up," she screamed. Eventually she apologized and he left for California, but now, as Trauma Group continues, and the day comes closer when it will be Adam's turn to talk, to "detect everything about you," as Fred put it, "because it isn't when it went boom," Saskia's pleadings are only increasing. Texts. Phone calls. Letters.

"I'm so sorry, I dont know whats going on with me anymore. But nothing I seem to do seems to be helping. I'm just melting in my own self pity," she writes one night in the longest, saddest message yet. "I walk downstairs and look at that stupid fish and all I can see is you sitting there, shaking, with a gun to your fucking head, fighting you for it and not even thinking about the possibility of myself getting hurt or the fact that our son is upstairs crying or that our daughter could walk in at any moment and find her daddy's brains splattered all over the basement. That moment I was forever changed . . ."

She is making herself sick with what she's becoming, but that doesn't mean the messages stop.

Finally, one of the family counselors at Pathway calls her to explain what Adam is dealing with, that if he comes home too soon he'll almost certainly turn suicidal, but Saskia has some things to say, too.

"I'm pretty much tired of doing it myself," she tells the counselor as she sits in her living room, while Jaxson naps and Zoe is in the backyard, splashing around in an above-ground swimming pool they had bought during one of their good stretches. "My daughter cries every night . . . His leave is pretty much gone . . . I'm sorry. I'm not trying to be rude . . ."

Her voice is rising, enough for Zoe to come in from the pool and see if something is wrong, and Saskia goes to the front porch. She lights a cigarette as she keeps talking—her newest habit.

"I'm sick of it. I really am. I did not have kids, I did not get married, to be on my own . . . It doesn't matter. If I lose my house, if I lose my car . . . What I'm getting really pissed at . . . I *understand* . . ." she says, as one of the dogs comes into the living room and Zoe gets on the floor with him.

"My entire family is falling apart because of this . . . There's only so much I can take . . ."

Her voice is shaking now, and she's wiping her eyes. "Eddie, lay down," Zoe says.

"I have not gotten *any* help. From anyone . . . That isn't the point. I shouldn't have to be doing this twenty-four-seven while he's out there having fun . . . I can't . . . I *can't*. I can't afford it . . ."

"Lay down," Zoe says.

"*I'm so angry because he's not fucking taking care of what he's supposed to* . . . I am *done*. I am *done*. I am fed up. I am *sick* of it. I am tired of being made to feel guilty. Poor Adam. It's always poor Adam . . ."

Zoe starts giggling as Eddie licks her neck. "Okay. More kisses," she says when he stops.

"I can't do it anymore. I cannot do it anymore . . . Why is it fair? . . . So when he comes home in two and a half months, I can't even leave for the weekend . . ."

"Not in the eyeball!"

"Because the whole time I'll have to worry about whether he hears my son or not . . . Once you drop a baby, it kind of takes the trust out of it . . ."

Saskia gets up and comes back into the living room. She stinks of cigarettes. Her eye makeup is a mess.

"Okay . . . Okay . . . Bye."

Zoe, dog-kissed and grinning, looks at her.

"Oh my fucking God. I'll fucking kill him."

Zoe keeps looking.

"*Go! Play!*" she says, and when Zoe goes, she sits on the couch, trying to figure out what just happened. "If he comes home, he's going to kill himself. If he stays there, we're done.

"What am I supposed to do?"

Her phone buzzes with a message.

Adam.

"I'm almost packed. Leaving in an hour."

He must know about the conversation.

"Well she thinks I need to let you stay," Saskia writes back.

"Just let it go," he writes. "I'll be home in a few days."

"How am I supposed to let it go? I either suck it up and you stay or I get threatened with you killing yourself."

"I'll be fine. I know what I need to do."

"No. Just stay."

"Too bad," he writes back after a few minutes. "I already left."

"Turn around."

"No. You live with it now."

Where is he? she wonders. Did he really leave?

"You get what you want now," reads his next message.

What does he mean by that? She calls him. He doesn't answer. She calls again. No answer.

"He didn't leave," she says. "No way he left."

But he did.

He emptied out his room, threw everything in the car, said goodbye to no one, just left, and now, as he heads east, away from Pathway and back to his traumatized wife and craving daughter and son he dropped who may or may not be okay, he is once again a man out of control. He is shaking and crying and wishing to be dead. Saskia calls and he ignores it. She calls again and he ignores it again. Now it is Fred calling and he swallows hard and answers. "Did you leave?" "Yeah." He tries to explain, and instead of telling him to come back, Fred simply says the choice of what to do is his. "You need to take care of yourself," he says, and when he hangs up, Adam feels as alone as he did when he was in Iraq, waiting in line for the helicopter out of the war and the soldier screamed at him, "Next one's yours."

Four years later, he is still waiting for it.

He doesn't know what to do.

In Kansas, Saskia doesn't know what to do, either.

He keeps driving. She keeps waiting to hear from him. Both of them know that something has to be done, that this has become unbearable, and it is finally Adam who makes a decision.

He swings the car around and heads west, away from Saskia and back to Fred.

He will tell him everything. His guilt over Doster. His guilt over Emory. His guilt over Jaxson. His guilt over Zoe. His guilt over Saskia. His guilt over the way he grew up. His guilt over all of it, all the way back to the beginning. That's his decision, to finally stop dying and instead turn himself over completely to someone who has been dealing with fuck-ups like him forever.

Somewhere in Fred's office is a video of him when he first started. It was, by his own estimate, seven thousand mentally wounded veterans ago, on a day in 1981 when Jim George was about to aim a gun at himself and Adam was about to be born. Fred had a mustache then. His hair was longer. His voice was a little higher.

Other than that, only the landscape has changed.

"There is no magic here. Okay?" he said that day to ninety young combat veterans from Vietnam, thirty-four of whom had tried to kill themselves. "The magic is you."

Now Fred waits in his office to start the next session of Trauma Group. There's goodness in everyone. The moment has arrived to let Adam know.

14

During the war, every day would begin the same way. The soldiers would tuck lucky charms into their pockets and joke about their final words. They would gather in quick circles to pray and smoke the last cigarette of their lives. They would tighten their body armor, push in their earplugs, lower their shatter-resistant sunglasses, and tug on their burn-resistant gloves, and when someone called out, "Let's go," they would climb into their Humvees and go, knowing full well what was waiting for them down the road. They had seen Harrelson's Humvee rise into the air and burst into fire. They had seen Emory get shot in the head and collapse in his own spreading blood. They had seen soldiers lose legs, lose arms, lose feet, lose hands, lose fingers, lose toes, and lose eyes, and they had heard them, too, in the aid station, in whatever pain is enough pain to make a nineteen-year-old scream. They had heard a soldier ask, "Is anything sticking out of my head?" after a mortar attack. They had heard a doctor say, "I'm hoping, I'm hoping," about a soldier who in a few minutes would be dead. They had heard a soldier tell a dying soldier as he stuffed what was left of him into a Humvee, "You're gonna have to move your feet so I can close the door." They had heard a soldier who had lost his right leg and left leg and right arm and most of his left arm saying, "Ow, it hurts. It hurts." They had heard a sergeant who was watching something skid across the floor of the aid station, which had fallen from a shredded soldier who was about to die, say with sadness, "That's a toe." They had heard Aieti ask in the most hopeful voice a soldier could ever muster, "What happened to Harrelson?" They had heard Golembe say to Schumann, "None of this shit

Shawnee Hoffman

would have happened if you were there." Most of all, they had heard explosion after explosion and seen dozens of Humvees disappear into breathtaking clouds of fire and debris, and by the end most of them had been inside such a cloud themselves, blindly feeling around in those initial moments to determine if they were alive, or dead, or intact, or in pieces, as their ears rang and their hearts galloped and their souls darkened and their eyes occasionally filled with tears. So they knew. They *knew*. And yet day after day they would go out anyway, which eventually came to be what the war was about. Not winning. Not losing. Nothing so grand. Just trying until it was time to go home and discovering that life after the war turned on trying again.

"I'll try anything at this point," as Adam Schumann had once said.

"I try so hard . . ." as Nic DeNinno had written.

"Another damn day," as Michael Emory had said, waking up one more time.

"Catherine . . . Catherine . . ." as Tausolo Aieti had said, staring so hard at the photograph of that woman, and then, not ready to give up, he said it again.

"Catherine . . . Catherine . . ." he said, because what was the alternative?

It was five minutes in the Gardner Room.

It was becoming a lesson learned.

And so their lives now: trying to recover from the trying they did during the war. Emory may have bitten a wrist. DeNinno may have overdosed. Aieti may forever hear Harrelson. Schumann may have come the closest of all. But the fact is that three years after their war ended, all of them are still here and still at it, as are all of the soldiers from the unit, as is every other affected person in this cluster of war wounds. They are, if nothing else, all still alive, and it is something they hang on to like some kind of battle victory, right up until they hear about Danny Holmes and realize that as hard as they try, the war keeps trying, too.

He had been in charge of all the weapons for the company for a while, so all of the guys knew him that way, and then as things worsened he became one of the guys who grew increasingly reclusive and spent his down days huffing a lot of cans of Dust-Off, and then he went home from the war with a sleep prescription and an honorable discharge, and now he is the one who shifted what's possible for all the others, leaving behind a fiancée named Shawnee Hoffman and their twelve-month-old daughter, Aurora. It has been ten days since Danny Holmes killed himself. It happened in Dodge Center, Minnesota, population 2,600, the newest point of light in a country aglow, and as soldiers keep sending out messages—"I don't believe it"; "RIP bro"; "Please forgive"; "sorry you went out like that"; "you served your country well"—Shawnee is remembering the first conversation that she and Danny ever had, a year after he'd come home.

"What do you see in my eyes?" he asked her.

"Nothing," she said.

"Pain?" he asked.

"Yeah," she said.

They were at a party. She was nineteen years old and he was thirty.

"We just clicked," she says now. "I didn't feel pity for him. I didn't feel bad for him. I felt like I could relate to him. I recognized that look." And so began a relationship that, like Kristy Robinson's, steadily began to deteriorate and eventually turned her into the newest version of what James Doster's commander had once said of Amanda: probably the saddest woman yet. She is twenty-one years old now, broke, jobless, and on her own to figure it out for herself and Aurora, who at the moment is teething and feverish and gumming her dead father's dog tags for relief. As for her own state of mind, she hasn't been sleeping very much because she sees Danny hanging in front of her whenever she shuts her eyes.

There isn't much furniture in the apartment she and Aurora are left with, but there is a couch that she sits on to look once again through Danny's old computer. Hidden away in a file called Iraq/Graphic are a series of photographs that she would find him staring at sometimes, his lower lip twitching. They are of a day when the entire battalion was out on an operation to clear an area of insurgents who had been way too successful in blowing the soldiers up. At one point, a helicopter gunship opened fire on nine men clustered on a street corner, some of whom had weapons and two of whom turned out to be journalists covering the war. A video of those people being blasted to pieces became infamous when it was posted on the Internet by the antisecrecy group WikiLeaks and watched more than ten million times by people around the world, many of whom would comment on it in absolutes and certainties, as if war could be comprehended fully by a high-speed connection to the Internet and a carefully edited video clip. The footage from the video, in somewhat grainy black and white, was hard enough for anyone to stomach, but the views of that day that Danny would look at were the views that no one had seen except the soldiers themselves as they swarmed in, at least one of whom took pictures to document what had happened for after-action reports.

Heads half gone, torsos ripped open, spreading blood, insides outside.

Close-ups, auto-focused, sunshine lighting, perfect color.

The war, in other words, as it was experienced by the soldiers who were in it and asking what had happened to Harrelson and wondering after a mortar attack if anything might be sticking out of their head. The pictures were supposed to be classified, but many of the soldiers brought them home anyway as trophies of a sort, and as Shawnee looks at them now, she remembers when Danny showed them to her soon after they met, which was two years before he died.

"Do you judge me?" he asked. "Do you think of me any different?"

"How many people have you killed?" she asked him.

"Quite a few," he said.

"Did it bother you?" she asked.

"No," he said.

"Not ever?" she asked.

"No," he said.

"Not even the worst one?" she asked. "Did you walk up and look at him?"

"Yeah," he said.

Now she is remembering another conversation, soon after that.

"He said they were in a Humvee, or whatever they were called, and they were driving, and they were taking fire, engaged, whatever, so they stopped to return fire, and Danny said there was an Iraqi with a girl in his arms, and he was shooting, and he was holding the little girl, and Danny said, 'I had no choice, I had to shoot him,' so Danny shot and killed him and also killed the little girl. That's the story I was told."

He told other stories, too. The day he was in the shitters during a rocket attack. That one he laughed about.

The women who worked on the base who you could pay for sex if you used the code word. "Apples," he said, and he laughed about that, too.

But it was his killing of the little girl that he kept coming back to and retelling, especially after Aurora was born. Some of it was specific. She had dark hair and looked at him and seemed about three years old. Some of it was vague. No date. No time of day. No exact location. Making it even hazier: none of the soldiers he was with remembers such a thing ever happening. "That *never* happened," one of his sergeants insists. But Danny dwelled on it more and more. "I see children everywhere," he would tell Shawnee, waking up from another nightmare. He mentioned it to his mother, too, although only briefly, and only after she had asked what it was like over there. Like most soldiers, he preferred not to talk about what he had experienced, and with his mother he'd been extra-protective of her ever since helping her through what she thought would be the worst days of her life: when her oldest child, severely bipolar, stopped taking his meds, then hanged himself. For several weeks, Danny held her hand until she was asleep and was there waiting for her when she woke up. That was eight years earlier, though, before the war, when he was still capable of such things.

"You need to get help," Shawnee urged Danny from time to time.

"I'll get help," he said.

He didn't, though. Shawnee says he told her once that the VA wanted to do a workup on him at the hospital in Minneapolis to see if he had TBI, even offering to get him there by van, but that it would take all day and he didn't want to waste his time. Toward the end of his life, he told her he called a crisis line of some sort, but she doesn't know if he actually did.

Instead, as his decline continued, he began ignoring Aurora, whom he had doted on when she was first born. He stopped cleaning up after himself, leaving his dishes wherever. He stopped showering every day. "He was constantly tired," Shawnee says. "He was constantly in a bad mood." He told her it might be a good idea to hide his knife collection, so she tucked it under the couch.

More conversations:

"Are you sure you want to be with me?" he began asking.

"Yes," Shawnee said, feeling increasingly overwhelmed.

"Are you sure we're going to stay together?" he asked over and over.

"Yes."

"I just need to hear you say it," he said again and again.

Two weeks before he killed himself, around the time of Aurora's first birthday, he went to see his mother, who lives in a tiny town in northern Iowa called Chester. "I'm not worth nothing. I'm not worth nothing," she remembers him saying to her, and later that night, she remembers watching from a window as he stalked in the dark around the yard, finally disappearing into a garage toward the rear of the property. After a while, she heard a couple of gunshots. A few days later, she would see a broken window and realize it was Danny, but lots of people have guns where she lives, and at the time she figured it was one of the neighbors, up to whatever.

Before saying goodbye to her the next morning, he fished his old dress uniform out of the attic. Back home, he put it on and asked Shawnee to take a picture of him.

A few days later, after another fight about her feeling smothered by him, she woke to the sounds of Aurora crying and Danny screaming, "Shut the fuck up!"

"Danny?" she called, and immediately his voice changed.

"Are you ready to get up?" he asked Aurora.

A week or so later, she woke to the sound of scissors and Danny saying in the dark that he just wanted to cut off a little piece of her hair.

"You're doing crazy stuff," she told him.

"I'm sorry," he said. "My head's not right."

She needed a break. It was getting too weird. She could no longer look at those pained eyes that had attracted her in the first place. "It would make me sick to my stomach," she says. She made plans to go out with some friends who weren't thirty-two years old and always coming home from a war. He didn't want her to go.

"I need to talk to you," he said as that day began.

"I gotta do the laundry," she said, and she went to do the laundry.

"Please talk to me," he said when she was done. His lip was twitching like it would do when he looked at the photographs. She knew she was ignoring him but just wanted to get away.

"I'm gonna go tanning," she said, and she went tanning.

"I want to talk to you." She cleaned the house. She cleaned their old car. "Will you please talk to me?" She showered and got dressed and kissed Aurora goodnight.

"I wish I had stayed home," she says, but instead, she went out, drank a few beers, got pulled over for speeding, failed a breathalyzer test, spent the night in the booking area of the jail, couldn't call Danny because she had the cell phone they both used, called some friends to take her home when the police released her, and remembers how the sky was just beginning to lighten and the birds were chirping up a racket as she opened the front door. The light above the stove was on, but otherwise the apartment was dark. Still, there was enough light for her to see Danny in silhouette, just to her left, lying on the steps leading to the second floor, with his neck and head somehow suspended in the air.

Another conversation:

"Is this 911?"

"Yes it is."

"911?"

"Right."

"I'm freaking out."

"What's the matter? What's the matter?"

"I think—I think that my baby's daddy killed himself," Shawnee wailed. "He was watching my daughter and I came home and he was hanging from the steps and I don't know if he's dead I think he's dead I don't know I don't know I don't know . . ."

"Okay stay on the line for me. You're at 106 Fifth Street Southwest?"

"Yes . . ."

"Apartment thirty?"

"Yes apartment thirty Dodge Center the Crossroads please *please* please please send someone please right now please. Please. *Please.* I don't know if he's dead . . ."

"You said he might have hung himself?"

"Yes he's hanging from the steps . . ."

"Are you able to cut him down?"

"I don't know how long he's been like this I just got out of jail I . . ."

"Okay, I'm going to page you an ambulance. Stay on the line. Don't hang up. Try to cut him down if you can, okay?"

"Okay . . ."

"See if you can get him down."

"Okay I'm gonna try to get him down you really want me to do it, okay, I'll try . . . oh my God . . ."

How exactly did he do it, she is wondering now, standing at the base of those steps and looking up. There are fourteen steps, a banister, and a small landing at the top, beyond which is Aurora's room, where a pillow had been placed on the floor next to the crib, and Shawnee wonders: did he lie there for a while and say goodbye? He used his military-issue parachute cord. It's a shoelace-thick cord, made mostly of nylon. He knotted one end around the top of the banister and the other around his neck. And then what? "The rope was so tight, I'm thinking he had it all measured out," Shawnee says. "I'm thinking he tied it at the top of the steps and just jumped. Just jumped and rolled down the steps. Or he jumped straight down, and it jerked him back, and he probably sat there and struggled and tried to get it off his neck." He was wearing boxers. Just boxers. When she touched his leg, it was cold. The coroner, she says, told her that it probably had happened before midnight, which meant that he had been there all through the night while she was drying out at the jail and watching TV with a sign underneath it that said "No Soap Operas." "You motherfuckers are funny," Shawnee told the jailers when she saw that, and meanwhile, Danny was hanging cockeyed on the steps and Aurora was in her crib. So she's been thinking about that. The coroner also said it probably took him ten minutes to die, so she's been thinking about that, too, and also about what a neighbor said to her just after

Danny had been placed in a red velvety body bag and taken away. The neighbor, who Shawnee had seen from time to time, introduced herself by saying she was a medium. "'I can see what he did—he was pacing back and forth from the kitchen to the living room to the kitchen. He decided, fuck it, I'm just going to do it,'" Shawnee remembers the neighbor telling her. "She said that as he did it, he heard Aurora cry, and he spent his last minutes struggling and regretting it. That's what she was getting from Danny on the other side."

Shawnee keeps looking at the steps, which she has been trying to go up and down as little as possible.

"Maybe he took a running start," she says.

Here's what she knows for sure, that when the 911 dispatcher asked if she could cut Danny down, she went to the kitchen and got a knife and felt sick to her stomach and thought she might pass out, and that as she sliced the cord, it made a sound—"a boing," she says—that she has been unable to stop hearing since.

Now she looks down at Aurora, who is trying to crawl up the steps. "No, you can't," she says gently. She lifts her and moves her away, but Aurora comes right back and starts up the stairs again, and so Shawnee takes her outside and sits with her on the front stoop.

Someday, she is going to have to pass on to Aurora the legacy of her father, that he went to a war, that he came home, that he tried, that he stopped, but first she will have to understand it for herself. "How could you do this to me and Aurora?" she says she screamed at Danny just after he died, and then, overwhelmed with guilt for asking such a question, whispered to him, "I take it back."

Another day: she went to visit her own father, who, as she was leaving, leaned in the car window and asked her, "What's the lesson learned?"

Another day: "Valium. A ton of Valium. Take some. Go to sleep. I wouldn't be brave enough to jump down the steps," she says of the lesson she's learning, while in Chester, Iowa, Mary Holmes, whose own learned lesson is her inability to stop asking questions, is sitting at her dining room table with the black plastic box that contains Danny's cremated remains.

"Why did you hang yourself?" she asks him, crying and furious.

"How could you hurt Aurora this way?"

"What happened over there?"

"What was so bad?"

Meanwhile, in Kansas, on what for her is day 1,395, Amanda Doster decides to send Saskia Schumann a message.

"Hey there Saskia," she writes. "I was wondering if you had thought about ways you could start paying me back the money I loaned you so long ago."

She is sitting by a pool when she writes this, waiting for the kids to finish a swim lesson. There's no particular reason for the message. It's not like she's running out of oops money. She and the Schumanns haven't been in touch in months. But she thinks often of them, sometimes wondering how they are, sometimes wondering why they cut her out of their lives, and so she sends the message to the last address she had for Saskia and is surprised a few minutes later when she gets a reply.

"Yah of course. Right now its kinda tough. I'm not working and adams in a ptsd facility. We're hoping to get social security and back pay from that. If they backpay from the day he filed i could just do it all at once."

She rereads the message. A facility? Adam? She knew he hadn't been well when he came home. But the "one guy in particular," as James had once put it?

"I'm sorry to hear that," she writes back, and is suddenly in a conversation she didn't expect.

"We've been through a lot and had to witness many horrifying things with him," Saskia writes. "I hope to god this program works and he comes home somewhat 'normal.'"

"I can't even imagine what he must be going through. And you guys having to see/deal with all of that must be difficult," Amanda writes back.

"Sounds terrible, but i've lost a lot of sympathy for adam. I guess u get cold after being treated like crap for so long," Saskia writes.

The conversation keeps going, off and on, through the rest of the swim lesson, and it continues at home now, where Amanda should really be starting dinner.

"How r the kids?" Saskia asks at one point.

"They struggle and I struggle," Amanda answers. "It usually hits out of nowhere."

"Poor kids. Have you had them in any kind of therapy? I'm starting it with zoe now, she has seen and heard too much."

"No. I've spoken to my counselor about them and they are having normal grief reactions. When they are a little older maybe . . ."

"That's good your seeing someone. Has it helped? I just started seeing a therapist bout a mth ago."

"I'm not sure. There are days I take the kids to school then go back to bed and cry all day."

"I know how the crying all day thing is, there are days when it feels like everything around me is falling apart and I have no control over anything."

"I couldn't save James—it was out of my control. So I try to control everything I possibly can."

"Have you started dating at all?" Saskia asks at another point. "It wont replace him but it may help with the loneliness you have."

"I still only want my James," Amanda answers.

"It seems like everything just happened yesterday," Saskia writes at another point, and to Amanda those words are the most gutting of all.

For a while, she was wearing her wedding ring on her right hand, but now it's back on her left hand. She is no longer seeing James behind the wheel of a pest control truck, but she might have recently spotted him on TV. As for Grace's perfect acorn, it didn't work out so well, but she will collect more when she next goes to clean James's headstone in order to try again.

So she is trying, too.

"Yah, the day b4 he left he threatened to hit me, that was the last for me, thats why hes in a facility right now," Saskia writes now.

"I'm grateful that he didn't hit you," Amanda writes. "There's no excuse for that behavior."

"No," Saskia writes. "i talked to a lady whose husband is in the same place and she said he tried to kill her and shes still with him. How does someone ever get past that?"

"My mom stayed with my dad for years and put us through that. It took 25 years for her to leave and it damaged me forever. His was PTSD from Vietnam . . ." Amanda writes, and then brings the conversation to an end because Grace is at her side, showing her a recipe for some kind of raspberry dessert.

Time to get busy with the lives they've moved on to, which for Amanda involves loading some new dishes she bought into the dishwasher. "I hate that they don't fit the same way," she tells the girls. "It's making me crazy."

Saskia, meanwhile, is left to wonder where she will get the money to pay back Amanda when her pressing concern is a house with broken air-conditioning during a summer heat wave and Adam nowhere around to fix it.

At least there's the swimming pool in the backyard to cool off in, but the house is blistering, and the next afternoon, Dave from across the street comes over to see what he can do. Donna, his wife, comes, too, and they all head down to the furnace room to look at the air handler. Saskia hates the room more than ever, with its smudged light and sickening echoes, and when Jaxson gets in the way, she points him toward the hallway and tells him to go play with Zoe in her room.

A few minutes later, Zoe comes in.

"Where's Jax?" she asks.

For a moment, Saskia is confused. Hasn't he been with her? She gets up and checks the laundry room. He's not there. She looks behind the freezer. "Jax?" she calls. "Jax?"

Now she and Donna head upstairs, and while Saskia checks the kitchen, Donna goes out back to see why the dogs are barking.

Just some birds.

Then something catches her eye.

"He's in the pool!" she screams, seeing him on his back, floating near the four-step ladder he somehow managed to climb. His eyes are closed, his lips purpling. She grabs him by a leg and yanks him out as Saskia comes running, and soon another conversation is under way:

"911, what's your emergency?"

"My son just fell in the pool," Saskia says, crying, "but he's breathing, so I think he's okay."

"Okay do you need an ambulance to come check him out or anything?"

"Yeah."

"How old is he?"

"He's going to be two in November."

"Did he go underneath the water at all?"

"Yeah, he was under."

"And he's breathing okay?"

"Yeah. I think so. He won't open his eyes."

"He won't open his eyes? Is there chlorine in the pool at all?"

"Yeah."

"Okay. I want you to stay on the phone, I'm going to get an ambulance in route to you, okay?"

"Okay, thank you."

"Are you in the front yard or the backyard?"

"The backyard."

"Okay. Hold on just a moment."

"Jaxson. *Jaxson! JAX!*"

"Saskia, how's he doing now?"

"He threw up a little bit. He's really tired. He won't open his eyes."

"Okay you're gonna have to calm down for him, okay? 'Cause if you calm down, he'll calm down, okay?"

"Oh my God . . ."

Later, after riding in the ambulance with Jaxson to the hospital, after telling the doctors that she didn't know how long he was underwater, after tests and X-rays and listening to a doctor lecture her about pools and in the middle of everything getting a message from Adam asking, "You okay?" and writing back, "Phone's dying," and shutting it off, she is home wondering what to say to him.

For the second time in his life, Jaxson, somehow, is fine. Breathing evenly. Not even a mark. How can that be? But it is.

She gives him spaghetti for dinner and listens to him laugh as he makes a mess of it, and then she sends Adam a long message telling him what happened.

She feels a little dizzy. The house is so hot. The forecast for tomorrow is 110 degrees. There's no way they can sleep upstairs. Zoe leads the way down to the basement, and Saskia follows with Jaxson in her arms. They go past the furnace room and into Zoe's room, and as they lie next to one another in bed, Saskia's mind drifts. How long was he underwater? How did he get back to the surface? What if Donna hadn't been there? What if the dogs hadn't been barking at some birds? It would have been her fault. It *is* her fault.

She thinks of what Adam finally wrote back to her, after they had talked on the phone and he heard for himself that Jaxson was okay:

"Well, we're even now."

She sets her alarm to wake up in an hour. She will get up every hour, all night long, to check on her lucky son. She will put her hand on his chest. She will listen for his breaths. It's a plan that gives her enough relief to shut her eyes, but she is still wide awake when at 2:00 a.m. her phone buzzes with another message.

What mean thing is he going to say now?

"I can't sleep. All I can think of is all the death I've seen, caused."

"You didnt cause any of it," she writes back after a while. "You cant have that kind of guilt. Thats the cost of war."

"Yes I did," he replies.

In California, he lies in the dark, in need of forgiveness. In Kansas, so does she.

Everywhere, the war keeps trying.

"Love u," one of them writes now.

"I'm so sorry," the other writes back.

As they keep trying, too.

15

Hey, you wanna come in here and work some menus?"

General Chiarelli's aide says this to General Chiarelli's chef, who at the moment is on shoeshine duty in the basement of General Chiarelli's house. It's a position with perks, vice chief of staff of the United States Army. One of them is to live in a huge brick house on Fort McNair along Washington, D.C.'s waterfront, another is to always have good-looking shoes, and another is the ability to invite important people in Washington to dinners overseen by a chef and an aide.

"What's the topic?" asks the chef, an army sergeant first class, because the dinners always have a theme. "Readiness" was one. "Budget" was another. "Modernization" was another.

"Suicide prevention," says the aide, an army master sergeant.

"Okay," says the chef, sucking in his breath.

"I already told the chorus," the aide says. "Gave them a few ideas."

Another perk: a chorus, usually the U.S. Army Strolling Strings, whose members surround the guests after dinner and serenade them.

"We should probably have some kind of greens," the chef says, starting with the appetizer, which will be a pistachio sea bass that will need to be topped with something. "Or frisée."

"How do you spell that?" the aide asks.

"e-e," says the chef, as the aide types into a computer. "Render down the bacon," the chef continues, "use the bacon itself as a crunch in the frisée. With vinegar."

"What do you call that?" the aide asks, wondering what to type.

"I'd call it warm bacon dressing," the chef says.

Adam Schumann, on his way home

"Could we call it vinaigrette?" the aide says.

"Yeah," shrugs the chef.

"I like that," says the aide, typing it in.

Members of Congress come to these dinners. So do "Thought/Action Leaders," "Military/Government" types, and "Media/Opinion Shapers," according to the lists that Chiarelli's staff starts assembling a few weeks before each dinner. The goal is twelve people minimum and sixteen people tops, because more than sixteen means two tables and everyone wants to sit with the Vice.

Next course: a soup with butternut squash, parsnips, and mushrooms.

"You could call it an autumn vegetable bisque trio," the chef says.

"Seasonal?" asks the aide, noting it's not quite autumn yet.

"You could do seasonal," the chef says. "That would be safer."

"Seasonal vegetable," types the aide and pauses. "What'd you say? Trio?"

"Yeah. Trio," says the chef. "But you might put it at the front."

"Tri? Tri-seasonal?"

"You could use three."

"Tri-Seasonal Vegetable Bisque," types the aide. "Now we're in the main. What's it going to be?"

"Lamb," says the chef.

"What are we going to call it?" asks the aide.

"Lamb," says the chef.

There is choreography to these dinners. Chiarelli dresses casually, offers a toast and during appetizers might tell the story of John Wilkes Booth being buried for a time not far from the house. Beth Chiarelli might mention the strange way the flowers grow on the spot where Booth was eventually exhumed. Members of Chiarelli's staff and a civilian protocol officer will be just out of sight, sending texts and updates. "The dinner has formed well." "Everybody seems happy." "No issues so far." The Strolling Strings will always play an encore, and the encore is often a song called "Rocky Top."

"Herb-crusted," the chef says now about the lamb.

"Herb-crusted," the aide types. "With?"

"I would put fig demi-glace."

"And?"

"Green beans," the chef says.

"Put some color on the plate," the aide says. "Carrots?"

"I'd just go with the green beans, man," the chef says.

The dinners are formal. Gold-rimmed plates. Many, many forks. This is what certain people in Washington expect, and Chiarelli has seen its effects, such as the dinner a few months before when a U.S. senator clasped her hands in delight as the Strolling Strings launched into the song "I Can See Clearly Now." The senator's importance at the dinner was highlighted in the dossier assembled beforehand by Chiarelli's staff, where, under "Reason for Inviting," they had written, "An influential member of both the SASC and SAC." That was shorthand for the Senate Armed Services Committee and the Senate Appropriations Committee, two committees vital to Chiarelli's interest in getting every single person in official Washington to pay attention to soldier mental health issues. So it wasn't the worst thing when at the end of the song, after the last chorus of "It's gonna be a bright-bright, bright-bright, sunshiny day," the senator, beaming, said to Chiarelli, "Thanks to your efforts, there will be more soldiers having bright, sunshiny days."

"S'mores," the chef says, about dessert.

"We gotta make it sound good," the aide says.

"We'll use the new gelato machine and make a chocolate gelato, a meringue for the marshmallow, a graham cracker, and give it a crazy name."

"Newfangled?"

"Uh . . ."

"The Chiarelli s'mores? S'mores . . . s'mores . . . Suicidal s'mores?"

"No."

At the same dinner, another of the guests, the incoming army surgeon general, spoke of her father, who had fought in World War Two, Korea, and Vietnam. He had been nominated a few times for the Medal of Honor and awarded a Silver Star, a Bronze Star with Valor, and three Purple Hearts. In World War Two, under fire, he had run across an open field, climbed a cliff, and, as he had described it at one of his award ceremonies, "I just started eliminating the Germans one by one. After the fifth one, six more came after me. They kept spraying with automatic weapons, but I just kept running around to different spots, popping up and shooting." That was her father sixty-seven years ago, and now he lives with her, and she said she begins every day listening to him scream- ing in his sleep. So yes, she said, as surgeon general, she would be paying extra attention to issues involving mental health.

"How about reconstructed?" the chef says.

"Reconstructed s'mores. That's fun," the aide says. He types it in. He changes Reconstructed to Deconstructed. He adds, "w/Caramel Sauce and Macerated Raspberries." He prints it out and looks it over. "That's a pretty good menu," he says.

So go things in Washington, where in a few days some of the people who authorize wars and fund wars will gather with someone who ran one for a while and now is obsessed with healing some of the people who were in it. "This is a problem we're going to be suffering with for many, many years," Chiarelli often says at gatherings with those pleading eyes of his, trying to convey the urgency of the moment, the depth of the prob- lem, the need for action, and now he will have the chance to say it again.

Except soon after the menu is done, one of the congressmen who had promised to attend pulls out because of some kind of conflict with some other event. Chiarelli's staff scrambles to find a replacement, but now another congressman pulls out, too, for some reason, and when another might be wavering, the scramble is to get an e-mail out to all of the others on the guest list. Was it the topic that did it? Something else? Doesn't matter. "It is with regret that I inform you the Suicide Prevention Quar- ters Dinner scheduled for 21 September at GEN and Mrs. Chiarelli's quarters has been cancelled due to unforeseen scheduling conflicts," it says. "The office of the Vice Chief of Staff of the Army will attempt to re-schedule this dinner at a date yet to be determined."

It will never happen. In a few months, Chiarelli will retire from the army. The monthly suicide meetings that he began will become some- thing different under his successor, on whose watch the number of sui- cides will keep rising until it is exceeding the number of combat deaths and averaging almost one a day. The Pistachio Sea Bass w/Frisée and

Warm Bacon Vinaigrette will never have its moment, and neither will the Tri-Seasonal Vegetable Bisque and Deconstructed S'mores.

That's how things can go in Washington, too, up at the high levels, and meanwhile, two days after the suicide dinner would have taken place, on the other side of the country, down at the low levels, another gathering goes on as scheduled.

"You okay?" Saskia asks.

It's graduation day at Pathway.

"Mm-hmm," Adam says.

In Trauma Group, he had done what he promised himself he would do when he returned that day in surrender. He started with his childhood and went all the way through the war. He must have spent twenty minutes just on fucked-up Emory, whose blood he could taste as he spoke, and thirty minutes on dear dead Doster, whose every word to him he could hear. He talked about losing his footing as he tried to get Emory through that doorway, about what Golembe had said after Doster had died, about coming home ashamed, about dropping Jaxson, about going down to the furnace room, and about his years of suicidal thoughts. He talked about all of it, every humiliating thing. Some great soldier, he said, and when he was done, he wiped his eyes and waited to hear the others confirm what he already knew about himself.

"You've got nothing to be ashamed of," one said.

"You did more than enough," another said.

He loved those men in that moment, and he loves them now as the ceremony begins and they are called one by one up to the stage.

"Are any of your family members present?" Fred Gusman asks the first of them as he walks uncertainly to the podium. A hundred or so people are watching—family, friends, some of the Rotarians who take everyone bowling on Monday nights to help them get used to being out in public, a woman who will give each person a yellow long-stemmed rose.

"Nobody came," he says.

"Well, that's why you have us," Fred says, and stands to the side as the soldier describes three deployments and two suicide attempts and says, "This is the happiest I've been in a long, long time."

There is applause for him as he gets his yellow rose, and then Fred calls up the next one, who is wearing dark sunglasses and is so nervous he begins gasping his words. "My family thought I was crazy. I was ready to give up," he says. "All I knew is I wanted to kill myself . . ."

"I wrote something, but I don't know if . . ." number three begins and then stops. He bows his head, leans on the podium, and looks as if he might collapse. He walks off without saying another word and disappears out a door.

"My God," Saskia says quietly, starting to cry.

"Okay, he'll be back," Fred says, and calls up number four, who has decided to wear his uniform for the occasion. "So, yeah, this is the next step for me in my life," he says, and as he keeps talking, Saskia is crying so hard her makeup is running.

Number five:

"I haven't wrote anything," he barely gets out because of nerves. "I appreciate your coming, and I appreciate your support."

Number six:

"I thought everything was going good, and then all of a sudden" is how he begins, and how he finishes is "Now I know how beautiful life can be."

"Well, we're getting right down to the end here," Fred says.

Number seven:

"Frightening, shameful, and humiliating" is how he describes his war, and then he says of what he learned at Pathway: "I know now that everything matters because everything has to do with everything."

Number eight:

He speaks of the day he wanted to kill himself and called his grandmother, whose husband had killed himself after Vietnam. "She told me if I did it I would break her heart," he says.

"Okay, last but not least," Fred says, and for the slightest moment gets uncharacteristically emotional. Maybe it's because of pressure: he is nearly out of money and had begun making contingency plans to shut down, and then came an unexpected donation of ten thousand dollars in the morning mail, which means he will still be open when fifteen new guys arrive next week. Or maybe it's something else. "These warriors are truly brave people," he continues after a moment. "I've had the privilege now to meet and know all of them, and the last one that's going to speak today is Adam. So come on up, Adam."

Adam goes on up.

He looks at the other graduates with their yellow roses. "A few months ago, someone asked me what does it mean to graduate from here. Is it proof that you're cured? I'm not cured. I don't think any of us are or ever will be," he says. "But I'm definitely in a better place than I was six months ago. Even a couple of months ago for that matter. It feels like in the last couple of weeks, a million pounds have been lifted off my back. I can breathe again. I can wake up in the morning and smile. For the first time, I'm not thinking about killing myself every day."

He looks toward Fred. "I want to thank you for saving my life."

He turns to Saskia. "I'm going to be home," he says. "Finally home."

He keeps looking at her. She watches him get his rose, which he lays across the crook of his arm like a shotgun.

"Okay, here we go," she says under her breath.

Clothes: packed. Fishing rods: packed. Rose: packed. Big TV: leave it for the next guy.

"If I'm ever in Kansas," one of the others who is leaving says to Adam.

"It was nice to meet you and your shitty wife," another says, to which Saskia smiles, pretty sure it's a joke.

"Go be home," another says, and as the last words Adam will hear at Pathway, at least they're more encouraging than the last time he started a journey home, when a soldier told Adam in his final moments of the war that he'd walk with him as far as the shitters.

That was the walk after Saskia had said to him over a scratchy phone connection, "I'm scared of what you might do," and Adam had told her, "You know I'd never hurt you." Now, as they head onto the highway, Adam says, "This is the first time I've seen clouds in California."

"Really?" Saskia says.

"Yeah. It rained that first week, and it's been clear blue skies ever since," he says.

The plan is to drive through the night, stop in Denver to see relatives, and go home from there. He turns on the radio.

She doesn't change the station.

"Like it?" he says. He reaches over. He pats her on the leg.

She doesn't push his hand away.

They head north toward Sacramento as the sun sets, and east toward sunrise in Utah.

"There's nothing to be nervous about," Adam says at one point, when Saskia has been quiet for a while.

At another point, he telephones one of his old soldiers, who he found out is at Fort Carson, just south of Denver. "It's Schumann," he says, and gives him the address of where he'll be stopping, just in case the soldier feels like going for a drive.

"Are you nervous?" he asks Saskia again, a little bit later.

She is. She smokes now. She is in counseling. She is on antidepressants. She is unsure about whether their marriage can last. She sees herself sometimes bolting with the kids to North Dakota. She still tailgates at 80 miles per hour. "If people would move the fuck over and get the fuck out of the way, I wouldn't have a problem," she says when she takes the wheel for a while and a slow-moving car won't move to another lane.

But when Adam is driving and flies over a bump in the highway he hadn't seen, instead of screaming, or seething, or glaring, she instead rubs the back of his head until he calms down, and in this way they arrive peaceably in Denver.

They have been driving for eighteen hours. In Reno, at two in the morning, they had stood in line at a convenience store along with an Elvis impersonator. In Wyoming, at a gas station outside of Laramie, an old man had yelled to Adam, "Come here. I want to show you something," so Adam went over and found himself looking at the freshly decapitated head of an elk. Once, long ago, just back from the war and trying to figure out what had happened to him, Adam had said, "I was a normal guy who got sent to Iraq and became crazy, so they sent me back to America to become sane, and now it's America that's driving me crazy." But something about this drive through America is reassuring to him, and in the best of moods, he hugs his aunt, and then turns his attention to his grandmother, who spent so many silent years married to her war-wounded husband and now looks over Adam from head to toe.

"How are you?" she asks.

"Better," he says.

"Much much better?" she asks.

There are others here, too, including a kitchen full of people cooking barbecue and a patio full of people drinking beer, and now, pulling up out front, ringing the doorbell, making his way toward Adam, here comes the soldier from Fort Carson.

He has a tattoo on his right arm in honor of James Doster.

And a memorial bracelet on his left wrist, also in honor of Doster.

"When's the last time you two saw each other?" one of Adam's relatives asks.

"In Iraq," Adam says.

"That's when I hated you," the soldier says.

"I know," Adam says.

It's Christopher Golembe.

"None of this shit would have happened if you were there," Golembe had said after Doster died and meant it as a compliment.

"None of this shit would have happened if you were there," Adam had heard and nailed it into his soul as blame.

Now, nearly four years later to the day, ever so carefully, he listens again as Golembe is talking about some of the things that happened over there. The time they were running along the roofs in a firefight. The time a guy found a scorpion in his pants. The time they barreled into a house and past an Iraqi on his knees with his hands up except it turned out he wasn't on his knees, that he had no legs and was balanced on his stumps and went flying across the room. The time . . .

"How do you remember all this shit?" Adam asks him. "I don't remember anything."

"Good times, man," Golembe says.

They are standing in the backyard next to a fire pit. The sun is dropping. The temperature is falling. "I'm so fucking sick of this army shit," Saskia says, walking away. Golembe drinks a beer, and Adam drinks a Mountain Dew. Golembe drinks another beer, and Adam drinks another Mountain Dew. "Remember that day you shot that guy in the ass?"

"Yeah. I probably shouldn't have shot him," Adam says, but as he looks at Golembe what he is really remembering is why, in the war, Golembe had been one of his favorites. He had been one of Adam's team leaders, and after Emory was shot on the roof, and Adam draped Emory across his back, and Emory's blood filled Adam's mouth and stained his teeth as he carried him down those stairs, and Adam got Emory into the Humvee and then headed back up to the roof, Golembe was right behind him. They reached the top and scanned for the sniper, who still was out there somewhere. What they saw instead, there where Emory had fallen, was his helmet. It had to be retrieved. Golembe volunteered, and as Adam popped a smoke grenade, Golembe bear-crawled across the roof and brought back a helmet that Emory would one day fill with candy and use on Halloween but at the moment was partly filled with his blood. That was the moment Adam began truly loving Golembe, as they took cover and figured out what to do with the helmet, finally emptying out a flour sack and putting it in there so no one else would have to see it when they brought it downstairs.

"Let's go out tonight," Golembe says now to Adam as they stand by the fire.

"I just drove eighteen hours," Adam says, shaking his head.

"We'll get on motorcycles. We'll get on dirt bikes," Golembe says.

"No," Adam says.

Emory happened in April, and after that Adam depended on Golembe more and more, right up until a night five months later when they ended up screaming at each other over some sunflower seeds in Adam's Humvee. It wasn't just a few seeds. There were handfuls all over the seats and floor, which Adam had discovered after his Humvee had been used by soldiers on guard duty at the entrance to the outpost. It was, to Adam, the latest example of sliding discipline in the platoon, and when no one would take responsibility for the mess, Adam took his concerns to Doster, who agreed to put the entire platoon on guard duty one night as punishment. Body armor on. Helmets on. Gloves, eye pro, and knee pads on. The full battle rattle, all night long around the Humvees, to make sure, as Adam put it, "no fucking ghosts climb in." "This is stupid shit," Golembe told him at one point in the night, and when Adam walked over to him to hear what else he might have to say, he thought he smelled alcohol on Golembe's breath. "Go back to your room and sleep it off," he ordered. A few hours later, Golembe was back outside, still smelling of alcohol. "The last fucking time I'm gonna tell you, go back to your room," Adam said. Then it was morning, and they were loading up the Humvees to go out on a mission, and Golembe still reeked. "I'm considering firing your fucking ass," Adam told him. "Go ahead," Golembe said, "fire my fucking ass." So Adam fired his fucking ass, and Doster reassigned him into his own Humvee as his gunner, and that was how, a couple of weeks later, when a roadside bomb went off, Golembe came to be blindly feeling around in order to determine if he was alive or dead as his ears rang and his heart galloped and his soul darkened and he heard Doster, who was a few inches from him, scream, "I'm hit."

"I never thought I'd talk to you again," Adam says now, easing closer to the fire, the evening air turning chilly.

"Shit happens, man," Golembe says, working on another beer.

They were the final words of Doster's life. "I'm hit," he screamed, and soon after that Golembe was helping to load him into another Humvee for evacuation to the aid station, him and his severed left leg, and meanwhile, back at the base, where Adam had stayed behind because of the video link with Saskia, the rolling boom of an explosion and resulting radio chatter had brought him to the aid station as well. He stayed outside, at one end of the blood trail, as inside, at the other end, doctors and nurses did what they could. He remained outside as Doster, minutes away from death now, was brought out motionless on a stretcher and loaded onto a helicopter. He was there as the soldiers who had been part of the convoy emerged from the waiting area, and he kept waiting by himself until the final soldier came out. "You doing okay?" he said to Golembe, but Golembe couldn't talk, fearing if he tried to he would break down, so in silence and fighting back tears the two of them walked side by side back to their rooms. Eventually, Golembe went to a bathroom to try to scrub the soot off his face. Eventually, Adam took Doster's body armor to another bathroom and nicked his hand on the shrapnel he would give to Amanda Doster. Eventually both of them found out Doster had died, and Golembe said, "None of this shit would have happened if you were there."

But it did happen, and now they are here.

"Did they ever check you for TBI?" Adam asks. Dinner is over. The others have broken off into separate conversations. Saskia is still around but getting tired.

Golembe shakes his head. "I'm not good," he says. "I'm still fucked up. But I drive on."

Later: "That place was horrible," Golembe says. "I don't know how you did it three times."

"I didn't," Adam says.

Later, when Adam is standing off by himself, smoking a cigarette, Golembe goes over to him and wraps his arms around him in a hug.

"Schu," he says.

Adam stands there uncomfortably, his arms at his side, and Golembe drops his arms when he realizes Adam isn't hugging him back. He steps away. Neither says anything. Then he steps forward and tries again, and this time Adam wraps his arms around Golembe, too.

Later.

It's just the two of them now.

"James was better than us," Adam says.

"No he wasn't," Golembe says.

"I love that guy," Adam says.

"That's why we gotta get fucked up for him tonight," Golembe says.

But they don't. Instead, they try to get unfucked up as they stand together under a sky so clear that when they look up they must be looking at five hundred thousand stars.

That's how glowing it is. As if the sky over America this night isn't the sky at all, but a mirror.

The next morning.
    Saskia is driving.
    They fight in eastern Colorado.
    They make up.
    They fight again in western Kansas.
    They make up again.
    A car won't get out of the way.
    She gets close.
    It won't move.
    She gets closer.
    It still won't move.
    She honks her horn.
    It still won't move.
    She is so close she can read the bumper sticker.
    "Pray For Our Troops," it says.
    Now the car moves over, and Saskia guns it.
    They're almost home.

16

One day in the after-war, Shawnee Hoffman wakes up in Minnesota, carries Aurora down those fourteen steps where Danny Holmes launched himself, wants to go somewhere, can't because of a car with a dead battery, has nowhere to go anyway, and settles onto her couch. For a brief period, she thought she was doing better. She started seeing someone new but stopped after they fought and he hit her hard enough to cause a bruise and the police were once again at the apartment she wished she had the money to leave behind. She is tired all the time now. She tried sleeping pills, then switched to an antianxiety medication, then to an antidepressant. The night before, she tried drinking, and now she is hungover. "Eventually, it's like you just give in. I don't know. Time? I don't know," she says. She plays a video game called *Modern Warfare 2* for a while, just like she and Danny used to do, and then she and Aurora go back up those stairs.

In Georgia on this same day, Michael Emory says, "I see life now as a second chance to correct all my mistakes," and that second chance allows a man who should have been dead, who shouldn't be talking, who shouldn't be standing, who shouldn't be walking, to make plans for another day. Soon, he will telephone Texas and speak for a minute to his little giraffe, and after that he may walk over to Radio Shack, and maybe he'll hear from that woman who once wrote to him, "Thank you for serving our country," but for now, he waits by himself for his aide to arrive so he can get dressed.

At her house in Kansas, Kristy Robinson is having a birthday party for Summer, who on this day is turning three. Her walls remain half

Home

painted and the kitchen floor remains nicked. The door at the end of the hallway remains gouged. The texts from Jessie remain in her phone. Reminders of what happened remain everywhere, and yet two weeks ago, she was missing Jessie so much that she laid her head on Kent's shoulder and wept. She has been wondering how to say more to Summer than what she already has said, that "Daddy's head got hurt," and "Daddy was sad," but not today. This day is about Summer seeing some party hats and balloons and getting all wide-eyed. "Are those for my birthday?" she asks.

On Fort Riley, where Suicide Prevention Awareness Month is about to end and Apple Days are about to begin, Nic DeNinno on this day is meeting with his case manager. After nearly two years in the WTB, two trips to Pueblo, and two suicide attempts, he's waiting to receive his final disability rating, and then he'll be done with the army. His biggest struggle continues to be guilt, he says—"the guilt is just kind of over how we treated people"—but he's concerned about his medications, too. He asks his case manager if there's a way to get off the pills upon which he has become so dependent, and she promises to come up with a plan.

On another part of Fort Riley, Tausolo Aieti leaves math class, heads past the sign announcing Apple Days, and goes into Walmart. He has no idea when he'll be getting out of the WTB—no time soon, they've said—but on this day, Tausolo is feeling better than he has in a while because of the dream he woke up from this morning. "It was about my son," he says with relief, and tries not to worry about what will happen tonight.

In her house, meanwhile, Amanda Doster is composing a message to Sally. The anniversary of James's death is three days away. Four fresh acorns are on the kitchen counter after yesterday's trip to the cemetery at Fort Leavenworth. The new flag has been bought and is ready to be hung, but what is on Amanda's mind this day is a lump in her neck that her doctors want biopsied to see if it's cancerous. Suddenly, there are so many things to do. "I want you to finish the girls' quilts if I can't," she writes to Sally, feeling more out of control than ever. "Grace's is very very close. I quit working on Kathryn's the day James was killed. You would do it with love. But I'm going to start working on them tonight again."

Everywhere on this day, the after-war continues, as eternally as war itself, and now it comes to a house that Adam and Saskia arrive at after a daylong drive through the crimson-gashed grass fields of Kansas. It's late afternoon when they pull up, almost four years after Adam came home the first time in shame. This time, no one is rushing toward him asking him what happened. Instead, he pauses in front of the house and squeezes the outstretched hand of his son.

For a thousand days, he had been the great Sergeant Schumann.

Then he was injured.

Then he was dead.

Then he was done.

Now, another thousand days later, he points toward the front steps of a home that in this one moment anyway seems like the most peaceful place in the world. The wind isn't gusting. The clouds aren't skidding. The bushes aren't bending. The birds aren't cartwheeling. "Ready?" he says to the boy he had once dropped, releasing his hand.

He feels so alive suddenly. If only the moment could last.

"Go go go go," he says.

A NOTE ON SOURCES AND METHODS

This book is a work of nonfiction journalism. All of the people named in the book agreed to participate with the understanding that whatever happened would be on the record. I withheld the name of one family because of charges involving sexual crimes with a minor. I also agreed at the request of the army to not name soldiers whose suicides were being discussed at Suicide Senior Review Group meetings unless I had a specific family's permission. While most of the book is based on events I personally observed, the book also contains some scenes for which I wasn't present. In those instances, the details, descriptions, and dialogue used in the book come from interviews, U.S. Army records, Department of Veterans Affairs records, court records, 911 recordings, historical documents, photographs, videos, and personal letters, e-mails, text messages, and diaries of the participants. Primary reporting for the book took place between January 2010 and September 2011 in Kansas, Washington, D.C., the Pentagon, Colorado, Minnesota, Iowa, and California. Additional reporting took place between April 2007 and April 2008 in Baghdad, Iraq.

ACKNOWLEDGMENTS

First, I am indebted to the people I've written about in these pages for trusting that their stories matter.

I also want to thank the following people and organizations for their generosity, confidence, and support:

Sarah Crichton, my believing editor at Sarah Crichton Books / Farrar, Straus and Giroux. Also at FSG: Jonathan Galassi, Jeff Seroy, Brian Gittis, and Daniel Piepenbring.

Melanie Jackson, my literary agent, without whom there would not be this book.

Don Graham, Katharine Weymouth, Marcus Brauchli, Liz Spayd, Marty Baron, Shirley Carswell, Peter Perl, Kevin Merida, Cameron Barr, Eli Saslow, Stephanie McCrummen, Greg Jaffe, and Julie Tate at the Washington Post.

John Nagl, Nate Fick, Kristin Lord, Sara Conneighton, Shannon O'Reilly, Meg Harrell, Nancy Berglass, Ellen McHugh, Phil Carter, Bob Kaplan, and Tom Ricks at the Center for a New American Security.

The John D. and Catherine T. MacArthur Foundation.

Sheri Quarfoot, Ken Quarfoot, Cathy Speight, Ralph Kauzlarich, Brent Cummings, Tim Hester, Francie Hester, Bob Barnes, Lynne Perri, Steve Adler, Lisa Grunwald, Phil Bennett, Steve Coll, Lucian Perkins, Karl Vick, Dana Priest, Anne Hull, and especially Katherine Boo.

Julia, Lauren, Jon, Adam.

Lisa, most of all.

A Note About the Author

David Finkel is the author of *The Good Soldiers*, the bestselling, critically acclaimed account of the U.S. "surge" during the Iraq War and a *New York Times* Best Book of the Year.

An editor and writer for *The Washington Post*, Finkel has reported from Africa, Asia, Central America, Europe, and across the United States, and has covered wars in Kosovo, Afghanistan, and Iraq.

Among Finkel's honors are a Pulitzer Prize in 2006 and a MacArthur Foundation "genius" grant in 2012. He lives in the Washington, D.C., area.